Mr. Trump's
Wild Ride

ALSO BY MAJOR GARRETT

The Enduring Revolution

The 15 Biggest Lies in Politics
(with Timothy J. Penny)

Common Cents
(with Timothy J. Penny)

Mr. Trump's Wild Ride

THE THRILLS, CHILLS, SCREAMS, AND OCCASIONAL BLACKOUTS OF AN EXTRAORDINARY PRESIDENCY

Major Garrett

ALL
POINTS
BOOKS

MR. TRUMP'S WILD RIDE. Copyright © 2018 by Major Garrett. All rights reserved. Printed in the United States of America. For information, address St. Martin's Press, 175 Fifth Avenue, New York, N.Y. 10010.

www.allpointsbooks.com

The Library of Congress Cataloging-in-Publication Data is available upon request.

ISBN 9781250185914 (hardcover)
ISBN 9781250185921 (ebook)

Our books may be purchased in bulk for promotional, educational, or business use. Please contact your local bookseller or the Macmillan Corporate and Premium Sales Department at 1-800-221-7945, extension 5442, or by email at MacmillanSpecialMarkets@macmillan.com.

First Edition: September 2018

10 9 8 7 6 5 4 3 2 1

To Lara,
with whom I find grace,
peace and joy

Contents

Mr. Trump's
Wild Ride

What I Should Have Learned

"Major. Fantastic. I watched you with President Obama two weeks ago. He was not thrilled. I'm sure I'll be more thrilled."

Those were the first words Donald Trump spoke to me. And they should have told me so much more than they did.

At the time, they told me nothing. I was surprised by what sounded like informality and an odd sense that somehow my presence at an August 2015 press conference with Trump in Birch Run, Michigan, mattered.

As for the "thrill," I have been a journalist in Washington since 1990 and attended thousands of press conferences in the Capitol, in the White House briefing room and in campaign venues across the country and "thrill" had never been part of the politico patter. Who gets thrilled or not thrilled? Angry, sure. Evasive, of course. Bored, sometimes. But thrilled? That was a circus word. Not a campaign word.

Had I taken time to analyze that sentence, I would have learned a lot about Trump. But I didn't. I foolishly thought it was silly rhetoric from a silly reality TV celebrity running a silly campaign for the presidency.

How silly I was. How silly almost all of us were.

If I had taken the time, if I had been more curious and paid Trump more respect, I would have diagrammed that sentence—in literal and psychological ways—and found a trove of information. Like so much with Trump, it was all out in the open. Trump at times made it hard to listen—hard to fathom him, hard to take him and his "movement" seriously. Experienced political reporters like me have grown accustomed to being spoken to (perhaps even stroked) in certain ways by politicians and those who serve them. By that I mean our experience left us sensitized to and desensitized by the sick pseudoscience of campaign strategy, focus groups, wedge issues, bank shots, double bank shots, feints, dog whistles, doublespeak, okeydoke and flimflammery. Trump didn't play that game. He spoke beneath voters, never down to them. He bypassed political reporters entirely and scorned the process of engagement, disarmament and flattery. When I say Trump spoke beneath his supporters I mean he met them at their level and then made them feel smarter—as if what they had long been thinking was now the truth of our times. This mystified traveling reporters and enthralled Trump supporters. Trump lifted his supporters up and tossed skeptical reporters on a metaphorical pyre of their own skepticism. I don't think many of us, in the moment, saw Trump for what he was or is. We never bothered to seriously study the strutting, trumpeting id that was transforming American politics before our very eyes—and paving the most improbable path to the Oval Office ever.

Ever.

If we had paid closer attention to Trump—what he was telling us and how he was harnessing the passions of millions—we would have understood the campaign better and been less surprised. And we would have had a leg up in comprehending the chaotic maelstrom that became his first year as president.

Here is what Trump was telling me—and what he was indirectly promising to bring to the presidency:

"Major. Fantastic."

Of the 30 or so reporters there in Birch Run, I was the only one so regarded by Trump. I never saw him say anything like that again to another reporter. This was Trump signaling his obsession with adjectival exuberance—even with reporters. Trump's infatuation with linguistic inflation is comically consistent. It's a window into his psyche—how he craves and seeks attention, how he boasts and tries to impress and intimidate, how adjectives are frequently placeholders for thoughts. In this case, the craving revealed Trump's desperation for and delight in media affirmation. As much as he pretends to hate reporters and journalism, Trump is uncommonly addicted to publicity—an affliction that followed him straight into the White House.

Whatever you think of Trump as a person or president, he is the most media-savvy political figure since Ronald Reagan. Reagan was a master of the medium of his time—network television. Trump is a master of the medium of his—Twitter, Facebook, Instagram and the like. The key is to use the medium to dominate the narrative and confound your opponents by forcing them to chase your story arc. Reagan's stage management achieved that when network news coverage set the nation's editorial and psychological tone; Trump's twitchy Twitter habits serve him much the same way now. Trump has a canny sense of the entire media universe because he has spent more than 30 years churning it. In Birch Run, Trump cared more about who was covering him than how he was being covered. As Corey Lewandowski, Trump's first of three campaign managers, told me, Trump was excited because he viewed me as a "big-time" network correspondent. That meant Trump's campaign was big-time now, too. "Up until we saw you, we had campaign embeds [traveling producers from TV networks and cable channels] and a London correspondent from NBC [Katy Tur]," Lewandowski told me. "With you there that meant we were being taken seriously." "Fantastic" was also part of Trump's crude method of seduction. He was ladling attention on me in front of other reporters en route—he hoped—to fawning coverage (we would revisit this tactic before he left Birch Run).

"I watched you . . ."

"I watched." How I regret not paying more attention to "I watched," the sine qua non of Trumpian interpretation. Trump watches an inordinate amount of television, or as former White House lawyer Ty Cobb told me "a shitload of television." From Cobb's charitable point of view, that makes Trump "a great multitasker." The first year of his presidency would be defined by the multiple tasks he set in motion and the many mistakes he committed because he watched a shitload of television. What he sees and what he watches—about world events and him—can drive policy.

The first Syria missile strike is a classic example. The images horrified Trump. He wanted to rapidly flip the chemical weapons script inherited from President Obama. He launched Tomahawk missiles and for his first year that became a plot point illustrative of his decisive leadership—courage in a cocoon of cable coverage. His worldview is not only shaped by TV; his judgment of and reaction to events—true or false—are reinforced almost entirely by TV. Trump gathers information in other ways, of course, but TV is Trump and Trump is TV. He is not as docile or as shuttered as Chance the Gardener (who becomes Chauncey Gardiner as the story continues) from the 1970 Jerzy Kosinski novel and 1979 Oscar-winning movie *Being There,* but there are similarities. Chance has his own simple orientation to the world and it has never evolved. Chance absorbs life largely through his relentless attention to the tube and has an oddly nimble way of cataloging its collapsed time, pulverized nuances and parade of banalities. Compared with Chauncey, Trump is louder, larger and worldly. And Trump is less kind, humble and courtly. But in terms of their inner truth and how the world is presented to them—and how it mesmerizes them—the TV comparisons are valid and unnerving. Throughout, simple sentences from Chauncey, non sequiturs in most contexts, are invested with a shattering sense of common wisdom and clarity. At the end of the movie, Chauncey is whispered as a potential president and those taken in by his imagined brilliance allow themselves even to believe he can walk on water. See what I mean?

During the transition, the way to win consideration for a top Trump administration job was to have been on television—preferably Fox News. Trump hired K. T. McFarland as his deputy national security advisor on that basis (McFarland was so ill-suited for the job that those asked to replace fired National Security Advisor Michael Flynn refused to take the post if McFarland remained deputy). The same was true of Monica Crowley, who was to be Trump's frontline advisor on communications strategy at the National Security Council before she had to withdraw amid a plagiarism scandal. During the transition, Trump considered former San Francisco first lady and Fox News' *The Five* personality Kimberly Guilfoyle as press secretary—he was talked out of it by incoming Chief of Staff Reince Priebus. Priebus demanded Trump hire Sean Spicer, his former spokesman at the Republican National Committee, so Priebus could have an ally at the podium.

Spicer's briefings became a tragicomic midday TV phenomenon, drawing car-chase-quality cable ratings and the rapt attention of the 45th president. Trump often built his schedule around watching Spicer's briefings—frequently sending notes of clarification or instructions to end the Q&A sessions. TV animates Trump's consciousness; he drifts to sleep with it on, and it rouses him to mental action before dawn. Trump's reaction to TV frequently darkened his mood early in his first year, prompting aides to hand-deliver laudatory press coverage, some of it of dubious or even fabricated origins, just to improve his outlook. TV is an important window into the world as he sees and responds to it . . . not as it may actually be.

Back to Birch Run and Trump to me:

" . . . with President Obama two weeks ago."

That is Trump registering his awareness of my celebrated showdown with Obama over the Iran nuclear deal. It was also the first time I should have noticed Trump has no sense of time. Trump either lives in the moment or in his memory. Both constitute his reality and almost nothing can shake Trump from his reaction in the moment or how his memory recalls events. What Trump said happened with Obama "two weeks" ago had actually occurred a month earlier. For Trump such precision is useless. What matters is he remembered it his way.

This was another phenomenon reporters had a hard time with. Rising politicians like to prove their smarts by dazzling reporters with their ability to synthesize facts, history and policy. The best ones later add self-deprecating humor, smoothing out their smarts with synthetic humility. Trump made no such effort and that made reporters wonder if he was serious. For months, reporters kept trying to understand how Trump could be so wrong about dates, times, facts and history and get away with it. He brought this mania to the White House—even though precision is among the most important presidential commodities and sources of power.

Trump had and has a roundabout sense of things—an indifference bordering on hostility to pesky facts. What Trump (and as I learned many of his supporters) cared about was the *larger* truth—the essence of things. The simpler the better. Little did I know at that moment how foolhardy my pursuit of precision would be when it came to Trumpian hyperbole. He never cared if I corrected him or if dozens of other journalists corrected him. Our obsession with accuracy was his proof of reflexive bias. We were addicted to proving him wrong while he was compelled to tell voters rude truths the political class and its media allies were unwilling or afraid to speak. It was all right there in front of me. But I was too blind to see. Trump created an illusion of imperviousness—the sense that he-who-could-not-be-touched in the heat of the campaign would not be bowed by the pressures of the presidency. That hunch—like all Trump hunches born of gut instinct, arrogance, limited knowledge and experience—has been severely tested each week of his presidency.

What Trump saw about me and Obama, though, did matter. At a July 15, 2015, press conference, I asked a clearly ebullient Obama how he was content with the Iran deal when four American hostages still languished in Iranian captivity—and in light of the 11th-hour concessions Obama made to Tehran on ballistic missile and conventional weapons while Iran conceded nothing on the hostages. Obama berated me, accusing me of implying he did not care about the hostages—knowing full well I implied no such thing.

Obama had downplayed the hostages in the negotiations and knew they were the most glaring weakness of his rapprochement with Iran. He rarely mentioned the hostages in the final months of the negotiations. Standing in the East Room empty-handed, as far as the hostages were concerned, Obama took special umbrage at my description of the four—three held, as I said, on trumped-up charges while the fourth's whereabouts were unknown—as representing the "conscience of this nation, the strength of this nation unaccounted for." I covered Obama's campaign and interviewed him many times. We clashed, as politicians and reporters do, but it was never personal. And it wasn't in this case. But Obama lit into me as he never had before.

"I got to give you credit, Major, for how you craft those questions. The notion that I am content, as I celebrate, with American citizens languishing in Iranian jails . . ." Obama looked down and paused for five seconds. I was in the front row, just a few feet from the podium and Obama's withering glare. I knew the hammer was about to fall. I returned Obama's glare impassively and told myself "Don't twitch. Don't move a muscle. Don't smile. Don't frown. Don't look away." The

East Room felt as if it were tightening around me, the lights closer and brighter, the sound of Obama's voice rising in my ears. "Major. That's nonsense. And you should know better. I've met with the families of some of those folks. Nobody is 'content.'"

The president did what every politician does when a question exposes an uncomfortable truth or pokes at a vulnerability—he erected a straw man. Straw men come in handy because they are easy to build and easy to knock down, usually with a flick of the rhetorical wrist. The creation and destruction of a straw man allows a politician to create a show, a distraction from the nagging truth or open wound. A well-crafted question can do both: reveal a nagging truth that becomes an open wound. When this happens, even the best politician can lose his or her temper and the straw man's destruction is no longer a brief diversion but a psychological looking glass.

Rare was the moment Obama flashed anger. His anger at me over the hostages generated as much attention and debate as any question asked during his presidency—an estimated 42 million tweets and a week of scrutiny (not all of it favorable) by media critics and reporters. Moments after the press conference, I appeared on the CBS News digital network CBSN and was asked what it felt like to be "spanked" by Obama.

> My question did not suggest he was content with the captivity of those four Americans. My question was about the contentment or the satisfaction or the realization that it was necessary within the context of this deal to leave them unaccounted for. That was the essence of the question. Clearly, it struck a nerve. That was my intention, because everyone who works for the president and the families of those four Americans say he's not content and they will work overtime to win their eventual release. That does not appear to me to be a sideline issue in the whole context of this conversation about this Iran nuclear deal. Was it provocative? Yes. Was it intended to be as such? Absolutely.

The next day, my former CBS colleague Charlie Rose asked me during an appearance on CBS This Morning if I wished I had phrased the question differently.

My answer: "No."

The question was designed not only to contrast Obama's unwilling-ness to push for the hostages' release in the final hours of the nuclear deal talks (even as Iran fought for and won new concessions) but also to make the hostages a central issue in consideration of the deal itself. Despite withering criticism from Obama, I soon heard from emissaries for the hostages' families, and all relayed their gratitude. After he was released, *Washington Post* reporter Jason Rezaian and I met for coffee in downtown D.C. and he told me the happiest news he received in prison was word from his mother that Obama blew up after I asked my question. It is also worth noting that, after our confrontation, Obama referred to the hostages—all four of them—by name in every subse-quent speech about the Iran deal. Obama had never done that before.

Iran was not ISIS but it did have American hostages and seemed to take them without fear of reprisal. The U.S. government legally for-bade families from negotiating ransom for the release of their loved ones. This aspect of Obama's approach enraged some families. They questioned the logic of blocking ransom negotiations while simultane-ously keeping a hostage's name out of the spotlight. Who benefitted? A cynic might reasonably conclude the White House did—by shield-ing itself from constant pressure to deal with the hostages (see Carter, Jimmy) and by placing the hostages' fate at the center of negotiations. If families can't negotiate and the White House deems it important to downplay their release, political risk is minimized.

The summer of ISIS. That was the summer of 2014. Kidnappings. Beheadings. YouTube terrorism. It was a new dimension of post-9/11 horror. It begat anger and powerlessness. What America suffered psy-chologically that wretched summer in part primed voters for Trump's declaration that the time had come to "bomb the shit" out of the Islamic State. "Bomb the shit out of them" sounded better than having another one of ours beheaded. ISIS bred fear and represented what seemed like a new nightmare. Trump had an answer. Bomb. Kill. Win. When Trump spoke of generals he admired he named only two: George Patton and Douglas MacArthur—both famous for daring, vanity, a win-at-any-cost ethos, contempt for political subtlety and hostility to multilateral diplomatic niceties. For Trump supporters, Bomb-the-shit + Patton + MacArthur equaled a return to American muscularity, confidence, brashness and dominance. When mixed with "America First," it was for Trump supporters a call to reason.

And Trump knew it. How I wish I could have figured that out back then.

My clash with Obama over the Iran deal, more than anything else, brought me to Trump's attention. The contrast between Trump's demeanor, language, intellectual approach to campaigning and life could not have been more different from Obama's. It was this jarring difference that also kept me off balance. I had spent 14 months covering Obama in 2007–2008 and nearly six years covering his presidency. That may have been about the worst preparation for Trump imaginable.

"He was not thrilled. I'm sure I'll be more thrilled."

This was Trump contrasting himself to Obama and trying to put me on the spot. Obama wasn't thrilled because my question was right. That is what Trump was telling me. He was also saying he was "sure" he would be "more thrilled" because in Trump's mind he is always right and reporters, even good ones, are always wrong or at least less correct than him. Trump conveys a sturdy superiority that psychologists fret is excessive narcissism. His confidence in public rarely wavers, and he is not prone to self-reflection or self-doubt. It is a form of belligerence and he loves to taunt those who consider his ego misplaced.

Based on my own experience, I have come to believe that with Trump every encounter is about demonstrating power and balancing power as the dynamic shifts—reclaiming it if Trump has momentarily lost some or unexpectedly parceling out a small sum as a kingly gift to a pauper.

Later in the campaign, I saw this phenomenon up close. On January 11, 2016, Trump criticized me on Twitter—the one and only time that has occurred. "@MajorCBS Major Garrett of @CBSNews covers me very inaccurately. Total agenda, bad reporter!" By Trump's standards, it was pretty mild. But it jostled my Twitter feed just the same. I ignored the flamethrowers and let the moment pass. Trump and I saw each other several days later at the GOP debate in North Charleston, South Carolina. Trump worked the line of reporters in the post-debate spin room. Let me describe how differently Trump handled the spin room. Most candidates, if they come to the spin room at all, walk in and are surrounded by reporters on all sides. If the candidate doesn't go to the spin room, his or her campaign dispatches surrogates who are trailed by an aide holding a sign aloft with that campaign's logo and the surrogate's name. It's all a sweaty, noisy and ill-mannered scrum and it's where print reporters get their best post-debate quotes. On the edges of the spin room, TV networks have their stages and interview spaces. Front-runners typically head for those locations.

Trump almost never did any of this. At most debates he entered the spin room down a separate aisle made for him with space for his family and traveling aides. Metal rails that looked like bike racks would separate reporters from Trump. We would often lean over the bike racks and wave to Trump or his bodyguard, Keith Schiller; his head of advance, George Gigicos; or top communications advisor Hope Hicks. The waving could be comic. You simply had to get Trump on camera or record some post-debate sound. Stories without Trump after the debate were substandard. The bar was always the same. Land Trump. Get him on camera. Get a quote. Wave like a maniac. Shout your head off. Jump up and down. Get his attention and get the quote. Don't leave without it.

Typically, I didn't have to beg. Trump knew me. We had our "Fantastic" moment and he always made time for me—I had a big network audience and he liked the banter. Twice he had introduced me to Melania as the "CBS guy . . . my CBS guy." But this was our first encounter after Trump had bashed me on Twitter. He saw me and his face soured. He was going to walk right past me.

"You're not truthful," he said in a low whisper. "You're not truthful."

He slowed but was heading down the line of reporters.

"What are you talking about?" I asked.

Trump slowed.

"You are terrible. You are terrible."

He kept moving.

"That is not true," I said.

"You really are terrible," Trump said as he stopped to glare at me. I had him stopped. That was progress. Now I could engage.

"You don't mean that," I said.

"No. I do mean it," Trump volleyed.

"No," I said. "You don't mean that."

"I think you are very unprofessional. But go ahead."

We did the interview. Trump made news. Skirmish over. Lesson learned. Don't give Trump an inch. He's always testing you and the testing moved seamlessly from the campaign to the White House. If you back down, you can lose the moment and possibly more. If you stand up, you have a chance. But he knows he can set the terms. You need your wits and your guile about you. I saw a variation of this when Trump became president and held press conferences. I would watch him carefully at the podium and saw him wink at reporters and give them nods of approval. He did that a few times to me. This didn't mean he was going to call on you. Frequently, it meant the opposite. It just meant Trump knew you were trying to catch his eye, leaving him in even more control. In those press conferences, some reporters oddly hungered for his attention—as I did at the North Charleston debate— even though Trump had denounced them or their news organization. As personal and bombastic as Trump got, reporters kept coming back. Biased. Fake. Liar. Dishonest. Dumb. Lazy. Those jabs from Trump were just part of the job and only he knew how serious he was. Trump knew his relationship with the press was constant, that reporters were captive to his every move, tweet and action. He sought maximum leverage, yelling and bullying and then, with a wink, offering a momentary reprieve to keep the target of his aggression, as an individual and as part of the collective cadre of journalists, off guard.

Again, back to where it all began. Birch Run. There was one other encounter that should have taught me more than it did.

The rally had ended and the crowd (an eye-popping 2,000-plus . . . which also should have made a stronger impression on me than it did because it was a fund-raiser for two county GOP parties and tickets went for $25 apiece) began to file out. I jumped through the throng to position myself in the parking lot by the arena's rear exit in hopes of grabbing Trump for an interview.

Trump walked straight to me and the camera.

"How was that? Have a good time?" he asked.

I told him, "It's your show."

He smiled approvingly.

"Yeah, and we certainly had a good time. We had a great crowd. You saw that, right?'

I asked about the long haul ahead.

"Is this an endeavor you're going to carry all the way through to the convention and into November?"

"Absolutely"

"There's no hesitation?" I asked. "There's nothing that would drive you out of the race?"

"No hesitation whatsoever. Yeah, if my numbers drop down to nothing. But I think right now I'm leading by so much. The only thing that can really drive me out, if my numbers drop down. I'm a realist. But I don't see that happening. I think the response, you see the response tonight: standing ovations all the time, sold-out crowd, turned away hundreds and hundreds of people. But, if the numbers went down, it would be different. But I don't see them going down."

I asked about new polls that showed after the first GOP debate in Cleveland some voters said they were less comfortable with Trump than before.

"Do you think you turned any people off?"

"I don't think so. I think that actually if you look at Fox and you look at what happened I think that people probably agreed that not only did I win but I won by a large margin. Look at all of the polls. If you look at Drudge, if you look at *Time* magazine, all of the polls have me winning by significant numbers. But those are not the important numbers; the important numbers are the ones that happened after the debate and you see Iowa, you see New Hampshire, you see South Carolina."

I interjected. "But that's what I was just asking about—in all those states—voters were less comfortable with you after the debate," I said, citing polling that backed up that assertion.

"Well, I haven't seen that, my numbers went up," Trump said, holding tightly to affirming some facts while discounting others.

I quoted a Suffolk poll and another in New Hampshire.

"Well, I haven't seen that. My numbers went up."

He then furrowed his brow and took a slight step toward me to close the distance.

"Excuse me, did I win?"

"That's for you to decide," I said.

"Excuse me, if you don't say yes then you're not an honest reporter. Good-bye."

Trump stalked away and climbed into a waiting black SUV.

I stood as the vehicle idled, state troopers astride motorcycles waiting to escort Trump to the airport, and was struck how, even at this embryonic stage of his campaign, Trump had the beginnings of what looked like a presidential motorcade.

Trump motioned to have his driver roll down the window.

He beckoned me to draw closer.

"You see what I just did there, right? You saw that. Call me. We'll have lunch. Call me in New York. We'll get together."

What Trump wanted me to notice was that he drew close, asked his bottom-line question, didn't get the answer he wanted and walked away. That's part of his negotiating style. So was the "call me" line. With Trump the negotiation and seduction, always accompanied by the threat of an angry conflagration, is rarely ever over—especially with a reporter.

He drove off with entourage in tow.

We never had lunch in New York.

Or anywhere else.

ONE

Does Trump Matter?

The first year of the Trump presidency ended as it had begun: a cauldron of confusion, legislative disarray, international disbelief, Democratic rage and Republican bewilderment—all simmering over the coals of racism. That's one perspective. Every part of it objectively accurate. Another is Trump's first year ended with a smashing legislative victory that lowered individual and corporate tax rates and simplified the tax code for the first time since 1986. That capped a year of accelerating economic growth, a hefty populating of the federal bench with judicial conservatives, a new European conversation edging toward Trumpian precepts on immigration and military burden-sharing and revamped federal regulations as unabashedly pro-business as any administration since Ronald Reagan.

These vastly different interpretations of Trump's first year, both accurate, illustrate the conundrum that is Trump and his confounding presidency. It accomplished as it appalled. It was chaotic, confusing and, despite itself, historically competent. Much of the hand-wringing that was visited upon Trump's first year was, justifiably, focused upon this unique new president's effect on American institutions—the White

House, Congress, the courts, the free press, even the resilience of America's identity—and what shape they would find themselves in at the end, however long it might be, of Trump's reign.

Trump matters more than we can currently comprehend. His very presidency still startles because it's real, and the reality TV part is both a joke and a truism. Historians have long debated how much the president reflects the country or the country comes to reflect the president. Trump is the first president never to have held public office or to have led armies to victory in battle. Already this tells us something about a new American idea of what makes a president. Personally, Trump disdained politics and avoided active duty military service. He is a hero and an antihero at the same time. His long history of self-promotion and fascination with tabloid culture fits more seamlessly than we might want to admit into our current selfie and social media mind-set and mania—a place where relentless self-branding can be a path to notoriety, infamy, riches and at times all three.

From the moment of his election, Trump was a force for and a crucible of division . . . and devotion. His presidency, quite apart from its record, is already original. No one has been more publicly tempestuous, dare we say stormy, with the words and mannerisms of the presidency. Trump is recklessly authentic—a living, breathing, orangish and hairsprayed Rorschach test of what early-21st-century America wants and expects from politics and the presidency. Importantly, Trump is also a barometer of how much we as a nation are prepared for this highly personalized and vocalized presidency to permeate—through the minor miracle of digital technology—every moment of our waking lives. Eleven days into Trump's presidency, one of the great satirists of our times, Jon Stewart, read aloud on *The Late Show with Stephen Colbert* a mock executive order: 'I, Donald J. Trump, do declare by executive order that I, Donald J. Trump, am exhausting.' It has been 11 days, Stephen," Stewart said to the host. "Eleven fucking days. Eleven! The presidency is supposed to age the president, not the public. We have never faced this before. Purposeful, vindictive chaos." Part of Trump's originalism exists within that humor, that truth and that collective (and possibly exaggerated) anxiety.

And yet on Inauguration Day, my CBS colleague Dean Reynolds was in Kenosha, Wisconsin, one of the crucial states in Trump's electoral map. He was surveying voter attitudes and expectations at Frank's Diner. "I think you got a country that's fed up with the establishment and they wanted change and they didn't want a politician," said Jim Roberts, a Kenosha city worker. Glen Woods, sitting at the diner's counter, summed up the Trump mystique. "He's a pit bull. He swam upstream against both parties. I've never seen that before." Reynolds asked if Woods considered Trump a disruptive force. "Oh, absolutely. Tear 90 percent of it down. He was the only candidate who seemed to really hammer in that you can't tell people to go get a job if there aren't any."

All presidencies arrive with lofty expectations. Historic ones leave behind big ideas and big changes. What kind of presidency is Trump's? What kind of president is he?

Legislatively, Trump's first year was both active and inert. He failed with the legislative goal that started his presidency—repealing and replacing the Affordable Care Act—and succeeded on his biggest legislative push, to reduce corporate and individual tax rates and simplify the federal tax code for the first time since 1986. He also nominated and saw confirmed a Supreme Court Justice, nominated another Supreme Court Justice in 2018, peppered the federal judiciary with constitutional originalists and allied with the GOP-led Congress to dismantle many Obama-era regulations.

In between this activism lay months of headline-grabbing nothingness—another novelty. Here is a short list of campaign promises that became vaporous memories: paid family leave; infrastructure; criminal justice reform; combatting the opioid crisis; price controls on prescription drugs. Even in the second year, these promises received token attention or none at all. What Trump did achieve came by virtue of two tools: executive orders (which he had scorned Obama for) and simple majority bludgeoning in the Senate. If legislation required compromise or a modicum of cleverness, it often eluded Trump and the Republican-led Congress (a problem that persisted in 2018). Throughout the first year, Trump would rage about the glacial pace of Washington, about how little Republicans accomplished on his behalf and how much of his agenda was stalled. He papered over these anxieties with cartoonish tweets—also a new presidential coping mechanism.

This reminded me of an interview I did with Trump in Myrtle Beach, South Carolina, a few days before the primary. The main topic was Trump's unexpected spat with Pope Francis over immigration. But I sensed Trump was heading for a big victory in South Carolina and from there had a bead on the GOP nomination. I wanted to talk about the massive crowds that came to see Trump at almost every step along the way. Their expectations for Trump appeared limitless. I knew well the frustrations of past presidents I had covered and how the office could consume them and how frustrations with the slow pace of change could make the most powerful person on the planet feel hemmed in, stuck and always, always, always underappreciated and overcriticized. I reminded Trump of Dwight Eisenhower's predicament as president, the very one President Harry Truman predicted with reporters from the Oval Office shortly before Eisenhower's inauguration: "He'll sit right here, and he'll say 'do this, do that'! And nothing will happen. Poor Ike. It won't be a bit like the Army. He'll find it very frustrating."

I stood with Trump directly behind the blue drape separating him from the stage and the thousands of people who had been standing in line in the parking lot outside since before dawn.

"Do you ever worry if you're elected president you will let them down, that you can't accomplish all the things you're hoping to accomplish?"

Trump looked at me appreciatively. This was a question about being president. Now, he was really getting somewhere.

"I will be so disappointed in myself," he said. "We're going to have strong borders. We're going to have a great military that hopefully we won't have to use. We're going to take care of our vets. We're going to get rid of Obamacare, replace it with really good and much less expensive care. We're going to get rid of Common Core and have local education. There are so many things to do. Our country's so far behind. We owe 19 trillion dollars and we're going to start chopping away at that. No, I don't want to let these people down."

"Do you feel," I asked, "like that's a burden, though, if you become president?"

"It's a burden," Trump said. "It makes it tougher, but I don't want to let these people down. And you're right. People come here seven, eight hours in advance. I say, 'What are you doing?' They want to come. And I won't let them down."

At the end of his first year, Trump made some inroads on border security and military funding, but not nearly as much as he had promised or anticipated. He failed to repeal and replace the Affordable Care Act and by 2018 that goal had completely vanished from his agenda or long-term aspirations. Some states left Common Core but at their initiative and not at the behest of Trump's Education Department. As for the national debt, it rose on Trump's watch to more than $21 trillion. The gulf between reality and those Myrtle Beach promises—as well as others—haunted Trump and he became much like his predecessors, irritated with the inability to move matters along. Those frustrations were taken out on White House staff and cabinet secretaries, many of whom resigned or were fired. Trump found the job, at times, bigger than he had imagined. Interestingly, that appeared more often with domestic matters than with his initial encounters with foreign leaders.

During Trump's first year, world leaders came calling in droves. They were as startled as half of America. They quickly realized how nationalistic Trump was and how much of his rhetoric was real. Washington was shifting and many leaders, at least rhetorically, began to adapt. As the year wore on, heads of state adopted some code words on trade, immigration and burden-sharing (spending more on military operations to take the pressure off the United States). Whether this reflects a genuine change or temporary tactical adjustment is unclear. What is clear is that Trump forced the country and the world to study what "America First" meant. Trump stepped away from multilateralism. He stepped toward tariffs. He resurrected the word "reciprocal" to describe new trade arrangements. In Europe and Asia, these words crept into the conversation. The Trump effect on language was real.

Politically, Trump inspired a political backlash that imperiled Republican majorities in the House and Senate. In numerous elections in 2017 turnout among Democrats exceeded projections while Republican turnout met historical projections or fell short. Even in special elections Republicans won, the victory margins were startlingly small. Democrats won races in unexpected places like Alabama (U.S. Senate), Wisconsin (state legislature and supreme court), Oklahoma (legislature) and Virginia (governor and legislature). Republicans consider this midterm cycle (2018) the most daunting since the party lost the House and Senate in 2006. History shall be found in the action and reaction of this year's midterms—will pro-Trumpers rally to the president's cause? Will Democratic-leaning voters storm the polls in an act of post-2016 primal scream therapy?

Trump also transformed media coverage of the presidency. Trump arrived at the White House as a political novice, a billionaire (at least on paper), a full-blown media celebrity, global merchandiser, golf course developer, hospitality brand and real estate mogul. He checked more media boxes than any previous president and brought reporters from politics, business and entertainment crashing through the White House gates. New rituals developed. I began showing up to the daily White House briefing 15 minutes ahead of schedule to avoid having to swim through the daily standing-room-only crowd clogging the aisles of the James S. Brady Press Briefing Room. News organizations like mine had to set up elaborate, multilayered work shifts at the White House to keep pace with Trump's news-making activity. Some organizations went on hiring binges to meet the demands. White House reporters who used to take meetings and leave the White House to return to their newsrooms became like hermits, staying for hours in the cramped press room or in the briefing room theater seats—fearful that if they left they might miss something. The press room is small. This wasn't a workable option for everyone. Other reporters began camping out in neighboring coffee shops—staying close so they could run over for a just-announced press conference or statement or to seek comment on the latest blunderbuss Trump tweet.

White House coverage has for years been built around TV coverage. The pictures told the story. Well, it takes time to position cameras and connect all the cables that bring the sweep of the presidency to the world. Every White House I have covered built its schedule around this reality and gave the networks and cable channels ample time to prepare. This was not an act of supplication but a realization that properly staged shots and calm technicians produced higher quality pictures. The planning burden thus fell upon the White Houses. Trump reversed that. He sprang events on journalists, knowing they would jump when he commanded and those who did not jump fast enough would be lost—and then better prepared to jump faster the next time.

Another new ritual developed: small hordes of reporters would perform an awkward walk-dance, their cell phones dangling from outstretched arms, chasing White House officials for the scrap of a quote or some nugget of news whenever they emerged from the West Wing for a North Lawn TV interview. (The North Lawn is where all TV stand-up locations, wired for light and sound, have been permanently constructed.) On Capitol Hill, still more hordes of walk-dancing reporters shuffled up and down the hallways, asking lawmakers about Trump's latest tweet or news development. Everything about Trump felt newsy—even when it wasn't. It was a feeding frenzy and I'm sure it felt that way to harried viewers and news-alert cell phone readers.

The Trump story did not deliver the same ratings gold as the campaign, but it was a hell of a journalistic ride just the same. News organizations had a 24/7 story with a charismatic central character, the grandeur of the White House, big issues, real change, politics, celebrity, scandal, soap opera personalities, firings, resignations, humiliations, vicious White House intrigues and an unpredictable parade of slipups, tweetstorms and meltdowns. To be in the middle of it day-in, day-out felt like what I imagine it would be to witness Cirque du Soleil on acid.

Trump also called into question what journalism is and should be. It became an emotional topic in the press room and across the country. What is fake news? Who is dishonest? Does the media hate Trump? Was coverage skeptical or loathing? Many Trump supporters noticed how aggressive reporters became about administration travel expenses, agency staffing, internal bureaucratic clashes, policy disagreements and wondered, not unreasonably, where that intensity was during Obama's or Bush's presidency. To Trump supporters, inquisitive reporters appeared to have a vendetta; their scrutiny seemed disproportionate. Opponents of Trump's found new vitality in the press and rediscovered a lost appreciation for the Fourth Estate. Big newspapers like *The New York Times, The Wall Street Journal* and *The Washington Post* vastly increased their staff size and erected investigative teams to bloodhound the administration—gaining subscribers and market share along the way. Trump pushed back with harsh denunciations. The free press fought back and after a year the forces remained implacably at odds. Trump and his supporters were certain they were getting a raw, biased deal. Journalists and those reassured by their hard work rediscovered the power and purpose of a free press. This clash carries the whiff of history.

An equally important question is whether Trump is changing the Republican Party. This matters greatly while the GOP controls Congress and possibly just as much if Republicans lose control of the House and/or Senate depending on the degree of loyalty to Trump after what might be a 2018 midterm deluge. Another important question: during his first year was Trump a force for domestic policy or did he hitch a ride on the ideological bandwagon Ronald Reagan built and that finally came of age when Trump was elected? On a series of issues, the answer is patently clear: Trump was a means to a predetermined Republican end. He was the final actor and that makes him historically important. Without his signature and advocacy nothing becomes law. In every other sense, though, in 2017 he was a bystander who rarely provided original legislative direction or durable political cover. His achievements reflected not so much his political acumen, guile or clout as the Reagan and Tea Party influences that sought to harness Trump after his unexpected triumph.

"We don't need a president to tell us what to do," Grover Norquist, head of Americans for Tax Reform, told me. "We have a House and a Senate and a Reagan agenda. The House and the Senate are 80 percent essence of Reagan. We know what to do. We need someone with enough working digits to sign the bills. Reagan brought the party with him. Trump didn't elect anybody. We had the House and Senate. After the election we had him. He did us the favor of winning the election. But he didn't bring anyone else in."

After the first year, Trump's touted accomplishments fit more closely Norquist's and Reagan's worldviews than Trump's own. Trump rattled a lot of cages on immigration but succeeded mostly in enforcing existing law. On trade, he imposed a few tariffs but never labeled China a currency manipulator and made scant headway in the renegotiation of the North American Free Trade Agreement (NAFTA) with Canada and Mexico—both conspicuous campaign promises. In fact, the U.S. trade deficit increased by nearly 13 percent in 2017 to $568 billion, a nine-year high (the U.S. trade deficit with China also rose, to $375 billion, a record).

What Trump did reflected less of his will and more of the will and procedural muscle of his GOP majorities in Congress. His biggest achievement—reducing corporate and individual tax rates and simplifying the entire tax code by eliminating dozens of tax breaks and loopholes—was achieved through a legislative process known as reconciliation (which we will discuss at length later), through which only a simple majority was required in the Senate. The same was true of all 15 Congressional Review Act bills Trump signed to nullify federal regulations put in place during the last year of the Obama presidency. It was also true of Trump's confirmed federal judicial nominations. Simple Senate majorities all. Outside of incremental changes on veterans' policy, Trump forged not one significant bipartisan compromise in his first year. There is ample evidence to argue that Trump merely jabbed his presidential pen across a Reaganesque paint-by-numbers canvas.

"The things he actually touches and does, they are mainstream Reagan Republican," Norquist said. "Every place where he could turn the dials himself, he's done exactly the right thing. I didn't think he was going to win. But he did. He gets a lot of credit for getting across the finish line when McCain and Romney didn't. He's the quarterback. He gets touchdowns. Do you like him? He scores touchdowns. Reagan had a movie. Trump has still photos. He's like, 'I talk to people who like me.' His experiential learning moves him in the direction of a Reagan Republican on issues like regulation and taxes."

The persistent question of the Republican primaries—Is Trump a conservative?—turned out to be irrelevant. It didn't matter. Trump wanted bills to sign. Republicans had bills they wanted to pass and, for the first year of his presidency, the wherewithal to get a certain kind through Congress and to Trump's desk.

Even so, throughout the campaign and his first year, Trump forced Republicans to build a Jenga-like skyscraper of rationalizations that began at times to look like an act of link-armed mini psychosis. In private conversations with top White House officials, current and former, there are pained descriptions of bad or terrible ideas that were sidelined or stopped. These are regarded as accomplishments as important as the ones the White House trumpets. Trump would even complicate or knock off track good ideas or suddenly reverse himself and leave Republicans wondering how to respond and how to cope with the next unanticipated turn of events. It led to odd coping mechanisms.

"The ways these guys work around Trump," said one Republican who works regularly with the White House and congressional

Republican leaders, "it's like they are running a government behind his back."

Trump had therefore introduced new philosophical questions into GOP ranks. The first and possibly most important was—Do you serve Trump at all? Hundreds of experienced Beltway Republicans waiting for a new GOP administration simply refused to enter a Trump administration. During the campaign it was called #NeverTrump. Trump and his advisors tracked GOP hostility during the campaign. After Trump claimed the presidency, some in #NeverTrump were denied jobs. Most would not apply for or accept jobs—their #NeverTrump hostility bigger than a role in his government.

This may seem like a simple clash of philosophies and preferences, but it was much more—it deprived the incoming administration of skilled bureaucrats with institutional knowledge and some manner of political experience to help Trump. That Trump was largely unaware of and at times indifferent to this problem highlighted his inexperience as a president and political leader. Throughout 2017 and well into 2018 the Trump administration operated without a cadre of experienced cabinet undersecretaries, deputy secretaries and mid-level bureaucrats who could have increased functionality.

The vacuum was never filled but it did shift power toward career civil servants who may not have shared Trump's agenda, and that enabled lower levels of the federal bureaucracy—what Trump supporters sometimes darkly referred to as the "deep state"—to engage in something you might call slow-motion sabotage. Whose fault was it that Republicans refused to serve? Was it Trump's? Was it theirs? Was Trump so repulsive that the needs of the nation and the call of a president were insufficient? Again, this may seem like a nerdy, politico navel-gazing topic, but what Trump lacked in terms of capable bureaucratic advocates and functionaries contributed to some of his biggest problems—rivalries, leaks, inconsistent decision-making, poor communication and policy zigzags. For those who did join the White House or administration another question arose. What was the higher duty? Was it to resign and shout indignantly about Trump's short attention span, unpredictability and hot temper (among other tendencies) or was it to stay close, keep harmful things from happening and try to move productive ideas or policies forward? It was a question asked routinely and many different answers emerged. Some stayed. Some quit. Some stewed in an indecisive in-between. These questions, I think it is fair to say, have not been so routinely or so seriously considered since the final paranoid days of Richard Nixon.

With Trump the questions are cosmic in size. They persist. What matters? What doesn't? Will there be war? Who has the president's ear? Is the president under investigation? Did his campaign commit a crime? Is there a pro-Obama cabal undermining him? Who has power in the White House? Should a daughter wield so much power? Should that daughter's husband? Is Trump about the country or himself? Who has been fired? Who has resigned? Why so much turmoil? Is any of this normal? What are norms? Most fundamentally of all, does anything matter anymore?

These and other questions, but especially the last one, became grist for *Saturday Night Live* and, undoubtedly, will be debated for decades by presidential historians.

Stormy Daniels. Robert Mueller. Michael Cohen. Karen McDougal. *National Enquirer*. Three national security advisors. Two secretaries of state. Two chiefs of staff. Two national economic advisors. Two Home-land Security secretaries. Hundreds of senior staff vacancies. Dozens of unfilled ambassadorships. White House advisors hawking Trump products on television. Sloppy security clearance procedures. Trump berating the FBI and intelligence agencies. Trump branding commin-gled with White House business. The head of the Centers for Disease Control and Prevention owning and selling tobacco stocks. Cabinet secretaries hiding public schedules and lying about flying corporate jets and government helicopters. Lobbyists in government deregulat-ing the industries they used to represent. A son-in-law who is also a se-nior White House advisor repeatedly submitting incomplete financial disclosure forms while being given access to classified information—then temporarily losing this top-secret clearance even as he continued to lead Middle East peace efforts.

In mid-September 2017 Hillary Clinton released a book—a *débâcle à clef* on the 2016 campaign called *What Happened*. Where Trump is concerned, "It Happened" is more apt. It did. And it does.

It was a wild ride. It still is. "Wild Ride" is a metaphor Trump would probably love. It's catchy, memorable and based in truth. It works because that's what it feels like and is therefore true. What's odd and oddly fascinating about this Wild Ride is that it was constructed and is being constructed on the fly. There is no finished ride. The curves, dips, loops and everything else are being built as the national car of experience approaches. Some of the superstructure was built by Trump's decisions—many of them improvised and therefore with more jarring twists and turns. Other sections were built by the GOP Congress as it conformed its blueprints with Trump's politics, where possible, and took the country on a policy ride of its design—with many downward zags on health care and a celebratory splash landing in tax reform as examples. Still other parts of the ride were built by outside subcontractors—such as the conservative Federalist Society's hand in the Neil Gorsuch nomination to the Supreme Court and other federal judicial nominations. Still other parts of the ride, namely regulatory reform, were handed off to conservative think tanks, pro-business groups and lobbyists, another form of Wild Ride outsourcing. Thrills, chills, screams and blackouts came unexpectedly and continue to this day. Critics of the president—many on the outside who feel powerless and some on the inside who are trying to exert calming control—sometimes use the same disparaging roller-coaster rhetoric: off the rails, out of control, unhinged, reckless and careening. Collectively, the national stomach churns—tens of million in anticipation and tens of millions in dread.

Back to the cosmic questions.

What is a lie? What is a white lie? How many of either can a president tell? What can our institutions withstand? Is democracy dead or being reinvigorated? Who is an enemy of the American people? What is the higher political calling—criticizing a president you know will ignore you or standing nearby, protecting the presidency and the nation from the worst of Trump's erratic whims? Is Trump killing philosophy or reviving it? Ask yourself, has the question of American democracy ever felt more urgent? Has its essence ever felt more contested? Have the institutions bequeathed to us from, as the saying goes, landed-slave-holding-white-men ever felt more relevant and protective? Have you ever felt more energized—positively or negatively—about the idea and future of the American republic?

These questions stalked almost every week of Trump's first year and they were certainly there, potent as ever, as his administration sped erratically into its second year. That didn't seem possible. So many things during Trump's first year didn't seem possible. After one year, politics under Trump felt primal—as if American destiny was at some unimagined crossroads, a demographic and conceptual place of past, present and future that Trump perfectly and abhorrently personified. We were there. And we are here. It is very real.

Trump personalized the presidency in ways utterly consistent with his novice past but utterly inconsistent with the office to which he was elected. On November 3, 2017, Fox aired an interview with Trump in which he explained why he didn't care about filling senior-level State Department vacancies. "The one that matters is me," Trump said. "I'm the only one that matters because when it comes to it, that's what the policy is going to be. You've seen that, you've seen it strongly."

Trump truly believes this. It is this stubborn perspective that raises fundamental questions about his knowledge of, reverence for and interest in the office and the powers it wields.

Trump has been known to derail policy discussions formed over weeks and moved through key agencies—humiliating senior White House staff or cabinet officials in the process. Sometimes he would decide an issue abruptly, skipping over that same policy process, because he grew bored or impatient. Both tendencies left senior White House advisors and cabinet officials wondering how to approach their core mission, uncertain how to present or move options through a rational process. Trump's approach was dismissive of almost everyone around him and the very jobs they did in service of his agenda and his government. Fundamentally, Trump believed most government jobs were useless and the process to create a solution too cumbersome and slow. When Trump did succeed it was because these tendencies were harnessed, either by him or by a cell of inside and outside advisors (the roster of which shifted), and he maintained focus and a modicum of discipline.

Importantly, Trump also feared being manipulated, even by those who worked for and with him. Frequently, Trump would, at the last minute, seek out an advisor who disagreed with a decision memo presented to him, just to test whether he was being set up or boxed in. If he couldn't find anyone, Trump would argue against the consensus position himself. At such times, he was known to describe himself as the "minority voice." The lack of bureaucratic Republican superstructure around Trump exacerbated these shortcomings. Trump's inability and unwillingness to disperse trust and have faith in his own policy-making process aggravated rivalries within the White House. Trump's hunger, even at the last minute, for opposing points of view could and sometimes did empower advisors with an alternate agenda—even advisors unfamiliar with the policy, law or politics—to torpedo a carefully constructed, multiagency policy. Not surprisingly, this at times triggered an odd competition of destruction that bred hostility and fueled nasty press leaks. This slowed down productivity and, oddly, made the president more isolated and less effective. The point here is not that a well-coordinated process always produces the best result. Plenty of seamlessly constructed and politically buffed government initiatives have failed. The point is, Trump's peculiar style, and the weak bureaucratic team around him, at times undercut his agenda and exasperated the few competent people around him who were trying to do his bidding.

The wreckage of senior advisors after Trump's first year was as historic as it was worrisome. By the middle of Trump's second year, his National Security Council was a shell, with senior directors and deputies fleeing marquee jobs to be rid of Trump's unpredictability and volatility. His new National Economic Council chief, Larry Kudlow, was, according to White House sources, overmatched by the pace of the job and jarred by the fractious internal economic debates, specifically over trade policy. Kudlow suffered a mild heart attack two months after taking the job. About this time, the top White House nuclear arms negotiator resigned, undercutting manpower needed for coming talks with North Korea. In the spring of 2018, Trump's top Homeland Security advisor, Tom Bossert, fled after being bureaucratically neutered by the arrival of new National Security Advisor John Bolton—the one whose arrival had sent so many NSC advisors fleeing.

Make no mistake, Trump's agenda is imperiled by this warped approach. In the first year, decisions on cybersecurity, trade, infrastructure, prescription drug prices, opioid intervention and criminal justice reform, to name just a few, were stalled or stymied by Trump's inability to trust his team, respect a policy process and give administration stakeholders space to do their work. These tendencies also complicated efforts to repeal and replace Obamacare and achieve tax cuts—the latter prevailed because the political imperative was so great; the former failed because it wasn't.

Trump's impatience undermined focus as well. Trump wanted issues solved immediately. He has so far done very little to study the federal bureaucracy and even less to understand what it takes to move ideas through Congress. Assignments therefore trickled down to ad hoc White House teams—often populated by nongovernment amateurs—working on Trump's pet projects.

Early in 2017, Jared Kushner's policy team tried to jump-start a push for criminal justice reform. Many policies fall under this umbrella term, including those reducing federal prison populations, changing federal sentences for drug crimes, addressing issues of police brutality and training, restoring felon voting rights and improving juvenile crime rehabilitation. These are long-simmering, multilayered and politically fraught issues. Kushner announced to the team assembled in the White House—from relevant departments, agencies and Congress—that the goal was to have Congress complete action within six weeks. Insane does not begin to describe the time line. The few experienced legislative hands in the room rolled their eyes in disbelief. The Office of Legislative Affairs became known as the depressing dead zone where great Trump ideas went to die. In fact, it was one of the few shops with political and legislative guts and guile—the place where ideas survived but nutty time lines died.

When things slowed down, Trump did not sharpen his focus but tended to lose interest. The day-to-day chores of governing have not yet come to him nor did he appear to be in search of them. Impatience, lack of curiosity and mistrust mixed toxically. On occasion, they led to temper tantrums and impolitic outbursts that became global spectacles—as when Trump made headlines by referring, during a contentious bipartisan negotiation on immigration policy, to Haiti, El Salvador and parts of Africa as "shithole countries."

The dichotomy between cannot-be-possible and it-just-happened defined Trump's first year. The shutdown was the last of many tornados. The difficulty in writing a book about what *actually happened* during Trump's first year is you write in a frenzied state of dread. What the

@#%*& is next? Is what I'm writing what really matters? I have asked that question relentlessly for the past year. The pages to follow represent my best retelling of the things that occurred that, years from now, will be regarded as pillars of Trump's legacy. Legacies can be grand or hideous. Such judgments I leave for the passage of time.

On policy, Trump in one year did many things to transform the nation. I will list some of them here, for they form the essence of this book's purpose.

1. Trump is the most aggressive deregulatory president since Ronald Reagan—changing the federal government's relationship to the private sector more fundamentally than even Reagan did. Reagan had the intent, but not the appointees; the ideological commitment but little backing in Congress. Trump had none of the ideology, beyond a businessman's hatred of being bothered, but he had the appointees (the most conservative in American history) and a compliant Republican-led Congress. From direct erasure of late-term Obama regulations to the wholesale overhaul of the Federal Communications Commission, National Labor Relations Board, Consumer Financial Protection Bureau, Food and Drug Administration and Environmental Protection Agency, Trump has not so much drained the swamp as stocked it with pro-business piranha. And they are scissoring the Federal Register—the repository of all regulatory language—with frenzied free-market zeal. Trump credits this approach with positive economic growth indicators during his first year and is probably right. He also argues that this inflicts no harm on consumer health or safety standards. He is probably wrong. Such is the tradeoff of ideology and power, however inexpertly managed.

2. Trump oversaw the rewriting of the U.S. tax code with the biggest permanent reduction in corporate tax rates in history. He cut individual rates but made the changes temporary—not to punish families but to weaponize the tax debate for the remainder of his presidency. Within days of passage even Vermont Sen. Bernie Sanders, the voice of *progressive* populism, was saying that the individual rate cuts had to be made to last. The tax cuts will either usher in an era of growth unseen since the go-go late 1990s

or starve the federal government of hundreds of billions on the eve of Baby Boomer entitlement repayments. The latter would likely trigger an intergenerational political clash and, possibly, a global debt panic. Either way—Trump's tax cut must be regarded as transformative. Interestingly, as the tax cuts took hold in 2018, one of the very few threats posed to upward economic growth was Trump's decision to threaten or impose tariffs on China, Europe, Canada and Mexico. This debate simmered inside the White House throughout 2017 but burst on the scene in the spring of 2018. If Trump presses ahead with tariffs and a trade war of any duration ensues, he will be transformational on this score as well.

3. In his first year, Trump put one justice on the Supreme Court and 12 on the federal appeals bench. No president before Trump nominated a Supreme Court justice in his first two weeks in office. Trump did. As you will learn, Trump toyed with the idea of nominating Neil Gorsuch *before* he was inaugurated. The 12 circuit judges nominated and confirmed represent the largest first-year addition to the appellate bench in presidential history. This story, as you will learn, is about 30 years of studious and politically astute work by a man you may have never heard of. The story is also about one of the most audacious gambles in American political history and the gambler that Trump often derides in private as weak and "not much of a leader." This is an early down payment on Trump's desire to remake the entire federal judiciary in the image of Antonin Scalia, the justice whose death gave Trump a political opening he shrewdly exploited on his way to the GOP nomination. It also gave him an issue—the future of the Supreme Court—that strapped even the flightiest of Republicans to the rollicking Trump Train. In June 2018, Justice Anthony Kennedy's retirement allowed Trump to add to his Supreme Court legacy.

4. Trump has changed the course of U.S. interaction with North Korea and China. For much of the first year, Trump's rhetoric threatened war—from the well of the United Nations and the dais of the South Korean National Assembly. By mid-2018, Trump had turned from warrior to summit host, producing by far the most TV-savvy summit in the history of world diplomacy. Trump defanged his

own rhetoric about North Korea—"depraved" and "wicked"—and substituted praise of Kim Jong-un the likes of which had never been uttered by an American president. Trump threatened war as no president ever had; then he made summit peace in a neck-snapping reversal for him and American diplomacy. No one can predict the success or failure of this high-risk gambit. All we know is when Trump returned to the White House from the Singapore summit he declared the nuclear standoff with North Korea "solved." This despite precious few advancements in American or international inspection of North Korea's nuclear weapons facilities. When I conducted interviews for this book, former House Speaker and frequent Trump advisor Newt Gingrich gave me this piece of advice: "Write the North Korea part last."

Until Trump, U.S. policy had been to avoid war at all costs—even enduring the deaths of U.S. sailors, other military personnel and civilians through decades of North Korean provocations. Trump's bellicosity appears to have changed China's calculus. Beijing began for the first time applying real economic pressure and supporting UN Security Council sanctions. It also shut off access to the Bank of China and limited coal sales—all unprecedented. On New Year's Day 2018, Kim Jong-un admitted that the sanctions were taking a toll—a painful and rare public concession. North Korea and South Korea began talks about cooperation and summitry at the Winter Olympics. On this issue, Trump moved the needle by increasing anxiety in Asia and the Pacific that war might be days away—or, if it was started by North Korea, mere moments away. In the fall of 2017 Hawaii reengaged its civil defense warning system to alert islanders about a potential North Korean missile launch. One week before the end of Trump's first year, that system was accidentally activated and for 40 stomach-churning minutes Hawaii wondered if nuclear war had come to paradise. The edginess was real, even though the warning was not. North Korea's reckless actions ratcheted up tensions. But Trump's own rhetoric intensified the sense of confrontation—a calculated maneuver to tell Kim he was different, belligerent and militarily unpredictable. With that tension as a backdrop, Trump conducted the kind of high-stakes, high-risk, face-to-face diplomacy with Kim that by itself labels Trump transformative. There is no undoing that moment or its portents. Trump bet on Kim's willingness to abandon two generations of repression and militarism. It was a jaw-dropping gamble, one Trump intensified by giving up at the summit joint U.S.–South Korea military exercises, which Trump, using a favorite North Korean adjective, described as "provocative." The outcome of Trump's extraordinary approach has quieted the sense of impending war but not resolved the underlying strategic threat. Oddly, war is less likely but peace more uneasy. Trump's approach, by turns caustic and cuddly, made North Korea the foreign policy story of 2017 and 2018.

5. Trump changed the American image on immigration. That's an unmistakable fact. Much of the 2018 election cycle will turn on what the country thought of that transformation, intensified as a topic of domestic and global debate by the family separation imbroglio of mid-June 2018. Trump used every power in his possession to speed up deportations, intimidate sanctuary cities into submission and force Congress to rewrite immigration laws in accordance with nationalistic definitions of immigration outcomes (to bring in already-skilled, pro-American workers with economic means of their own). This is an approach not seen since the turn of the 20th century. In the intervening decades, immigration policy sought those hungriest to leave their home (either because of ambition or persecution) or be reunited with their families in America. Trump clashed with federal courts repeatedly on the travel ban and DACA (Deferred Action for Childhood Arrivals). After fumbling the first travel ban, the details of which you will learn later, Trump eventually prevailed. You may have missed it but the Supreme Court has upheld Trump's travel ban. Trump also secured initial funding, $1.6 billion, to build a wall on the U.S.-Mexico border and threatened a 2018 government shutdown if he didn't obtain another $2.2 billion. Yes, Trump said Mexico would pay for it. It didn't and won't. Trump supporters don't care. In the campaign Trump offered them the wall and gave them a laugh ("Who's gonna pay for it? MEXICO!!"). All they wanted was the wall. As you will learn,

plenty of politicians had promised a wall. Many were Democrats. But it was all, as Trump might say, phony. Whether you love or hate the idea, Trump made the wall real and changed immigration policies and politics.

6. Trump pounded ISIS into territorial submission. He didn't single-handedly defeat the Islamic State, and he certainly didn't erase its murderous credo, but he was president when it lost vast tracts of land and tactically important cities. ISIS was already being pounded by Obama. But not relentlessly and not ruthlessly. Trump added both Rs. And he teamed up with unsavory allies who could make life difficult for the United States later. The best and most repellent example is the Iranian Shia militias who helped Iraqi forces eject ISIS from Mosul. Those ground fighters kept the United States out of the cross fire—observing from close range but not "in the shit," as the infantry says. U.S. bombs helped, but the door-to-door fighting was aided openly and with long-term aims by Iran's Shia militias. They now remain in Mosul and other northern Iraqi cities, laying the foundation for their own political future and Iran's influence in Iraqi presidential and parliamentary elections. Trump's tolerance came at the expense of the Kurds, who fought first and most fiercely against ISIS. Trump now joins a long and appalling list of American presidents who have seduced and then jilted Kurdish fighters. As it turns out, some conventions appeal to Trump.

7. Trump is doing more with less and less with less. He oversaw a reduction in the federal workforce of 14,400. Obama added 68,000 workers in his first year and 188,000 in two terms. At the end of his first year in office Trump had failed to send to the Senate nominees for 256 high-level cabinet vacancies—by far the largest number in modern presidential history. More than a third of Trump's senior White House staff were either fired or had resigned in the first year—another record. Trump left some of the positions unfilled. At the end of his first year, Trump had given four separate West Wing jobs to one person. Johnny DeStefano, a former aide to House Speaker John Boehner, headed White House personnel, public liaison, intergovernmental affairs and political outreach. Even in a

caretaker role this is impossible. In the history of the modern presidency, no one has held more than two of these jobs. In Obama's White House Valerie Jarrett and David Axelrod split them. In Bush the younger's, Karl Rove had two. Trump doesn't want to nominate non-Trumpers. That was difficult at first. It was becoming seriously problematic near the end of his first year. Trump would rather leave a position vacant than take the chance of empowering a back-slider or back-stabber. Consequently, vacancies persist. Trump had a cabinet secretary run an entirely separate agency: Office of Management and Budget Director Mick Mulvaney was, at the end of year one, also in charge of the Consumer Financial Protection Bureau with an eye toward dismantling or significantly narrowing its regulatory scope. Trump's approach to federal output is subtraction by subtraction. Its silent radicalism is also unique.

The wonder is that the Trump presidency has, as you read this in the fall of 2018, not collapsed under its own disorganized weight. Trump has already left his mark on the presidency and the nation, doing so despite vicious White House feuding, obstruction by Senate Democrats, massive White House personnel firings and defections, cabinet agency scandals and shake-ups as well as near-daily distractions from the investigation into his campaign and Russian meddling in the 2016 election. All the while, Trump's gall was changing the institution of the presidency and American politics. That laid before the country a midterm question as profound as any asked since the tumult of the Vietnam War and civil rights struggles: Is *this* the country you want?

I am a student of the presidency and Congress. The greatest privilege and responsibility of my professional life has been to cover four presidents up close—five if you count my coverage of George Herbert Walker Bush from the vantage point of Congress. This is my fourth book on American politics—the first two coauthored with a former Democratic member of the House of Representatives and the third a much-heralded analysis of the historic 1994 midterm election and the so-called Gingrich Revolution. I have traveled the world and covered war and peace, prosperity and recession and everything in between. The worst day of my life was being with George W. Bush in Sarasota,

Florida, on September 11, 2001, and witnessing the sense of paralyzed disbelief that gripped our government in the immediate aftermath of that terrorist atrocity. I covered the launch of the war in Afghanistan as well as the run-up and execution of the second Iraq War (much of that coverage from the Pentagon). I have covered six presidential campaigns, five as a reporter and one as an editor, and three takeovers of Congress—1994, 2006 and 2010–2014.

I have a reputation for asking tough, respectful questions of each president I have covered. Aides to Clinton, Bush and Obama have berated me for doing precisely this. Trump aides leave the berating to him. To walk onto the White House grounds is to know anything can happen—a terror attack, a stock market crash, a mass shooting, a new cabinet scandal, a fence jumper or a law-defining Supreme Court ruling. The presidency projects power and grandeur. It can free the imprisoned. It can rescue those dying in a natural disaster. It can create and destroy.

Every presidential narrative is fixed, or "rigged" as Trump might say.

A presidency has a thousand layers of success and failure, insight and blindness. Even the worst presidencies achieve some success and the best have their blunders. It is sometimes hard to know what matters while it is happening and how it might change events in the future. Having covered four presidents, I can tell you this is always challenging work. In the age of Trump, it is like trying to light a candle standing behind a jet engine. The Twitter turbines are deafening, the braying from the White House podium and the clamor in response are enough to make you wince.

This is part of the legacy of the 2016 election and a presidency unlike any other in American history because it divides the national consciousness over simple things—not big ideas like slavery, tariffs, child labor or civil rights. Americans turn savagely on one another over the meaning of voter fraud and collusion, wiretapping and fake news, surveillance and security, obstructing justice and seeking loyalty. America first or America ashamed? In mid-June 2018, the Homeland Security secretary and two White House officials were chased out of Washington-area restaurants or asked to leave because their mere presence was offensive to patrons, assembled activists or the ownership. Is there a story behind this story? Is it possible to render a credible, balanced and nuanced assessment of the first year and a half of the Trump presidency amid its cyclonic spasms?

I will try.

Kellyanne Conway, Trump's last campaign manager and then White House counselor, once told me she was surrounded inside the White House by emotionally insecure men (many of them long gone by mid-2018). Sounds like the makings of a soap opera. We already feel the presidency has become a reality TV show. We know it has infiltrated our subconscious in unexpected and unwelcome ways. People stop me in airports and sporting events to tell me they can't take it anymore, that they are exhausted and wonder how I can keep up with it all. Senior White House advisors tell me of nightmares they have about the unpredictability of Trump. Others in the White House have described jagged and emotionally taxing days that sometimes end in secret crying rooms in the Eisenhower Executive Office Building. Dozens upon dozens of Trump White House staff have fled to preserve their own sanity. It takes weeks and sometimes months for them to process their time in the Trump White House. We are processing it, too, at what feels like a slightly safer distance. And I mean the country, not me.

This is one universe. Another is peopled by Trump officials and cabinet secretaries who extol Trump's decisiveness, loyalty and love of country—how he surprises them with creative questions and takes in differing opinions, meshes them with his own assumptions and visibly learns. They speak of Trump's obsession with job creation and smaller government—both of which lead him to tolerate lobbyist-driven favors for industry and to a reflexive opposition to existing regulations and cost structures. Trump is belligerently pro-business because, as he said during the campaign, government policies have undercut Americans who lack a college education. One statistic speaks to this politically potent allegation. According to a 2016 study by Georgetown University's Center on Education and the Workforce, of the 11.6 million private sector jobs created after the Great Recession only 80,000 went to workers with a high school education or less. On questions of taxation, trade, spending or regulation, with Trump, the preference goes to the common man—the "forgotten" worker who can't reach college and needs to survive by his wits and his hands.

For this reason, those who love Trump react with primal, possessive satisfaction—"He's *my* president. I love *my* president." To these Americans, disproportionately white according to 2016 exit polls and surveys taken during 2017, Trump represented something visceral and true, nostalgic and nervy. He was an economic and political savior and the embodiment of an America they feverishly loved—whether that America existed in memory, myth or some combination of the two. This is an America of power and evangelical fervor, of cockiness and guile utterly untroubled by the mores of multiculturalism and uninterested in the strictures of multilateral decision-making. This America knows its mind and its center—knows its "heritage," to use a favorite Trumpian code word.

There is, of course, the counternarrative of a reckless president with character defects so profound and pathologies so obvious that the country's very future is in peril. Judith Lewis Herman, M.D., is a professor of psychiatry at Harvard University and wrote the following in the 2017 book *The Dangerous Case of Donald Trump*:

> In a court of law, even the strongest insanity defense cannot show that a person is insane all of the time. Delusional levels of grandiosity, impulsiveness and the compulsions of mental impairment, when combined with an authoritarian cult of personality and contempt for the rule of law, are a toxic mix . . . anyone as mentally unstable as Mr. Trump simply should not be entrusted with the life-and-death powers of the presidency.

The book carried the subtitle *27 Psychiatrists and Mental Health Experts Assess a President*. It was published in October 2017—less than a year into Trump's presidency—and constituted a 384-page indictment of Trump's mental health, arguing the presidency was in dangerously unpredictable hands. And yet Trump is entrusted with these powers. He functions every day as the 45th president of the United States. Those who work closely for him see some of the pathologies described in the book but consider them much less frightening because they are, in the main, manageable—because of *their* intervention and the countervailing powers of Congress, the courts and a free press. Those who work closely with the president also harbor a deep and abiding respect for the election itself. I have heard them say over and over that the country chose Trump. That is the will of the people. Trump may not be my idea of a president, his temperament may wear me down, his antics might test my patience but, damn it, the people elected him, and respecting that choice is my duty to the country and the Constitution. These conversations are not uncommon. And that is bizarre. Critics of Trump consider all of it a grotesque rationalization. Those who work for Trump consider it a profound act of patriotism. This is not a new construct around the question of power. What is new is how lacerating this debate is and how frequently it plays out in full public view.

Trump is the unstable axis between hate and love. There doesn't appear to be much middle ground. Trump doesn't want any. He craves the fight. He lives for it at close range and a distance—so long as it is about *him*. "Trump hates negative publicity," Lewandowski told me. "Unless he generates it."

It is worth noting, in this context of presidential fitness, that previous presidents have been described, even by those who supported or worked with them, as incompetent or volatile. Two examples strike me as possibly relevant. These are direct quotes spoken of two presidents now viewed favorably by presidential historians.

> I had heard much about [unnamed president]'s violent temper and paroxysms of ungovernable rage. . . . I realized I was standing at the apex of a situation that could make me the next victim of such an uncontrolled passion. It came with suddenness and violence. What a contrast with the calm dignity and control of President Lincoln . . . the great contrast between Lincoln and [unnamed president] was not of time only. As one of [unnamed president]'s most prominent critics summed it up, "Among President [unnamed]'s many weaknesses was his utter inability to discriminate between history and histrionics."

This was said of another American president:

> [Unnamed president] will still rely on a staff that has almost no White House or executive experience . . . the appointments process is a sea of confusion . . . [he] has chosen a chief of staff who has either been unwilling or unable to exert much discipline on the president or his staff . . . while the staff can be blamed for some of the confusion, even his closest advisors insist that [unnamed president] is a big part of the problem. . . . He has extended automatic walk-in rights to the Oval Office—a privilege that is heavily restricted by most Presidents—to nearly a dozen people . . . the open-door policy has forced him to be his own chief of staff and caused the White House to move in too many directions at once, with little coordination.

The first unnamed president was Harry Truman, his critic Army Gen. Douglas MacArthur, writing in his 1964 book, *Reminiscences*. The second unnamed president was Bill Clinton, described in a *Time* magazine story headlined "That Sinking Feeling" on June 7, 1993, less than six months into his presidency. *Time*'s cover showed a tiny picture of Clinton lost beneath bold black type reading, "THE INCREDIBLE SHRINKING PRESIDENT."

What kind of president is Trump? Are there any useful comparisons? Probably not. However, there is something discussed in the corridors of Capitol Hill about Trump that might surprise you. It is shared among veteran staffers who take seriously presidents who engage actively with Congress (in recent years there have been so few) and look for comparisons and contrasts. I have spoken with many of these students of Congress and the presidency (and the personal intersection of the two) who detect three similarities between Trump and President Lyndon Baines Johnson. Yes, LBJ. Forget Johnson's wealth of legislative experience and encyclopedic knowledge of and experience with the political players of his day. Forget Johnson's mastery of arcane Senate procedure and force of will to create legislative achievement when all appeared lost. Those are not apt comparisons.

These three are: Both gathered information independently through continual use of the telephone; both relied on TV as their window into America; and both used their physicality as a means of communicating charisma and power. Trump works the phone relentlessly, calling aides, friends, acquaintances and even reporters in zealous pursuit of information. Trump likes to flatter and butter up lawmakers by giving them his personal cell phone and urging them to call him *anytime* (knowing they won't because what backbencher in his or her right mind would just dial up the president?). Trump calls lawmakers all the time, and he did so with minimal success during the health care debate and better results during the tax reform debate. Johnson worked the phones in much the same way. The tapes of Johnson's phone calls may provide the greatest insight into a president's thinking and political processes in modern history—surpassed only by the Richard Nixon Oval Office recordings because of Nixon's baroque paranoia, conspiratorial malevolence and anti-Semitism. Johnson also had a bank of televisions installed in the West Wing so he could monitor network news coverage. From the tragic first moments of his presidency, Johnson kept a keen eye on TV imagery and its influence on America. The telephone and TV unite Trump and Johnson in unexpected and important ways.

Both also used their size and bearing to "own" a room and to intimidate. Both 6 feet 3 inches tall, both (where Johnson is concerned I rely on biographers) used their size to signal aggression or passivity and study the reaction of others in real time. Neither was physically fit, so it's not about muscle but rather about psychology and the sense they radiated that they are big people, big personalities and ceaseless workers (Johnson is said to have worked 18–20-hour days; so does Trump). In my experience, Trump is not one to jab a finger in your chest or tower over you as Johnson did. But Trump does give the sense that he could and that it would not be pleasant. Trump uses his physicality to convey he's the Alpha Dog in every room and everyone should react accordingly.

As for the phone, Lewandowski spoke to Trump at least a dozen times every day. Trump even spoke to Lewandowski three times the day before he fired him—when he had already decided to fire him. While chief of staff, Priebus got calls at all hours of the day and night;

so did all of Trump's attorneys. So did friends. So did lawmakers. So did heads of state. Gingrich described Trump's information-gathering via the telephone as "omnivorous." There is literally no time of day when a close Trump aide cannot expect a call. When and how Trump sleeps is a permanent mystery to those close to him. The nation knows at least one instance—the time when he nodded off mid-tweet, leaving behind the immortal "covfefe."

Trump rarely reads memos (Johnson did—an important difference) and he does not trust even his closest advisors to distill conversations for him. Trump goes to the source—and on the phone he persistently sifts the spoken and unspoken. He measures someone's voice and pauses—runs any hesitations through his own BS filtering system. It's not always truth Trump seeks. More than anything else, he wants the essence of the moment. If someone is trying to game Trump, he tries to detect it in their voice. Trump always wants to know—by himself—someone's game, how much guts they have, if they can be brushed back or how gullible they might be. He believes no one does that better than he does. Johnson did too.

"The president has a style of listening to a lot of people," Priebus told me, his sense of descriptive caution bordering on terrified. "He takes advice from all sources. That's not a negative. That's just who the president is."

"All sources" means *all* sources. Could be an elevator operator. The pilot of Air Force One or, more frequently, the pilot of his private jet (whom Trump suggested could be the next administrator of the Federal Aviation Administration). It could be lifelong friends. His bodyguard (as opposed to a Secret Service agent) or a famous athlete or celebrity. It could also be a policy wonk or CEO. It could . . . literally . . . be anyone. In this, Trump did not discriminate. He destroyed previous understandings of order, protocol or filtered access to the commander-in-chief. This tendency also helps Trump fight boredom and a sense of isolation. TV does the same.

"It doesn't frustrate me," Priebus told me when he was still chief of staff. "Initially, I'm a structuralist. I'm a check-box person. I do manage. And I do control. I have to deal with 50 inputs. Fifty serious inputs. He's willing to have more inputs than most presidents would."

The beginning and end of Trump's first year were marked by legislative chaos he created. As you will learn later, Trump chose the first travel ban from eight presented options. He chose—this may surprise you—the most modest and least restrictive. But neither he nor anyone around him made a serious effort—details coming in the pages ahead—to prepare agencies implementing the ban as to what it meant, how it would work and who was or was not covered. That was a presidential action born of inaction and indifference—owned entirely by Trump.

"They tended to do bold things badly," said Gingrich, husband to Callista, Trump's ambassador to Vatican City. "And that's partly because very often the amount of energy it takes to do a bold thing precludes you from doing it well."

Trump's presidency is so searing and noisy it is at times impossible to detect or discern its lasting impact. That is the only goal of this book. I seek to record events that represent genuine and lasting change. It is not the purpose of this book to persuade any reader these changes were beneficial or harmful; only that they happened and are very likely to last. I have also tried to learn why these things happened. This is always difficult work. In politics, points of view and points of emphasis vary even in placid times. Trump breeds distemper and even those closest to him possess not only rivalrous but vengeful agendas. Disagreements can flare over recollections and points of emphasis. This is always true in books about presidencies. Who said what to whom and when? What mattered? Who is playing themselves up at the expense of another? Which events were historic and which only appeared to be? Such disputes bedevil all political history. In the era of Trump those devils dance mockingly everywhere.

It was always incomprehensible to me to write a book on the entire first year of the Trump presidency. If you want a book devoted to the Russia investigation, this isn't it. I will delve into the firing of FBI Director James Comey and what sprang from it, much of it damaging to Trump *and* the FBI. But that's it. In late July 2018 I had no clue where the Russia story was heading. I know Special Counsel Robert Mueller wants to go to trial in the fall of 2018 against former Trump campaign chairman Paul Manafort. I know when Mueller was appointed, Trump talked openly about firing him—drawing hesitant nods from senior advisors who had no intention of following through because they knew Trump popped off about "firing" someone almost daily. Just as predictably, Trump would forget it and move on. Trump is mostly bark. Aides did nothing about the "fire Mueller" talk. They did talk Trump off the ledge and counsel him to leave Mueller alone and let his own legal team do its work without similarly reckless badgering. That's what Trump did.

"The president has some odd ideas," former White House lawyer Ty Cobb told me. "He was particularly confused about his power."

As for Manafort, perhaps by the fall of 2018 Mueller will have squeezed something out of him. Maybe there are more indictments. Maybe there is a separate special counsel investigating the upper echelon of the FBI and its approach to the Hillary Clinton and Trump investigations. I don't know. Don't look for that ticktock here.

As for the first year of the Trump presidency, there could be a volume devoted to each Trump month. If Robert Caro were young enough, it would be a task worthy of his formidable talents. Hell, there could be a book devoted to 10 days in May (the firing of FBI Director James Comey and everything else). There could be a novel or a rap song on the 11 days of Anthony Scaramucci.

I have tried to isolate and illuminate 10 moments in Trump's first year that are important and lasting in their own right—separate from White House spin and consistent with my sense of a presidency's first-year reach.

This book is not primarily about Trump's noisiness, rancor, lies or flamboyance. It doesn't ruminate about impeachment or 25th Amendment machinations. I am purposely evasive on—meaning I attempt to sidestep—the nation's emotional reaction to Trump. I know it is real and some believe our very institutions are being destroyed and that Trump is the most malevolent force ever unleashed on our republic. Trump supporters love his raw energy, pro-American swagger and contempt for elites. In important ways, Trump is their political idol. He is a proto-political force, bigger than party, bigger than ideology, bigger than everything but American . . . greatness. Trump supporters have never felt emotionally closer to a president. Trump critics can barely breathe, so strangled do they feel by his perceived selfishness, indifference to facts, contempt for institutional norms and haphazard management style.

This book is about the comparatively quieter side of Trump. It is intended to be about whether America will look back on Trump circa 2017 as a turning point, a way station or a dying experiment. Whatever the judgment, I have sought to bring the decisions and potential consequences to the surface.

TWO

The Lottery Ticket

There is a languid, gray calm on a national Election Night—a gap of national silence between the closing of polls, the fevered dissection of returns and the collective recognition of a president-elect. It is an odd, expectant interlude in which campaign speeches become sibilant whispers and the nation perks its ears for a governing credo drafted but not yet consecrated.

Inside the ballroom of the New York Hilton Midtown where Donald Trump introduced the nation to running mate Mike Pence on July 16, 2016, the crowd had yet to form. It was about 6 p.m. and low-level campaign staff nervously migrated from empty corner to empty corner, obsessively straightening white tablecloths hanging over waist-high bar tables positioned on the flanks, just below flat-screen monitors tuned to (what else) Fox News. Even in absentia, Trump's demand for perfection in presentation reigned supreme. Trump would never see those tables. But the fear that someone close to him might generated a sense of devotion and anxiety I had rarely seen in a presidential campaign. I remember once noticing Trump staff inside the lobby of Trump Tower, at an earlier campaign event, screaming at each other over the black drape covering the back of the press riser—a place Trump would never see. They argued and tussled to make sure the black cloth stretched all the way to the bottom, covering the metal posts and wood blocks beneath them protecting the marble floor. The issue: making sure no one passing by could glimpse any part of the supporting pole or wood block, lest Trump find out and fire them for inattention to detail. That Trump mentality and ferocity had trickled down by Election Day to volunteers twitching nervously over Velcro tablecloth fasteners.

One senior Trump staffer made a swift scouting trip through the room. Marc Short was Pence's top communications advisor and strategist. He had been Pence's chief of staff in Congress and through the creation of a new consulting company had, in the early stages of the 2016 campaign, been advising Pence's gubernatorial reelection campaign and Florida Sen. Marco Rubio's bid for the GOP nomination. Before working for Pence, Short was chief of staff to Texas Republican Sen. Kay Bailey Hutchinson and, before that, Oliver North's finance chair in his 1994 U.S. Senate campaign. Between his consulting company and work on the Hill, Short was a top operative and fund-raiser for the Koch brothers, serving as president of their conservative-backing political "charity" Freedom Partners Chamber of Commerce. Short had been on the Trump campaign since Pence was named running mate. Unlike Pence, who spoke of Trump as reverently and obediently in private as he did in public, Short at times sounded fatigued by Trump's histrionics. Short was among the first in the Trump world I encountered who spoke the tortured language of loyalist and hostage. It's a sound I would hear again when, a few hours later, the Trump world expanded exponentially under the title president-elect.

The ballroom was nearly deserted, except for reporters and technicians preparing for the long night ahead. Up on the TV risers, adjustments were being made, video and audio cables secured, communications channels confirmed. I was getting ready for a live shot for the CBS Evening News when Short beckoned me down from the riser and to the ballroom floor.

"We are very worried about what we're seeing in Florida," Short told me. "It's not looking as good as we hoped." I asked if the campaign was crunching numbers upstairs in Trump's penthouse room. Short shrugged. I quietly scolded myself. To the very end, it was impossible for reporters like me to remember there was no actual campaign.

It was idiotic to ask Short about data analysis across layered internal polling, door-knock surveys and volunteer bed checks on voter turnout (all masterfully constructed and executed in both Obama victories). Trump did not go to school on Obama's campaign in the way Obama went to school on George W. Bush's 2000 and 2004 campaigns, learning about his innovative pre-Facebook approach to voter identification, microtargeting through consumer habits and persuasion through so-called third-party verifiers (friends, neighbors and church-goers). It's not widely understood, but successful presidential campaigns typically go to school on those who succeed before them—regardless of party. Trump created a new school, a political School of Rock that unnerved fussy political parents (who knew how things had always been done) and enthralled the politically uninitiated.

At times, I was one of those fussy parents. To be honest, my training in presidential coverage dating back to 1992 disabled me. As strange as it sounds, I was hobbled by what I had learned. It was Election Night and I was still having a hard time remembering how different the Trump campaign was, how much of it took a sledgehammer to the scientific methods and voluminous data mining that had not only changed the way voters were engaged but, at least many of us had come to believe, increased the predictability of campaign outcomes.

Some may read this and conclude I wasn't trying to learn. I was. And I had told my network two weeks before the election Trump could win. I did not predict it. But I told our elections director Anthony Salvanto it was possible and that no one should be surprised if it happened. When it comes to unlearning that which you have studied for nearly 20 years, I will concede it is more difficult than I imagined. Ask yourself, what have you unlearned in your life that was completely different from the evidence and experiences of the previous 20 years? If this has happened to you, I'm willing to bet the shift from old to new did not occur overnight. Election Night was to become the biggest overnight ever.

From the beginning and at its core the Trump campaign had one organ and one organ only. Gut. Trump's instinct was the cauldron that cooked every calculation. Trump's gut told him the white vote was an untapped behemoth that Republicans ignored at their peril. He considered the RNC "autopsy" after the 2012 election pure junk because it ignored white voters and prioritized ethnic outreach and watered-down conservatism. To Trump and those close to him, it was less an autopsy than appeasement—a premature surrender to demographic trends that already favored Democrats. Trump's hunch was the GOP had ignored persuadable white voters; that John McCain in 2008 and Mitt Romney in 2012 had overlooked the possibility of building a broader base among evangelical, blue-collar or previously disengaged voters. Trump's first goal was to attract more whites and then, if possible, expand to like-minded nationalist, populist or conservative voters in African American, Latino and Asian communities. Unapologetically, Trump said: "This Is Where We Stand," take it or leave it. Gut also told Trump this about life: fear, anger and nostalgia are the most potent emotions. He pursued all three. Gut told him something important about his celebrity and success, namely that they were insufficient. Trump had to be grandiose about the size and scope of his success, hyperbolic about everything he achieved and indifferent to his many failures. Trump intuited that a scorned part of America was haunted by the decline of middle-class prosperity, was bewildered by rapid changes in race relations and sexual classifications and craved something—an ugly American in America.

Trump supporters did not describe their love for Trump that way. But it is a fair description of what they felt and the promise they saw behind the brashness, egoism and clownishness.

I met 70-year-old Betsy Wilson at a Trump rally in Ashburn, Virginia, in early August 2016. Wilson was hard to miss. She was wearing a red, white and blue American flag dress and floral hat.

"He says what's on his mind," Wilson told me of Trump. "He doesn't couch things like Hillary does. I think you can believe him. He also says things in sarcasm and today we have gotten away from sarcasm because we're trying to be too politically correct and I think that's a shame."

Almost exactly a year before I met Wilson, I interviewed Jorge and Alexandra Simones, of Topsfield, Massachusetts, at a Trump rally in Derry, New Hampshire. The Trump Train had barely left the station but the Simoneses were already aboard.

"Trump is different because he doesn't have to answer to any do-nors, any lobbyists," Jorge told me. "I mean, he has enough money to enter the campaign and run from the heart. I know he brags a lot. He has a big ego, but he means well. He's not a politician. He's one of the people. His only incentive of running is because he wants to do some-thing for this country."

Alexandra Simones then said something I have never forgotten. It may have been the best, most condensed expression of Trump sup-porter sentiment I came across at more than 100 Trump events, rallies and GOP debates.

"He says things that need to be said."

About what? I asked.

"The truth that nobody else says."

I had never covered a presidential campaign with three campaign managers. Trump had three, the third being Conway, the first woman manager in Republican history. Conway, in keeping with Trump's ap-proach, was not a typical campaign manager. By the time she took over, the nomination had been secured and what was needed most was not a strategic or financial wizard with the customary skill sets of a campaign manager, but someone who could appear regularly on TV and calmly and reassuringly reshape Trump's message. Conway buffed down Trump's rough edges and became his most important whisperer to the GOP suburbanites, an important but, in the late summer and early fall of the campaign, restive and anxious voting bloc. This repre-sented a new dynamic in presidential politics—a campaign manager who soothed voters made manic by *her* own candidate. In this, Con-way's contribution was doubly historic in importance and originality.

The job of a campaign manager had never been so constructed—work the cable networks like a drone self-toggled from one studio to another. Dave Bossie was the deputy campaign manager, his job also oddly significant and original. Bossie set the schedule. In most cam-paigns that is a side job full of numbing logistics and screaming phone calls with junior staff over event site minutiae—which VIPs sit where, what is the distance from stage to TV cameras, who introduces the candidate, how chairs are positioned, who is running security and who is handling food (or will there be any food at all). Bossie did that but much, much more. He ran the man and the man was the message. The message was the campaign. Where Bossie put Trump was where the campaign existed. The campaign was the show. The show was the campaign, a one-ring political circus with a lion tamer, fire eater, magician and trapeze daredevil rolled into one.

To run Trump's schedule was to run the entire Republican Party and, by extension, drive the narrative of Trump as the "change" candidate against Clinton. Steve Bannon was there to remind Trump to stay on message (and Trump followed the advice), another valuable contribution that required almost no actual work. Lastly, there was Brad Parscale, who analyzed pro-Trump social media chatter and Republican voter files to see which messages drove the most pro-Trump engagement and mobilization. Jared Kushner, daughter Ivanka's husband, had supervisory powers over fund-raising, press, travel and mechanics and used a light touch, owing to his inexperience and Trump's own sense of giving subordinates the freedom to make decisions and fail—so long as the failures didn't persist. Ivanka weighed in from the sides and was always among Trump's most important sounding boards. Bossie dispatched Trump's sons Eric and Don Jr. to small burgs (usually in the South) that their dad didn't have time for. It was well known in the campaign that Eric or Don Jr. would arrive without knowing much about the setup or locale. For most campaigns, this would have been a liability. In Trump world, the crowds materialized on their own and were attentive and forgiving. The pitch was basic: Trump, guns, God and football were good; Hillary was bad, liberal and possibly evil.

It was Election Night and after nearly 16 continuous months on the road, the epic journey was reaching its zenith. I was numb from exhaustion and genuinely unsure what the night would bring. I was standing near my camera position, guzzling probably my twelfth cup of coffee when Short beckoned me. As we chatted in that empty space nothing felt historic, nothing signaled we were about to walk through the most jolting political turnstile of our careers. Perhaps I was too tired to feel anything. Maybe the pounding campaign had dulled my senses. But deeply embedded lessons lingered. I had interviewed top presidential operatives on Election Night before. The winners knew they were going to win and the losers knew they were going to lose. No one ever said that, but I remember the telltale glint or cloudiness in their eyes. I had noticed the tilt or slump of their shoulders, the arc of their stride. With Short there was an odd emotional distance from everything—a dispassionate air of Trumpian "We'll see what happens" that I reminded myself to remember.

Short did not know if it would all work, this Trumpian burrowing into the marrow of dispossessed American patriotism, pride and racial alienation. I asked if it could be an early evening with a dignified Trump concession. Another shrug. It's not that Short did not care. It's that he did not know. No one in Trump's inner circle knew what would happen. Not even Trump. In these uncertain hours I was Trump's equal, just as anyone who brought a genuine sense of unknowing would have been.

What Trump did know is he'd seen the standing-room-only crowds in all the key states, watched TV coverage of lines that stretched seemingly to the horizon of T-shirt-clad Trump supporters waiting for his arrival through a blitz of six stops a day during his frenzied final weekend of campaigning. Nearly 10,000 showed up at a Minneapolis regional airport hangar for an event announced only 18 hours earlier. Many who didn't make it inside the hangar pressed their noses against chain-link fences, listening to Trump through rock-concert-sized speakers bellowing to the blue sky, empty runways and neatly parked Cessnas. Bossie added the stop not to win Minnesota, the only state Walter Mondale carried in his 1984 landslide loss to Ronald Reagan, but to gain blanket local TV coverage in northwest Wisconsin. Wisconsin would become key to the night ahead, as would Pennsylvania.

As I chatted with Minnesotans at the rally and snapped iPhone pictures of their wide-eyed children, I remembered a conversation I had weeks earlier with Ryan Mackenzie, a member of the Pennsylvania House of Representatives. Mackenzie's district includes Lehigh County, home of Allentown, the third most populous city in the commonwealth. "Individuals are taking it upon themselves outside of the Republican Party to go out and speak to their neighbors and tell them they are supporting Donald Trump, and that vocal base is a powerful thing. That person-to-person contact is something you can't replace." The last time Lehigh County voted Republican in a presidential election was 1988. Mackenzie told me a story about the Trump effect in his district that stuck with me. After the GOP convention, the Trump campaign and state Republican Party ran out of yard signs to distribute in eastern Pennsylvania. Yard signs, I have learned over many years covering politics, are one of the best indicators of durable—forgive me—grassroots support. They represent three important truths about political intent: the first is the homeowner is willing to take a public stand on a political question, which is rare; second, the yard sign invites scrutiny outside of the home, meaning neighbors are likely to bring up the subject at church, the grocery store or youth athletic events; lastly, it is a partisan identifier at a time of partisan animosity. These dynamics are true of every yard sign, which is why campaigns covet them so much. Signs alongside roads or on boulevards or taped to fences are about increasing name identification. Signs in yards declare strong support. This was doubly true for Trump in Democratic counties like Lehigh. Trump supporters there wanted yard signs and were growing frustrated. They stopped calling Trump headquarters and party headquarters and started calling Mackenzie. He didn't have any signs and kept telling them to wait. The calls kept coming. Finally, Mackenzie looked up the names of two local printers and began to give out their numbers. Soon enough, Trump supporters began to create their own Trump yard signs and paid for them out of their own pockets. "I have never seen that," Mackenzie said. "That is something you can't quantify. It is not in the data. It is not in the metrics. It is not in the number of offices that any campaign has going [Clinton had far more than Trump]. It is just the people doing this, taking it upon themselves." I can say in 25 years of covering presidential campaigns, I had never come across a story like that either.

In a very real sense Trump, the casino owner who went bankrupt on the New Jersey boardwalk (and elsewhere), had become a presidential lottery ticket—a gamble of long odds and dream-come-true payout. Trump's gut told him to sell a dream born on the anger and fear of economic chaos. Trump embodied garish, conspicuous wealth and sold himself as the seizer of riches, a new American Caesar who would humble the elites by siphoning their globalized prosperity into sluices of gain for "the forgotten men and women" of America's heartland. He was a traveling lottery billboard and tickets came for free. Take a chance. Trump said it most memorably to black voters, but he meant it for everyone: "What have you got to lose?" In the homestretch of the campaign, he told voters "This is your last chance" to recapture a lost America. Lose. Chance. Lottery. Gut. Gamble. Trump.

Outside of Trump, the campaign had no big brain, no central nervous system. There were a few ragged synapses linking polling data, focus groups, registration rolls, TV ad "warmth" meters and social media metrics. But most experienced campaign managers or consultants would have considered them inadequate in a competitive U.S. House race and frighteningly unfit for a modern ascent to the presidency. The Republican National Committee had all of the above and used it to Trump's advantage, but its focus was as much on down-ballot House and Senate races as it was Trump. Down-ballot is also where GOP-friendly groups like Americans for Prosperity (bankrolled by the Koch brothers) and The Club for Growth focused their attention. In most competitive Senate races, the Republican nominee ran ahead of Trump (Rubio in Florida, Johnson in Wisconsin, Toomey in Pennsylvania). This down-ballot effort may have propelled Trump to victory, even though both AFP and The Club, as they are casually known in GOP circles, could barely stand Trump (in the primaries The Club spent $15 million on ads against Trump, more than any other political player).

The RNC was the biggest resource at the campaign's disposal but it did not belong to Trump. It belonged to Chairman Reince Priebus and he rented it to Trump in exchange for a permanent seat at his table—loyalties delicately divided between Trump and the national party. More skillfully than most appreciate, Priebus kept the GOP machinery focused on all of the 2016 races while reinforcing Trump by minimizing intra-party rebellion.

"Reince was historically, unbelievably important," Gingrich told me. "We would not have won had he not been national committee chair. The scale of the machine he built and the fact that he held the party together in the spring when it was desperately trying to get to a civil war. I give Reince a lot of credit."

The RNC paid for more voter contacts than ever before in history—6,000 full- or part-time paid staff in 11 battleground states. The party began deploying paid staff in 2013 and during the general election used volunteers to overlay work of the paid staff. Internally, voter contacts were recorded by paid field operatives and refined—double-checked—by volunteers. This created the largest voter file in RNC history and in the pitiful early hours of Election Night was the only credible resource Trump advisors had.

In those glum hours about dusk when exit polls pointed to defeat, Priebus toed an optimistic line. "Let's stop spinning ourselves into depression," Priebus told Bossie, Bannon and Kushner. "We've got a plan. Let's follow the plan."

The "plan" was Priebus's general election strategy for all Republicans. Everyone in Trump's inner circle knew it was first devoted to the GOP and secondly to Trump. Throughout the fall, the needs of the RNC came first. The party decided what to prioritize, not the nominee—a reversal of every previous presidential campaign I had covered. This self-serving instinct is part of a gnawing resentment Trump operatives still carry toward Priebus and his crowd. The weekend before the election, top RNC aides briefed reporters that Trump was likely to lose and that it would be his fault—that the RNC did all it could to prop up a flawed nominee. The briefings might have been a head fake or wishful thinking.

Long after the election, Priebus told me that RNC polling a week before Election Day showed Trump down four to five points everywhere that mattered. In the final weekend, though, the internal polling showed Trump closing to within two points in every battleground state except for Nevada. That closing surge continued through Election Day as late-breaking voters collectively bought the lottery ticket. In the four states that mattered most the numbers were extraordinary: In Florida, 11 percent of voters decided in the last week and they favored Trump over Clinton by 17 points; in Pennsylvania 15 percent decided in the last week and favored Trump by 17 points; in Michigan 13 percent decided in the last week and they favored Trump by 11 points; in Wisconsin 14 percent decided in the last week and favored Trump by a whopping 29 points.

At 8 p.m. inside Trump "victory" headquarters the crowd was sparse, subdued and uncertain. Was this a pipe dream? Exit polls looked bleak. I was part of CBS News' continuous Election Night coverage. At 8:07 p.m. I gave the following live report: "There is deep and abiding anxiety within Trump Tower about what they're seeing in Florida because they know and have said over and over there is no Trump path to the presidency without Florida's 29 electoral votes. And they are deeply concerned about the Latino turnout for Hillary Clinton and a softening of suburban college-educated women for Donald Trump. And for that reason, Trump has urged supporters to get to the polls because it's a two-tiered system in Florida: 67 counties, 10 of them in the Central Time Zone. So that strategic urging from Trump has real value in those counties because Mitt Romney in 2012 cleared more than 190,000 votes over Barack Obama. Trump needs every vote he can find in Florida, hence the urging of supporters to get there before the polls close."

A few moments later, Brian Fallon, a top Clinton campaign spokesman, appeared on the CBS live coverage and spoke so confidently of Clinton's victory it almost sounded as if the night were over. Little did he and Team Clinton realize it was just beginning to turn.

"We really feel, based on what we're seeing so far today, is what you're seeing is a rise of the Clinton coalition," Fallon said. "What we're seeing in the early voting and then the turnout today suggests that Hillary Clinton has not just reassembled that Obama coalition but actually expanded on it." Fallon spoke confidently of increases in the Latino early vote in Florida and North Carolina, compensating for any softening of African American turnout. He predicted Clinton would carry white women with a college education. My colleague Norah O'Donnell then asked Fallon about Michigan. His answer spoke to the misreading of the data, the electorate and the mood of the upper Midwest. "Michigan, we've been pleased with what we have been seeing so far. In fact, I think that the day after this election one of the mistakes the Trump campaign will look back on is their failure to contest a state like Michigan earlier on. We never took it for granted even though it was late to the battleground map in the minds of some. We actually had 35 offices open there; we had a full staff in place there; we were always built to win a very close race and I think that's what going to happen tonight."

Priebus had his plan. But Trump needed a state—a big one to give him some genuine hope. Susie Wiles, Trump's Florida campaign chair, called Bossie and told him not to give up. Bossie put Wiles in charge of Florida in September (desperately late in the minds of nervous Sunshine State Republicans) as part of a campaign shake-up that reeked of disarray. Soon thereafter, Wiles discovered there was no statewide absentee ballot program. Trump was also tight-fisted about spending on TV commercials and mailers. Wiles pressed for more, fearful the Trump phenomenon wasn't enough—there needed to be an actual campaign. Not much of this materialized. Wiles spent most of Election Day crazed and tense. But there were glimmers. She had volunteers in two key counties—Pasco and Volusia—who reported what looked like surprisingly high Trump turnouts. Plus, she said, polls were still open in the 10 Florida Panhandle counties in the Central Time Zone. Already, heavy turnout indicated more white voters had shown up than in 2008 and 2012. This was looking like Trump Country Squared.

Bossie was in the crude Trump "war room" where he had been conferring for the afternoon with the core team (Priebus, Bannon, Conway, Parscale and Kushner). They were originally horrified by the first wave of exit polls. But they also did their own checks on operatives in key states. RNC staff in Iowa and Ohio said early Clinton leads would vanish when the rural vote came in. Trump was already assuming Iowa and Ohio were won. But word that Florida was competitive helped. It wasn't much but it was a hook for what could be described as conjured optimism. Focus on Florida, Bossie thought. Do what you can. Make every effort.

Bossie recruited Don Jr. and Eric to dial up every talk radio station in the Florida Panhandle. The boys kept the phones plastered to their ears until the polls closed, selling their father relentlessly and urging Trump voters to defy the odds. Ringing in their ears were the words Wiles spoke to Bossie before the last-hour phone marathon began: "It's not lost. We still have a chance."

South of the Panhandle, other good news was registering. Volusia and Pasco, counties where many snow-bird Democrats had migrated over the past 20 years, were surging, with Trump outpacing Romney. In the end, the two counties gave Trump more than 60 percent of his vote differential over Mitt Romney's 2012 performance, moving both from Democrat to Republican. This was a microcosm of an unexpected trend that would continue as vote totals came in for almost every important state. Clinton's campaign did not consider Volusia or Pasco vital battlegrounds. Instead Clinton's team focused efforts on urban Florida counties—Miami-Dade, Palm Beach, Broward, Hillsborough and Orange. Interestingly, Clinton outperformed Obama's vote total in

10 of the 12 Florida counties he carried in 2012. But Clinton lost what she thought were reliably Democratic counties like Pasco, Volusia and Pinellas. Trump's margins in the Panhandle also bested Romney, giving him a path to victory.

At 9:42 p.m. I filed this live report for CBS News Election Night coverage: "Early this evening there was a definite despondency within Trump Tower looking at the exit poll data and what they were seeing and hearing based upon reports from battleground states. That has turned into cautious optimism. One thing I heard repeatedly from senior Trump advisors was exit poll data doesn't look good, but we are going to overperform the exit poll data just as we predicted to you we would overperform public polls. How much? Maybe 1 or 2 percent. The trendlines we're seeing tonight, according to Trump Tower, reflect that overperformance in the battleground states. They are encouraged by Pennsylvania and Michigan but they have yet to see that breakout state where they can achieve a clear path to 270. Everything is very close. They are not nearly as discouraged as they were earlier this evening, but they are looking for a momentum builder, a battleground state that goes for Trump."

That phenomenon played out first in Florida, the most important early state to show Trump's surprising strength among white voters. While the Trump team waited for Florida, it saw Iowa and Ohio turn hard for Trump. Once Trump leapt ahead of Clinton in both states his lead only grew. That signaled urban strength was limited for Clinton and white rural voters were defying previous election trends and showing up in unforeseen numbers. That reinforced the growing sense among Trump's inner circle that close states like North Carolina, Pennsylvania, Michigan and Wisconsin might fall their way. It would be close. By 10:30 p.m. there was a path they could see more clearly. A path to victory. States had not been called for Trump yet but trendlines were visible.

Throughout Election Night I was texting Trump Tower and other sources I had developed throughout the campaign. One was former Pennsylvania Gov. Tom Corbett. Corbett lost his bid for reelection in 2014 and was not a particular fan of Trump. He wasn't an enemy but like many Republicans was a lukewarm bystander to the Trump fanaticism. But Corbett knew Pennsylvania politics and where the votes for a Trump victory could be found. As returns from Florida and North Carolina showed Trump running competitively with Clinton, I shifted my attention to Pennsylvania, because if Trump was going to win that was where the story was heading. Corbett kept scanning data on three counties—Lackawanna, Luzerne and Erie.

At 10:51 p.m. I was among the first reporters to quote key voices close to the campaign about the now-visible path to 270 electoral votes. I filed this live report: "They are feeling much, much better. They now see one or two, maybe three paths to 270 electoral votes. I was just texting with Paul Manafort, former campaign chairman for Donald Trump, still attached to this campaign, though not officially. He believes Trump is going to win North Carolina. I was just texting with former Pennsylvania governor, Republican Tom Corbett. He is not a Trump person at all but he is looking at Pennsylvania and says because Trump is winning in Erie County and Luzerne County and running just a little bit behind Hillary Clinton in Lackawanna County he said he believes Trump will win Pennsylvania."

In Trump Tower there was an awakening matched by disbelief. Wait. Could this happen? Trump had no victory or concession speech written. But the outlines of a concession speech were fully formed. A victory speech wasn't even sketched out. But the itch to sketch had begun.

When Manafort ran Trump's campaign, he built a loose organization of state operatives to help him in delegate counting before the convention and delegate discipline at it. He was still plugged in, though Trump Tower pretended otherwise. Manafort texted me that his top guy in Wisconsin reported to him there was no way Trump could lose. Priebus agreed and had been bullish about Wisconsin all night, primarily because Ron Johnson's Senate reelection numbers were exceeding expectations. Manafort passed his information on to Priebus and both relayed it to me. I reported this exchange on CBS, again being among the first to cite sources on the ground that Wisconsin was not only winnable but that Trump operatives believed the upset was at hand.

Shortly after 11 p.m. I filed a live report declaring the Trump inner circle was now sure it would win. It was based on reports from Wisconsin. "What I have been told via Paul Manafort . . . he texted me just a moment ago that Reince Priebus, the Republican National Committee chairman and a Wisconsin Republican of long standing, has told Manafort that he expects Donald Trump will carry the state of Wisconsin. Iowa Gov. Terry Branstad has told Manafort he expects Trump to carry Iowa as well and they are very encouraged by what they are seeing in Michigan. So in this upper Midwest aspect of the Trump campaign they are seeing exactly what they hoped to see and they believe they are now, for the first time, seeing a solid path to victory paved in part by the industrial Midwest."

The details of Trump's Election Night have been retold elsewhere—Trump and his inner circle shoehorning into his all-white, modern rectangular kitchen (not much cooking done by the Trumps) and watching returns on a flat-screen on the wall. One telling detail that would play out consequentially later is that not only were Robert Mercer and his daughter Rebekah (huge donors to Trump, Breitbart and other GOP-related causes) in Trump's apartment, but so, too, was New Jersey Gov. Chris Christie. It is said by some that Christie wheedled his way in and was unwelcome. Kushner held a deep grudge against Christie, who as a U.S. Attorney appointed by George W. Bush (named the day before 9/11, as he ceaselessly reminded voters in 2016) prosecuted Kushner's father for witness tampering and fraud. Someone let Christie into the apartment. Like so much in Trump world, alliances were kaleidoscopic—colorful, shifting and subject to vanishing. The Mercers and Christie would factor prominently in Trump's first year—Christie when the campaign botched the transition (by making him vanish) and the Mercers later in the political defenestration of Bannon.

The Trump circle that night drifted back and forth between the cramped kitchen and ornate dining room. According to Priebus, he knew Trump would win by about 11:30 p.m. but others were still unsure and Priebus was in no position to guarantee victory. But he was right and the trends kept moving in Trump's direction. At 12:32 a.m. Priebus high-fived Giuliani; the photo is still on Priebus's iPhone. Victory was at hand, though Clinton would not call Trump to concede for two hours. About this time, Trump asked speechwriter Stephen Miller to compose a victory speech. The first draft fell flat. It was harsh and full of I-told-you-so spite. Trump told everyone in the dining room the tone was off. "No. We're going to calm the waters and we're going to bring people together." Conway, Ivanka, Jared and Priebus gave the speech a serious rewrite.

At about 2:20 a.m. the Associated Press called Conway to say it would soon call the race for Trump, setting into motion the departure of him, Melania and entourage for the Hilton. The AP declared Trump the winner at 2:29 a.m. A thundering roar exploded in the ballroom while Trump, backstage, did something most politicians never think of but that was consistent with his approach to team-building. As he was about to address the world as president-elect, Trump spontaneously decided to have everyone in his retinue follow him on stage in one long line. There was one thing missing. Clinton still hadn't conceded. There was a sense the campaign should say something. Priebus prepared a short statement informing the crowd not to leave and to remain optimistic. He clutched the note in his hand, awash in the noise rising from the jam-packed ballroom floor below. There was some fear Clinton would not follow through on an earlier pact between the campaigns to concede within 15 minutes of AP's declaring the winner (a pact the Clinton team engineered with the expectation it would win and to force Trump into an orderly concession).

With the ballroom crowd still roaring, Clinton called at 2:32 a.m. Trump pressed Conway's cell phone to his ear, his words inaudible in the din even to those right next to him. Trump handed the phone back to Conway and, literally, everyone began to fall in line. It would be a long walk. Down a small staircase to a catwalk above the jubilation below. Then a left turn to center stage and podium. Before hitting the stairs, Trump made sure everyone was in loose alignment. He didn't really care about the order of entrance, except one small, or rather large, detail. Trump looked at Parscale, standing nearby at 6 feet 6 inches tall, and his wife, Candice, and said: "Brad, great job. Don't stand next to me on stage." This had been an issue at an earlier campaign rally and it stuck in Trump's craw—Parscale being three inches taller than Trump. The entourage was now ready for the walk on stage and Trump was at the front. Just before starting, the president-elect turned back and looked at Parscale. "Brad, I fucking mean it. Do not stand next to me."

During the CBS live coverage, long before the night was over but when Trump's momentum was building to his eventual victories in

Pennsylvania, Michigan and Wisconsin, I offered this observation: "You put Michigan, Wisconsin and Pennsylvania together and, ladies and gentlemen, that's the path. That's the path that Donald Trump has always imagined might be possible. An anchor in the industrial Midwest . . . a conversation with the country for the first time in a very long time, challenging the underlying economic assumptions of globalization and free trade because he believes, and these results tend to reinforce, that voters in those states either felt forgotten or out of the conversation or left at the economic margins of this country. And when he appealed to them they responded in numbers that did not show up in the exit polls entirely and certainly did not show up in the public polling before this Election Day occurred."

Trump's victory, his grand unraveling of a generation of presidential narratives, found its roots in overlooked places. One of those places is Grant County, Wisconsin—terrain so forgettable through history that three Native American tribes, the Spanish, the French and the British all left it utterly uninhabited. Almost no other place in early and inhabited pre-America or territorial America was so overlooked or forlorn. Grant County sits in the far southwestern corner of Wisconsin on the eastern side of the Mississippi River. For those who see the outlines of Wisconsin and imagine an oven mitten, Grant County is where a small cloth tie might be sewn for hanging on a refrigerator hook.

That image is useful—more useful than Grant County ever was from its founding in 1837 until 2016. Then it became the most representative Wisconsin county in Trump's victory, the hook upon which Wisconsin's 10 electoral votes and Trump's eventual 306-electoral-vote victory would hang. Republicans had not carried Wisconsin since 1984. Trump badly lost the primary there because Republicans considered him too erratic and moderate. Grant County became a pivotal crossroads of a transformed political landscape, a place where the tide of history finally arrived and foretold change that first shook Wisconsin, Michigan, Pennsylvania and then the world.

The county's population in 1970 was 48,398. It grew to 51,736 10 years later and hasn't grown since. It has been a stagnant part of the American heartland for nearly 40 years and solidly Democratic by inclination and habit for much longer than that. It shares this with other crucial Trump counties—like Trumbull in Ohio, Lackawanna and

Luzerne in Pennsylvania, Macomb and Ottawa (home of Birch Run) in Michigan as well as, you guessed it, Pasco and Volusia in Florida.

Priebus knew Wisconsin and sensed Trump was doing as well with disaffected, rural Democrats as he was with mainstream Republicans. Priebus grew up in Wisconsin and knew his rough-and-tumble relationship with Trump would only give him a chance at glory if he delivered or at least identified Wisconsin as winnable. Personally, Priebus kept Trump at arm's length early in the GOP primary process and was combative through Trump's "the system is rigged" phase. Their relationship almost collapsed in the panic over the Billy Bush *Access Hollywood* tape. Trump loyalists routinely—even now—retell Priebus's Trump Tower suggestion that weekend that Trump drop out and let Pence take over. It's not uncommon to hear a Trump loyalist, when referring to Priebus, begin with "The fucking asshole who told Trump . . ." Priebus sees it a bit differently and history will record he never lost his relationship with Trump, and in fact it remained intact in the crucial hours after the showdown over what Trump should do and say about "grab them by the pussy."

Priebus told Trump he could either get out of the race or lose in a landslide. "I was trying to make a point in front of everyone," Priebus said. "Not a single person challenged me. Nobody. It was what I was hearing." Explicit in this tough-love message was the sense that Trump had glossed over previous mistakes and could not, as he had in the past, blame someone else.

Priebus's main goal was to push Trump into apologizing at the second presidential debate with Clinton the next day in St. Louis. Before that, Trump, due to this and other prodding, recorded a video apology in the 13th-floor campaign studio, forever remembered by senior staff as "the hostage video." On the plane to the second debate, Priebus handled final debate prep, playing moderator and Clinton as he sat across from Trump. Priebus had told a hard truth the day before, and though Trump predicted he would overcome the Billy Bush tape, he took Priebus seriously and kept him close, as he was Trump's only link to useful political data and the only force preventing a wholesale party revolt (though many Republicans issued statements denouncing Trump and distancing themselves from his candidacy). Christie was in the residence when Priebus sounded off. He said little. But he refused to fly with Trump to St. Louis, a decision that would prove fatal to his relationship with the campaign. Giuliani agreed to do all Sunday show appearances for the campaign and arrived on Trump's plane for the trip to St. Louis looking haggard and exhausted. For his efforts, Trump told him he "sucked," looked "weak" and let the Sunday show hosts treat him "like a baby." Trump thought it was funny. Giuliani would not forget. Undetectable at the time, the seeds of a glaring division between the two had been planted.

Though Priebus remained vital to the campaign, he from then on wore a scarlet letter in Trump's inner circle of puritanical loyalty. When Priebus pushed for chief of staff after the election, Bossie and Lewandowski countered with Steve Bannon as chief strategist. Bannon was the late-arriving counterweight to Priebus, the embodiment of Trumpian antiestablishment, fuck-you politics. Bannon never considered the Billy Bush tape a serious problem and scoffed at "weaklings" who did. When Bannon was announced alongside Priebus, Trump wasn't splitting the difference. He was making the difference. Powerful establishment GOP forces (New York Jets owner Woody Johnson and Gingrich to name just two) were behind Priebus while insurgents (the Mercer family and Breitbart to name just two) backed Bannon. Trump sensed if Priebus was not checked by Bannon his entire White House might be staffed by RNC loyalists. Bannon was the counterweight. No White House chief of staff had ever been given an equalizer. Bannon was the voice of edgy, manic and uncompromising Trump populism— and immediate rival to Priebus's traditionalist, establishment pedigree and predilections. As for Lewandowski, Priebus, taking a cue from Ivanka and her husband Jared, showed no interest in bringing him inside the White House or giving him a role at the RNC. Lewandowski started peddling "Reince is going to be fired" stories less than a month after Trump's inauguration.

Back to Grant County. In 2012, with Mitt Romney leading the GOP, Grant County voted to reelect President Obama 13,594 to 10,255. That 56 percent–to–42 percent split exceeded the statewide verdict by more than three percentage points and continued a Democratic voting pattern that predated the Great Depression. Trump won Grant County 12,350 to 10,051—transforming a 14-point GOP loss into a 9-point GOP victory. It happened entirely with the votes of lapsed Democrats energized by a Republican the likes of which they had never seen. These overlooked voters in this forgotten county did not account for Trump's victory in Wisconsin. But they helped make it happen. These transformed voting tendencies shattered decades of political habits and the projections built upon them. This switch typified a Republican Party remade, at least for the moment, in Trump's image.

No one came to know that better than House Speaker Paul Ryan, also from Wisconsin and a veteran of statewide politics through countless backyard fund-raisers, cheese festivals, carnivals, fairs and town halls. Ryan clashed with Trump more than any other prominent Republican in Congress, aggravating Trump so much he endorsed Ryan's opponent in the 2016 GOP primary. Ryan prevailed, but the two disdained each other through the campaign.

After Trump won, the president-elect held a "Thank You" rally in West Allis, Wisconsin, just outside of Milwaukee. During the general election, Ryan refused to campaign with Trump (think about that for a minute: the Republican 2012 vice presidential nominee would not be seen in public with the party's 2016 nominee). Ryan had never attended a Trump rally before and knew he had to show up with the president-elect to try to thaw the relationship and ease the public tension. Trump and Ryan stood on stage before more than 7,000 jubilant, placard-waving Trump supporters—more than a thousand of whom stood in subfreezing temperatures for more than six hours to capture front-row space for the rally. It all looked familiar to Trump. For Ryan it was a political jolt. He looked out into the sea of Wisconsinites and found himself lost.

"I recognized maybe 10 people in that crowd," Ryan told me. "I've been doing Republican events practically all my life and I didn't know any of these people. These were not Republicans. They were Trump voters."

The same Trump voters that turned Grant County from deepest blue to Trump red. The ones who voted for what Trump said he would do—break up the Washington system and evict monied elites. The ones who bought Trump's lottery ticket. The ones who on Election Night might have been surprised to find Steven Mnuchin, a former Goldman Sachs partner, fund-raiser for national Democrats and movie producer, in the happy, bear-hug clutches of a victorious Trump. Mnuchin, finance chairman during the campaign, immediately became the front-runner for treasury secretary and many assumed the announcement would be among the first to come from the Trump transition. It wasn't. Trump became infatuated with other big-money names in high finance—precisely the types Trump supporters loathed. Still, Mnuchin had an inside lane, something reinforced the next morning when he received one of the very first Secret Service "senior staff" pins, a piece of political jewelry that carried more status and had more tangible value than any bracelet, ring or bauble sold across Fifth Avenue from Trump Tower at Van Cleef & Arpels.

THREE

Central Casting

As president-elect, Trump now commanded the ultimate in American security—full-fledged Secret Service protection and scrutiny of everyone in proximity. The "senior staff" pin given to Mnuchin designated those graced with unlimited access to the president-elect and those who warranted the least amount of security screening. Mnuchin was the only person not involved in daily Trump campaign operations at the most senior level so rewarded. The morning after election night, the Secret Service confiscated dozens of campaign security pins given to senior staff and others who worked regularly on the two Trump Tower floors devoted to the campaign—14 and 15. Top Secret Service officials provided about one dozen new "senior staff" pins, meaning many staffers who had enjoyed wide access to the building and Trump during the campaign would be cut out of the inner circle—at least for a short while and possibly longer, depending on their post-election status. Each pin had a number engraved on the back that corresponded to a new transition badge. Distribution of these new pins created the first bout of ego-driven acrimony. The first cut included Priebus, Bannon, Conway, Bossie, Mnuchin, Katie Walsh (Priebus's chief of staff), retired Gen. Michael Flynn (destined to become national security advisor), domestic policy advisor Stephen Miller, top communications aide Hope Hicks, Jason Miller (a campaign communications advisor who would soon resign for family reasons), social media guru Dan Scavino, Trump body man John McEntee and Trump bodyguard and longtime friend Keith Schiller. Mnuchin was conspicuous on this list. He wasn't a decision-maker on key transition matters or someone who, like McEntee or Schiller, traveled in constant and close proximity to Trump. He was, in fact, the top contender for treasury secretary and therefore should have had less access to a "senior staff" pin than one might reasonably assume. But Mnuchin had special status in the Trump orbit. He was thought of by some as Tom Hagen in *The Godfather*, a family member without Sicilian blood. Mnuchin was up for Treasury and while he waited was, for all intents and purposes, untouchable. Mnuchin and anyone with the coveted "senior staff" pin could breeze down any corridor or up any elevator, even to the top of the tower and Trump's three-floor penthouse apartment, without raising so much as a furrowed Secret Service brow.

After Trump addressed the nation and the world from the Hilton ballroom, Bossie escorted the First Family–to–be into the waiting Secret Service vehicles (the size of the Trump Secret Service detail more than tripled after he was declared president-elect, agents mobilizing from prepositioned locations in Midtown Manhattan). The black SUVs had waited for the Trumps in the alley behind the Hilton for the very short (five-block) drive to Trump Tower. It was about 4 a.m. The alley was, of course, dark and slick with water, garbage and kitchen scraps. The SUVs barreled down the alley and onto 54th Street. Bossie was left behind because he had to catch up with his family, still somewhere inside the Hilton with punch-drunk Trump revelers. Bossie stood in the damp, fetid alley and paused. He'd just watched the president-elect drive away. He was by himself in a dark Manhattan alley. It was quiet and slightly eerie. Was this the way it was supposed to be? Alone in the dark except for refuse, rotting food and rats? Was this what it looked like to elect a president? With Trump, splendidly and sourly, the answer was yes.

A few hours later, Bossie returned to his office in Trump Tower, overwhelmed by the confounding task of trying to prepare Trump for the presidency. As he walked into his office, Bossie recalled the first time he came to the 14th floor. It was late August. After surveying the scene and meeting campaign leaders Manafort and Rick Gates, Bossie plopped himself down in the hallway and just listened as staffers, most of whom had no idea who he was, walked by and gossiped. Bossie sized up the real estate. Bannon told him to take the office that had been occupied by Gates, the office between Bannon and Conway.

The next day, Bossie came to that office and checked the drawers. Except for stray paper clips and pencils, every drawer but one was empty. In the lower left-hand corner drawer Bossie found a thick book, bound around thick separate sections that looked as if they came from a binder. It was Mitt Romney's transition plan from the 2012 campaign. During his second presidential debate with Obama, Romney said that when he was governor of Massachusetts he sought to add more women to his cabinet and various women's groups "brought us whole binders full of women." This reference became a punchline used against Romney—a vague suggestion he didn't take such appointments seriously. As Bossie looked over the book that may have started as a binder, he quickly concluded it was serious and impressive. It contained transition tasks, flow charts, day-by-day checklists, agencies listed by policy and political priority and, most importantly, hierarchies for incoming White House staff and transition personnel. The book contained a line for every one of 4,152 presidential appointments. Beside each one was a name and next to that a list of alternatives. It also included job duties and an organizational structure for the White House and each cabinet department. Moreover, it identified each member of the incoming Romney White House staff and which offices they would occupy. It also listed every White House employee who worked in the adjacent Eisenhower Executive Office Building, with offices designated by task, area of expertise and floor. If Romney's campaign had more books like this, Bossie remembered thinking at the time, it had been ready to govern. Bossie also remembered thinking at the same time that Romney had spent too much time on this minutia. Win first. Govern later.

Well, Bossie and company had just won. He could easily quote Bill McKay, Robert Redford's character in the classic 1972 political movie *The Candidate*: "What do we do now?"

The principal author (there were three) of the "Romney Readiness Project" was Chris Liddell, who would later become a top White House advisor to Trump. Bossie flipped through it once during that summer of 2016. Impressive, he thought. And useless. Trump was a long shot who did not believe in transition preparation. Romney prepared and lost. Trump would focus on winning. He devoted no money, time or energy to a transition plan. Trump even forbade discussing it, even abstractly, in Trump Tower meetings about the campaign. Trump was deeply superstitious about the transition, considering it bad luck to plan for victory before it was achieved. Perhaps Trump was just running the campaign and his business at the same time—prepared for either to work out. What is frequently forgotten about Trump's presidential campaign is that the GOP nominee kept an active hand in his business throughout, tending to licensing, trademarking, lawsuits, product development and hospitality deals as he prepped for debates, wrote checks to his campaign, battled with lawyers for women who accused him of assault or harassment and had fixers like lawyer Michael Cohen put out fires (Stormy Daniels and Karen McDougal to name just two). Politics and business walked side by side for Trump. He could do one or the other. If he won the presidency, that would be epic. If he lost, the campaign would have enhanced his brand and made him a global sensation, promising more riches and marketing opportunities than before he announced in June of 2015. Either way, Trump would win.

To underscore the point, when Bossie arrived at Trump Tower the day after the election just after 10 a.m., Trump was already in his office on the 26th floor, working on Trump Organization business. You can take the president-elect out of Trump Tower, but you can't take Trump Tower out of the president-elect.

Bossie was discombobulated. He didn't know where to begin. How do we start the transition? Literally, what is the first step? Then he remembered the Romney book he had stuffed back in his desk in the summer. He retrieved it and held it in his beefy hands as he made his way to see Bannon, Priebus, Conway and Kushner.

"Hey, guys. Look what I found. It's a transition plan."

That is how Bossie told Bannon and others that morning they at least had a road map on how to proceed. Sure, it was four years old and none of the names were the least bit relevant—Romney Republicans in a Trump White House? Don't make me laugh! But at least it was a plan. Trump now had a rough outline of what to do. If Romney knew that morning that his plan was coming to Trump's rescue he, Trump and the campaign's most vociferous Republican critic, might well have fainted . . . or cursed.

As Bannon studied the Romney workbook, a call had to be placed to Washington to stop the scheduled shredding. It is well known that each nominee receives a government stipend and office space to prepare for a presidential transition. What is less well known is that the day after the election the government comes by to shred all the loser's documents to protect the identities of people in line for future jobs and to shield internal policy debates from public view. The trucks to gather Trump documents had already been dispatched to his transition offices at the General Services Administration. The Trump transition had to secure its paperwork. It was now the government-in-waiting. Trucks had to be sent to Clintonville. And were. Bannon had read Romney's transition book cover to cover three times. He had sections photocopied and distributed once he had set out transition responsibilities.

That was the one and only act Trump's team took to preserve the transition work that Christie supervised. In a decision Trump made but that was largely driven by Kushner, much of Christie's transition work was destroyed. It was Kushner's revenge but some in the Trump world now argue it did far more damage to his father-in-law. Christie was humiliated for a day. Trump was hamstrung, some loyalists say, for at least six months.

"You can fault Chris Christie for a lot of things, but I personally think he put together a plan that was similar to the Romney Readiness Project," Lewandowski told me. "What he did is he had a plan in place. The executive director of the transition team [Kushner] took that document and quite literally threw it into the trash. It set back the entire team. Christie in the eyes of many people . . . was tainted."

Bossie agrees. "Everything that Chris had done was thrown out. There was no 'Hey let's evaluate it.' It was, 'Let's start from scratch.'"

As with almost everything in Trump world, opinions differ. Other members of the senior transition staff, including but not limited to Bannon and Kushner, didn't think Christie's transition work was that solid.

In interviews with Republicans who served on the transition team, there is a general agreement that Christie built serviceable personnel files but that the policy sections were thin—in part because Trump delivered so few policy speeches and never empowered his policy team to develop white papers on federal policy. Trump just winged it on the road and after the election that left an atrophied policy apparatus. But that was not the biggest problem with Christie's transition work. The bigger problem was Christie. And the Billy Bush weekend. Christie had not gotten on Trump's plane for the second presidential debate in St. Louis. Kushner already disliked Christie. Old wounds and the Billy Bush weekend rendered Christie's transition work radioactive.

"I don't know that anybody went to the president-elect and said we're going to throw out everything that Christie did," Bossie said. "It was we are moving on from Chris and his people. He [Trump] didn't necessarily understand."

This would be a theme of the transition and Trump's first year. From that moment on, Bannon, Priebus, Jared and top campaign advisors Rick Dearborn (chief of staff to Jeff Sessions) and Katie Walsh (Priebus's chief of staff at the RNC) took control of all personnel decisions. All names produced by Christie's team as well as the vetting and research were ditched. There was little comprehension of the task ahead.

"You can't build a government in eight weeks," Lewandowski said.

But Trump had to try. His road map was four years old and he had very few names with which to build a cabinet. He had a handful of seemingly cabinet-ready loyalists including Mnuchin, Sessions and roadshow surrogate and former New York Mayor Rudy Giuliani. For his White House staff, he was less certain. There was Michael Flynn, former head of the Defense Intelligence Agency, and not much else. And Flynn, a firebrand on the trail who frequently whipped up crowds with shouts of "Lock her up," was losing credibility.

Two days after the election, Trump flew to Washington to meet President Obama in the White House. In their private meeting, Obama gave Trump specific advice about building his team. Obama warned Trump that he would get a lot of advice and hear from a lot of pleaders, many of whom would have agendas that didn't necessarily fit with his. Go with your gut, Obama advised. Don't be overly swayed by your advisors—even those closest to you. You won, Obama said. Your instincts served you well. Trust those instincts and pick people who you want and who you trust. Don't let people lead you in directions that differ from your original intent or desire. Trump took it all in and found it unexpectedly valuable. Then Obama paused. There is one thing I want to warn you about, he said. Stay away from Flynn. He's bad news. Do whatever you want with others, but my advice is to steer clear of Flynn.

I have not put quotes around Obama's words because I do not know the precise words he used. Only Obama and Trump know and neither has disclosed them. Both have relayed the conversation to others and numerous sources in Obama and Trump camps have told me this is an accurate summary. What matters is Obama took the unusual step of specifically warning him about Flynn.

By this time, Trump was already intending to pick Flynn as national security advisor. Trump wasn't exactly sure what to make of Obama's advice. Was he being helpful or manipulative? Trump knew Obama fired Flynn because the general openly criticized White House counterterrorism policy as weak and adrift. Trump agreed with that. He said so repeatedly on the campaign trail, often with Flynn as his frothy warm-up act. If Trump agreed with Flynn on terrorism, why would he agree with Obama that he should dump him? It was unsettling. Trump was new to politics and even newer to the presidential club. Was Obama trying to help him or hurt him? He couldn't be sure. Even so, Trump began to brood over Flynn. That did not prevent Trump from naming Flynn national security advisor on November 18.

Then came the unraveling. Within two weeks, news surfaced that Flynn's son and chief of staff, Michael Jr., had tweeted a defense of his father against allegations that he was pushing the conspiracy theory that Clinton was linked to a child molestation ring operating out of a pizza restaurant in the Northwest section of Washington, D.C. Neither Flynn nor his son directly endorsed the so-called Pizzagate rumors, but the younger Flynn's defense of his father against that allegation gave the molestation concoction more visibility. It never gave it credibility. Flynn the younger had, according to several sources, a Trump transition email and was on the payroll. When Trump saw TV coverage of Flynn Jr., who was already grating on the Trump inner circle for parading around Washington telling anyone who would listen how powerful he would soon be, the president-elect exploded.

Priebus was on the 14th floor in Trump Tower when, according to those present, Trump's call came in.

Trump said: "Is this fucking kid on our payroll?"

Priebus said he thought so.

Trump said: "You make sure that motherfucker is gone."

Flynn's flier was losing altitude and airspeed.

Within two weeks of the election, Flynn was in trouble. Senior advisors to Trump did not know what to make of the Obama warning but did give it serious consideration. The Pizzagate flap intensified the sense of unease. The growing consensus among senior transition officials was that Flynn, in the words of one, "was a dead man walking."

Flynn's hiring and firing cast a shadow over Trump's first year, undermining early policy development within the National Security Council on the Middle East and Asia—the consequence of which was to enlarge and expand the early clout of Kushner on both fronts. More problematic, Flynn had numerous contacts with Russian officials about future sanctions policy, United Nations resolutions and other issues. So, too, did Flynn's deputy, K. T. McFarland. Those conversations were not criminal, but they were incautious and betrayed a startling readiness within Trump's inner circle to shift U.S. policy more favorably toward Russia through rapid and repeated engagement. The contacts raised questions because they occurred just as Obama had announced a new round of economic sanctions against Russia for its interference in the 2016 election. Those contacts became fodder for Special Counsel Robert Mueller and foundational to Flynn's guilty plea for lying to the FBI. They also torpedoed McFarland when Trump dumped her from the White House and nominated her as ambassador to Singapore. The Senate Foreign Relations Committee decided her confirmation testimony on those Russia conversations during the transition had been untruthful. The Republican-led Senate refused to act on the nomination. McFarland was forced to withdraw.

When I asked numerous top transition officials why Flynn, amid Trump's misgivings, got the national security advisor job, I heard the same astonishing answer—he was around. That is both preposterous and perfectly representative of the Trump transition. Proximity mattered. So did the look. The look means looking the part, however Trump conjures it. Repeatedly during my research, when I asked top officials why someone landed a coveted cabinet spot, one phrase kept cropping up: "central casting." Or loyalty. Or military background. Those three formed the trinity of Trump considerations.

"Central casting" would loom large in Trump's choice of Neil Gorsuch as his Supreme Court pick (see Chapter Four). Trump's first big post-election meeting on filling the Supreme Court vacancy, the one Senate Republicans held open throughout 2016, took place in Trump's personal office. In attendance were his transition personnel brain trust and Leonard Leo, leader of the Federalist Society project on the federal judiciary, and Sessions. Leo played a vital role in the development of Trump's campaign list of potential Supreme Court nominees. He flew to New York to begin the process of narrowing the choices and starting the formal vetting. It was at this meeting Trump told Sessions he would be his nominee as attorney general, as fateful a decision as any Trump made during the transition. I broke the news of Sessions's expected nomination on *CBS This Morning*.

To build his transition from scratch, Trump needed to rely on existing networks of conservative activists, many of which neither supported nor opposed his candidacy. Trump turned to The Heritage Foundation as a resume mill for administration appointments. The Federalist Society ran all judicial nomination issues—Supreme Court, appeals and district courts. Pro-life issues were referred to the National Right to Life Committee and the Susan B. Anthony List. Crime and firearms issues were run through the National Rifle Association. Tax and immigration policy were kept in house.

"He basically outsourced it," said Dan Senor, a longtime Republican campaign operative who advised Romney's presidential campaign and remains close to Ryan. "On policy, Trump doesn't really believe in anything. So he was going to have to sell out to some faction. And we're just lucky he sold out to us."

Another common phrase during the transition was Trump "couldn't pick [him or her] out of a lineup." Trump knew very few Republicans and had very little sense of their loyalty, ideology or commitment. There were exceptions. Montana Rep. Ryan Zinke was an early backer who called Trump frequently during the campaign to offer encouragement. Zinke was commander of SEAL Team Six and served on SEAL Team One during a 22-year run as a SEAL. He was the first SEAL elected to Congress and was every bit Trump's "central casting" look of an interior secretary.

Trump had no such options for secretary of state. Giuliani wanted it badly, so badly he told Trump he would not accept any other cabinet position. One reason Sessions is attorney general is Giuliani turned the job down. He also turned down secretary of Homeland Security, prompting Trump's team to recruit retired Marine Gen. John Kelly. If Giuliani had taken either job, the first year of the Trump presidency would have played out far differently. Sessions would not be a recused attorney general in the Russia investigation and Kelly, because he would not have been recruited during the transition, would not have become Trump's second chief of staff. Trump and Giuliani had known each other for more than two decades. Trump expected Giuliani to take the plum jobs Trump offered and became infuriated when he refused. Giuliani believed he was more qualified and reliable than anyone else Trump might consider for secretary of state. Trump was furious with Giuliani. Bannon instigated the galling flirtation with Romney as secretary of state. It began as an insult to Giuliani and as a media circus to taunt reporters camped out in the lobby of Trump Tower. The Romney circus required restaurant stakeouts and other obsessive get-the-photo deployments in the blocks around Trump Tower. In Bannon's mind, part of the Trump message to Giuliani was—see, you dare turn me down and I will make you disappear by dining with my biggest GOP rival right here in Manhattan. Take that! It's worth noting Trump also interviewed Bob Corker, chairman of the Foreign Relations Committee, but Corker found the session, like every encounter he had with Trump, too driven by Trump's disorganized and indulgent mind and withdrew.

Romney was a larkish indulgence for Bannon. Then Trump became intrigued by the idea, prompting Bannon and others to say out loud, "'Hold the fuck on."

Yes, Trump was momentarily dazzled by Bannon's game. He started to think a bit more seriously about bringing Romney on board. Bannon, the voice of Trumpian populism, saw it as a billowing catastrophe and intervened, telling senior staff it was up to him to "un-fuck it."

These gyrations were common throughout the transition. Trump would seemingly make up his mind and then toy with another idea or set of ideas—or names. This tendency would follow him into the White House. The flirtations even beset Mnuchin, whom everyone considered the safest, surest bet of all.

Mnuchin kept waiting for his treasury secretary announcement. Where was the press release? It was late November now. Thanksgiving was approaching. He began to fear that things, inexplicably, might be slipping away. And for a demoralizing weekend before Thanksgiving, they were. Mnuchin was momentarily second fiddle on Trump's treasury secretary depth chart to Jamie Dimon, CEO of JPMorgan Chase. Gary Cohn, also with a Goldman pedigree, who would become Trump's top White House economic advisor, was also in the running—as was Bridgewater Associates co-CEO David McCormick. Dimon was the most alluring Mnuchin alternative. Trump was caught up in Dimon's Wall Street mega brand power and universal name recognition in world financial capitals. Dimon was bigger in financial circles than most presidents or prime ministers. He ate finance ministers on his breakfast toast, or so Trump imagined. Dimon expressed an interest and Trump was, for a time, flattered and hypnotized.

"One thing you can never forget about Trump," Manafort, Trump's former campaign chairman, told me at the time. "He's a star fucker. He can't help it. He loves stars and star power. Dimon has it. That's why he was in the running."

Ultimately, Mnuchin prevailed and emerged as spokesman for Trump on economic policy and as sherpa for other cabinet secretaries-to-be. Mnuchin's scrape with irrelevance—even after getting "pinned"—and the companion tale of Ray Washburne, a Dallas-based investment banker and restaurateur, encapsulated Trump's whimsical "central casting" preferences.

Washburne was in line for energy secretary. He was Mnuchin's chief deputy on Trump's finance team and guided him through his early days of befuddlement dealing with GOP donors, fund-raisers and bundlers (Mnuchin previously raised money from and gave it exclusively to Democrats). Washburne was fully vetted and clean as a whistle. Bannon told him after an interview, "When we appoint you energy secretary are we going to be hit with anything we haven't found? Are you going to embarrass us?" Washburne promised there were no hidden secrets or scandals.

Washburne waited for two weeks for the appointment that never came. He heard various names floated but was given repeated assurances he was the pick—that Energy was his. On the day of his expected nomination, Mnuchin plucked Washburne from a conference room on the 14th floor of Trump Tower and trundled him into the elevator for a ride to Trump's office on the 26th floor. Mnuchin was beaming and gave Washburne a reassuring slap on the back.

As they entered the office, Trump looked up. "Sorry, Ray, I just met with Rick Perry and I'm going with him as energy secretary. We'll find something for you."

Washburne wanted to recoil but stood completely still and did nothing—or as little as he could—to convey the shock and disappointment. Mnuchin let out a dry cough. He, too, was amazed and perplexed. He had no idea he was leading Washburne to his execution. It was supposed to be a celebration. Trump was on board—or so Mnuchin thought. But Perry was a bigger player, had more political clout and, importantly, the swagger to walk into Trump's office and demand a cabinet post already allocated to Washburne. In fact, Perry had done that very thing the day before, wiping out Washburne.

In the awkward silence, Trump looked absently around his office as if trying to remember something. Yes. That's it. He had to name a secretary of state and end the spectacle of playing Giuliani off against Romney. By this time, Giuliani had already withdrawn from consideration, knowing he'd miscalculated. But Romney hadn't. He just didn't know Trump had already landed on ExxonMobil CEO Rex Tillerson—a late entrant into the sweepstakes when Trump had grown tired of toying with Giuliani and Romney. Even though during the campaign Trump scorned the Republican foreign policy establishment, it was precisely those voices—James Baker, Condoleezza Rice and Stephen Hadley, secretaries of state or national security advisors during both Bush presidencies—who persuaded Trump to take Tillerson. The CEO had the "central casting" look, the business "star" quality so seductive to Trump and one other thing—fuck-you money. That's money that makes a Washington job, even a cabinet post, an afterthought. Trump loves that. Why? Because he believes money like that minimizes Beltway ladder climbing and allows him to judge loyalty and obedience more clearly. Trump chose cabinet secretaries with FU money credentials: Wilbur Ross ($2.5 billion) as commerce secretary; Betsy DeVos ($1 billion) as education secretary; Mnuchin ($385 million) at Treasury; Tillerson ($300 million) at State; Ben Carson ($22 million) at Housing and Urban Development; and Elaine Chao ($22 million) at Transportation. Gary Cohn, Trump's first head of the National Economic Council, was a former Goldman Sachs president and CEO. He came into his White House job with assets valued between $252 million and $611 million, according to his disclosure filing.

As Washburne and Mnuchin stared out Trump's office window, still adjusting to the stunning selection of Perry, Trump rustled papers and swung around to look over Central Park. Forgetting that Washburne and Mnuchin were still there, Trump swiveled his chair back toward his desk with a jerk and a "That's it" look on his face.

"Shit," Trump blurted out. "I gotta call Mitt and tell him he's not going to be secretary of state."

FOUR

Neil Gorsuch

President Trump strode down the Cross Hall on the first floor of the White House residence, live television capturing for millions each stride down the long, red carpet to the East Room. Trump's presidency was 11 days old and desperately in need of a presidential moment. In the right corner of the East Room, standing behind the audience seated in rows of chairs arranged in a semicircle before the majestic threshold, White House Chief of Staff Reince Priebus gnawed at the inside of his lower lip. White House Chief Strategist Steve Bannon stood alongside Priebus with a rumpled, greasy look of wonder. East Room. Prime time. Nationwide audience. President Trump. Nominating a Supreme Court Justice. Could you believe it?

The architects of this moment sat feet away from the Blue Goose, the informal name White House ushers have given the bulletproof podium presidents use for virtually all formal remarks. As Trump approached, Senate Majority Leader Mitch McConnell watched from second row center, just to the left, from Trump's vantage point, of White House Counsel Don McGahn. A few rows back sat Leonard Leo, an unassuming figure unrecognizable to most Washingtonians and utterly unknown to the rest of the country. As is sometimes true in history, when Leo, McGahn and McConnell began their work on this day many months earlier, they had no idea what would come of it—and every reason to suspect nothing much at all. As events unfolded, their interactions and decisions would, to even their surprise, help create this historic American tableau.

"This may be the most transparent judicial selection process in history," Trump said, reading from the teleprompter connected to the Blue Goose. "Months ago as a candidate, I publicly presented a list of brilliant and accomplished people to the American electorate and pledged to make my choice from among that list. Millions of voters said this was the single most important issue to them when they voted for me for president."

All true, which was somewhat unusual for Trump in his first days as president. Trump did offer a list. And it was vital to his election, so much so that many close to him doubt he would have been elected without it. The list bound uneasy Republicans to his cause, if for no other reason than to invest in his hands and not Clinton's the future of the Supreme Court. I met countless Trump supporters who, with no prompting, identified the Supreme Court as the reason they could live with Trump's volatility and lack of political experience.

Trump stood beneath a Bohemian crystal center chandelier, one of the three 1,200-pound marvels installed in 1902 by President Theodore Roosevelt to replace the first chandeliers hung in 1829 by President Andrew Jackson, a political figure with whom Trump likes to favorably compare himself. This was Trump's first East Room event. He spoke steadily, but the gravity of the moment and the grandeur of the surroundings got the best of him.

"Today I am keeping another promise to the American people by nominating Judge Neil Gorsuch of the United States Supreme Court to be of the United States Supreme Court."

Halfway through the sentence, Trump knew he was in trouble. After saying "of the United States Supreme Court," he paused ever so briefly and winced before reframing the sentence and patching the damage. For those in my world of television reporting, the crucial soundbite was the one that just got away. Trump supporters found it endearing; Trump opponents a sign he could not even handle basic elocution when it counted most. Before calling Gorsuch up to the stage, Trump began to describe the legacy he would soon cement on the federal bench.

"Depending on their age, a justice can be active for 50 years and his or her decisions can last a century or more and can often be permanent," Trump said.

Leo, a lawyer from Long Island; McGahn, a campaign finance expert born in Atlantic City; and McConnell, who as a boy of 13 overcame polio in rural Alabama, listened to Trump and beamed, knowing they had the tools to confirm Gorsuch and protect the 5–4 conservative majority on the high court. Gorsuch would replace Justice Antonin Scalia after the longest and most bitterly contested Supreme Court vacancy in American history. This trio—Leo, McGahn and McConnell (sounds like a law firm, right?)—reshaped the history of the court, the Senate and the presidency. It all started just less than a year before, on February 13.

McConnell had just landed in the Virgin Islands, arriving from Washington for the weeklong Presidents Day congressional recess. He looked at his iPhone (which he still refers to as a "machine") for a news update. What he saw stopped him cold. Associate Supreme Court Justice Antonin Scalia, 79, had died hours earlier in his room at a hunting ranch near Marfa, Texas. Much later, the Presidio County Sheriff's Office and Rear Adm. Brian P. Monahan, physician to the high court and Congress, would conclude that Scalia died of natural causes. The sheriff's office said nothing was amiss in Scalia's hunting cabin, where he was found alone in bed and with no signs of disturbance. Monahan cited Scalia's obstructive pulmonary disease and high blood pressure as contributing causes.

In these first, shocking moments, McConnell only knew Scalia was dead and there appeared in the early reports no indication of foul play or mystery. He and his wife, Elaine Chao, rode from the airport to their island hotel room. McConnell turned on the TV and immersed himself in the cable coverage.

"The first thing I thought about was my own interaction with him over the years," McConnell told me.

In the 1970s during the Ford administration, McConnell was a young Justice Department lawyer and once attended a meeting attended by Scalia, Robert Bork and Laurence Silberman. Scalia was assistant attorney general for the Office of Legal Counsel; Bork was solicitor general; Silberman was deputy attorney general. McConnell, who remembers shuddering at being in the presence of "giants," kept his mouth shut and took notes. McConnell was elected to the Senate in 1984 and voted, as luck would have it, to confirm Scalia to the Supreme Court in 1986; Silberman to the Court of Appeals for the D.C. Circuit in 1985; and Bork (in a losing effort) to the high court in 1987.

McConnell and Scalia were not personally close friends but knew each other well. After spending a few moments reminiscing, McConnell began plotting what to do about the Scalia vacancy. The plot he decided upon, next to Trump's decision to run, is by far the most consequential event of the 2016 election.

It was 3 p.m. There were about two hours, McConnell thought, to shape the future of the court, influence the battle for the Republican presidential nomination and deal one last humiliating blow to Obama. McConnell relished the prospect of all three.

McConnell convened an immediate conference call with his chief of staff, chief counsel and director of operations. His deputy chief of staff and communications consigliere, Don Stewart, would handle the statement McConnell would soon release. McConnell's staff had dispersed for the recess and dialed in from all manner of locations. McConnell did not seek advice. He gave orders. A statement under his name was to be released declaring the Scalia vacancy would remain open all year. He explained it to me this way.

"I turned to the practical situation and said to myself if the shoe were on the other foot, would the Democrats be filling this vacancy? And I knew the answer was no. So, sitting there by myself in the room, I sent out a statement saying the next president would fill this vacancy. Why did I do that? I had members scattered around the world and around the country. I was hoping to lay down a marker so when I got back [to Washington] a week later, I didn't have 51 different opinions on how to handle this. Everybody kind of froze until we got back."

McConnell's statement was released at 6 p.m. "Justice Scalia's fidelity to the Constitution was rivaled only by the love of his family. Through the sheer force of his intellect and his legendary wit, this giant of American jurisprudence almost single-handedly revived an approach to constitutional interpretation that prioritized the text and original meaning of the Constitution. The American people should have a voice in the selection of our next Supreme Court Justice. Therefore, this vacancy should not be filled until we have a new president."

Daring. Politically tenacious. The nation hadn't even begun to process the news of Scalia's death and McConnell declared no Supreme Court nominee—regardless of his or her qualifications—would be confirmed during Obama's presidency. No one knew who the next president would be. The constitutional authority to nominate Scalia's successor was Obama's. The constitutional obligation to advise and consent was the Senate's. With one statement and without consulting any Senate Republican colleagues, McConnell proclaimed Obama's authority and responsibility null and void.

The audacity is almost impossible to comprehend. Not only was it a power move without precedent, McConnell was taking on risks of titanic proportions. What if Senate Republicans rebelled and ignored McConnell's DOA pronouncement? The Republican presidential field was still in flux. Texas Sen. Ted Cruz had narrowly won the Iowa caucuses. Trump had won the New Hampshire primary in a landslide. The South Carolina primary was seven days away. What if the GOP nominee (Trump, Cruz, someone else) didn't beat Hillary Clinton, still the odds-on favorite? A victorious Clinton would surely punish McConnell and Republicans by nominating a fiery liberal replacement who would tip the ideological balance of the high court for at least a decade. Even if Senate Republicans fell in line behind McConnell, could they withstand inevitable White House denunciations?

McConnell knew the answers to precisely none of these questions. But he had the single-mindedness to turn risk into reality. McConnell knew he had to act fast because every Republican presidential candidate was in Greenville, South Carolina, for a prime-time debate on CBS. I was part of the debate prep team for John Dickerson and served as a co-moderator with John and Kimberly Strassel of *The Wall Street Journal*. The CBS team spent five days preparing questions for the 90-minute debate, a process that sounds easy but is excruciating in precision, research and management. Preparing for a debate is not just about the questions. It's about the premise behind the questions, the accuracy of the foundation beneath. It's also about the subject chosen.

Foreign policy can cover dozens of issues, ideas, places and circum-stances. Domestic policy—from economics to abortion, infrastructure to Social Security—can present myriad options as well. In the early stages, hundreds of potential questions are created. Each is then pains-takingly researched. Then the lists are winnowed in an eye-straining and at times mind-meandering process (Which Social Security ques-tion did we keep: the one about chain inflation adjustment or raising the retirement age?). This process only gets you halfway there. After you decide what questions to ask, you decide which candidate will re-ceive which questions. That's harder than it sounds. You can't ask the front-runner everything. How do you distribute a balance of domestic and foreign policy questions? How do you keep everyone as regularly involved as possible? Who is chosen for a follow-up? Does one question *there* naturally lead to a complementary question *over there*?

We wrapped our final cut on questions, research and distribution about noon that Saturday. Roughly four hours later came word Scalia was dead. The first 30 minutes of the debate we planned to conduct had just vanished. We had to recast the start of the debate to reflect the breaking news. That was our burden and it paled next to the exertions going on among the GOP front-runners. Trump's chief legal counsel, Don McGahn, called Leo and sought his advice for Trump's statement on Scalia. McGahn didn't come empty-handed. He was seeking Leo's specific advice about a particular way Trump wanted to talk about Sca-lia and his legacy—one that would amplify McConnell's declaration that the next president would fill the vacancy. Leo expected McGahn to say Trump would do the safe thing—pay homage to Scalia and say he would seek to fill the seat with someone like Scalia. Anyone could do that but Trump, as the race had already shown, had difficulty land-ing easy, conventional sentiments. Leo expected caution and a sense of timidity from McGahn. Leo knew McGahn well but had no sense of Trump beyond what came through the TV, which Leo did not find par-ticularly reassuring. What would Trump do in this moment? It was— to borrow a Trump word—huge. Leo knew Republicans generally and judicial conservatives specifically would scrutinize Trump.

McGahn was not cautious. He said Trump not only wanted to say he would appoint someone like Scalia, he wanted to give at least two names recognizable to conservative court watchers. Trump knew he would get the first question and wanted to steal the Scalia moment by doing more than expected. It was the first inkling Leo had of what would become a Supreme Court road map for Trump, one that would prove increasingly important to his pursuit of the presidency. This was also a moment where, McGahn told Leo, Trump wanted to show he was more than a showman.

By the start of the debate, Trump had already released a statement backing up McConnell's election-year "vacancy" strategy. Trump received the first question but Dickerson tried to turn it around in hopes of provoking an answer that conveyed more than talking points.

Dickerson: "If you were president and had a chance with 11 months left to go in your term, wouldn't it be an abdication to conservatives, in particular, not to name a conservative justice with the rest of your term?"

Trump: "Well, I can say this. If I were president now I would certainly want to try and nominate a justice. I am sure of that, frankly. I'm absolutely sure that President Obama will try and do it. I hope that our Senate is going to be able—Mitch and the entire group—is going to be able to do something about it. In terms of delay, we could have a Diane Sykes, or you could have a Bill Pryor; we have some fantastic people. But this is a tremendous blow to conservatism."

Dickerson: "So, just to be clear on this, Mr. Trump, you're okay with the president nominating somebody?"

Trump: "I think he's going to do it whether I'm okay with it or not. I think it's up to Mitch McConnell and everybody else to stop it. It's called delay, delay, delay."

Trump landed the first applause line of the debate. McGahn got the names of Sykes and Pryor from Leo. Neither was well known to Trump. Sykes served on the 7th Circuit Court of Appeals, nominated in 2003 by President George W. Bush, and was among those Bush considered to replace Associate Justice Sandra Day O'Connor in 2005. Pryor served on the 11th Circuit Court of Appeals, also appointed by Bush, and had been Alabama's attorney general. Unlike Sykes, Pryor's circuit court nomination was stalled by Senate Democrats. They branded Pryor an extremist and cited his description of *Roe v. Wade* (which legalized abortion nationally in 1973) as the "worst abomination in the history of constitutional law." Trump's mention of Sykes and Pryor sent an explicit signal to judicial conservatives and allowed him to occupy the post-Scalia high ground.

By putting names to a vacancy at the South Carolina debate, Trump moved gingerly from the general to the specific. The positive reaction gave Trump an early edge in the debate—making him appear more collected, focused and crafty than his opponents anticipated. Leo received only one other candidate call that afternoon and it was from Cruz. The Texas senator wanted to know how Leo thought the issue would play and how best it might be to proceed. But Cruz did not go as far as Trump, in part because he was, unluckily, the last GOP candidate questioned about the Scalia vacancy. He also lost momentum by confusing when Associate Justice Anthony Kennedy was confirmed. Cruz said he was nominated and confirmed in 1987, central to his point that a justice had not been confirmed in an election year. Kennedy, in fact, was nominated in November of 1987 and confirmed in 1988, as Dickerson pointed out. Irritated, Cruz plowed through this thicket but mentioned no possible replacements for Scalia. He gave a detailed description of Scalia's family (down to the 36 "grandkids") and the judicial stakes involved. It was lawyerly and dense—just as anyone familiar with Cruz might expect. In the Scalia sweepstakes, Cruz did not advance the ball or his cause. Trump did.

The mention of Sykes and Pryor planted a seed for the Trump campaign that would grow deep and durable roots. In ways not appreciated by McGahn, Leo, any of Trump's challengers or the legions of political reporters covering the race, the hours leading up to the South Carolina debate and the gathering of two specific names as potential replacements for Scalia led to Trump's Supreme Court list. That idea, viewed with the benefit of hindsight, may have done more than any other to propel him to the presidency.

Trump's debate performance was slightly daring. For the seemingly bloodless McConnell, his corking of the Scalia vacancy was bloodcurdling. McConnell had a world of variables in front of him and damn few talking points. Stewart and others began researching the history of Supreme Court vacancies in a presidential election year and found this was the first since 1932. Justice Oliver Wendell Holmes, a court giant, retired on January 12, 1932, and President Herbert Hoover nominated Benjamin Cardozo on February 15. The Republican-controlled

Senate confirmed Cardozo nine days later. There were two in-between scenarios. President Franklin Roosevelt nominated Frank Murphy on January 4, 1940, after Justice Pierce Butler died on November 16, 1939. Reagan nominated Kennedy on November 30, 1987, and the Democratic-controlled Senate, which had rejected Reagan's first nominee, Robert Bork, confirmed Kennedy on February 3, 1988. Stewart also found a 1992 quote from then-Sen. Joe Biden, chairman of the Judiciary Committee, suggesting President George H. W. Bush forgo nominating a replacement that campaign year if—IF—a justice retired. When Biden gave his Senate speech, no vacancy existed. He spoke on June 25, more than four months later in that campaign year than McConnell's no-consideration-of-a-nominee edict was laid down. Here is what Biden said:

> In my view, politics has played far too large a role in the Reagan-Bush nominations to date. One can only imagine that role becoming overarching if a choice were made this year, assuming a justice announced tomorrow that he or she was stepping down. Should a justice resign this summer and the president move to name a successor, actions that will occur just days before the Democratic Presidential Convention and weeks before the Republican Convention meets, a process that is already in doubt in the minds of many will become distrusted by all. Senate consideration of a nominee under these circumstances is not fair to the president, to the nominee, or to the Senate itself. As a result, it is my view that if a Supreme Court Justice resigns tomorrow, or within the next several weeks, or resigns at the end of the summer, President Bush should consider following the practice of a majority of his predecessors and not—and not—name a nominee until after the November election is completed.

McConnell called this the "Biden Rule." There was never a Biden Rule. It was a Biden speech. Nothing more. But McConnell was desperate for a hook, any hook to make his gambit look and sound grounded in precedent, no matter how flimsily. Biden's speech was a start. Biden didn't say no nomination in an election year. He didn't say the Senate shouldn't consider a nominee. He said that in the midst of nominating conventions and the ensuing campaign the atmosphere would be too belligerent to give a high court nominee due consideration. That was enough for McConnell. Biden's notion became a rule; his suggestion that Bush might delay nominating a successor for a nonexistent vacancy became a mandate for the Senate to ignore an actual nominee for a real vacancy. Such is the artwork of politics—macabre to some, merely inventive to others. Then Stewart unearthed a 2005 quote from Senate Democratic leader Harry Reid that said there was no constitutional obligation to confirm a president's nominee. "It says appointments shall be made with the advice and consent of the Senate. That is very different than saying every nominee receives a vote." In 2007 New York Democrat Chuck Schumer, who by 2016 was on the verge of becoming Democratic Leader, said "we should not confirm a Supreme Court nominee except in extraordinary circumstances." Reid's and Schumer's quotes came in nonelection years, buttressing McConnell's case (even though he had argued the opposite point of view under a Republican president).

Bits and pieces of evidence now gathered, McConnell could begin constructing the rickety scaffolding of his political argument. He surveyed Republicans over the next week and found only a few possible dissenters. The talking points helped keep order and gave politicians what they most need when a hot issue arises—a placeholder sentence that pushes off the hardest questions. All this was occurring in an environment without a nominee from Obama. And therein lay the beauty—or ugliness, depending on your point of view—of McConnell's stratagem. He didn't care who Obama nominated and didn't want Republicans to care either. He wanted them to help him change the rules of the game by focusing the argument on *whether* the vacancy should be filled, not by *whom*. He asked Republicans to stick with that and not budge. Historically, Supreme Court vacancy anticipation, a unique kind of Beltway fever, was about the nominee's identity and qualifications. Then the politics of advice and consent took over. Not for McConnell. This time, there would be no advice and consent. McConnell's attitude could be summed up in four words or one emoji: Talk to the hand.

"Here is what I was selling to my colleagues," McConnell told me. "The president is going to send up a well-qualified person. If you share

my view that this ought to be about who ought to make the appointment [rather] than who is appointed, then my recommendation is no
hearings, no action, no nothing. I didn't know for sure if it would work
for us politically. I thought it was a defensible position and could sustain a political barrage. If we'd actually had a process, we would have
been all over the place. But I had to sell that it was about who ought to
make the appointment."

While McConnell defied Obama and held his conference together
against editorial page and Democratic outrage, Trump won South
Carolina's primary and rolled up big wins on Super Tuesday and was
looking more formidable than any Republican could have anticipated.
After Super Tuesday II on March 15, Trump had won 19 primaries
and amassed 705 delegates. Jeb Bush was gone. So was Marco Rubio.
Trump had knocked 14 GOP challengers out. Only Cruz and Ohio
Gov. John Kasich remained. And yet Trump had only one U.S. senator
on his team—Jeff Sessions of Alabama.

Trump had to start thinking about being president and linking
up with key players in the conservative movement. In mid-March his
campaign organized an off-the-record lunch at the Washington headquarters of Jones Day, his campaign's law firm. McGahn was a partner there, as was William McGinley (who would become White House
cabinet secretary), and the firm would provide all of Trump's campaign
legal advice and handle much of the sensitive legal work through the
transition and Special Counsel Robert Mueller's investigation (more
on that later).

It was Trump's first trip to Washington as front-runner for the
nomination. Inside a conference room he met conservatives who were
already on his team and those who wanted to be. Sessions chaired the
meeting. Trump brought McGahn, Kushner and sons Eric and Don Jr.
Around the table he found: Gingrich, already a frequent advisor; Jim
DeMint, then-president of The Heritage Foundation, a conservative
think tank; Bob Tyrrell, publisher of *The American Spectator* and conservative curmudgeon; Arkansas Sen. Tom Cotton; and Reps. Chris
Collins of New York and Renee Ellmers of North Carolina.

McGahn invited Leo because Trump wanted to talk to him after
the lunch. Leo attended, but not as an endorser or advisor. After lunch
broke up, Trump and McGahn pulled Leo into a side conference room.

By this time in the campaign, Leo had learned from others that Trump did not like to be lectured and that the way to engage was to let him go first and ask questions. It was astute, and the heads-up served him well (as it does those who still survive in the Trump White House).

"He's not an intellectual," Gingrich said, describing Trump. "It's not that he's not smart. It's that he doesn't value words—he values words as a salesman. And he's pretty good at it. He doesn't sit around and think complex thoughts and read big books and put all of this together into paragraphs. Who needs a paragraph?"

For Leo, the moments between the luncheon and his first encounter with Trump were pregnant with possibility. Leo is head of judicial nominations for the Federalist Society and a case study in Washington influence and advocacy. He has spent three decades lobbying on behalf of a judicial doctrine known as originalism. Leo is a quiet, rotund man with gentle manners and a soft voice. He presents as a pushover but is a razor-sharp advocate for a federal judiciary that he hopes will halt what he regards as a progressive reinterpretation of the Constitution. Leo abhors the idea of a "living Constitution," but respects precedent enough to realize an achievable short-term goal is to maintain the status quo and, when possible, chip away at "liberal" court decisions of the past 40 years. Leo revered Scalia and has cultivated a national network of conservative lawyers in the hopes of populating state and federal benches with jurists in Scalia's image. It was just possible, Leo thought, that Trump could advance that cause. Little did Leo realize Trump would do it with bullet-train velocity.

Trump's ego demanded and demands an exchange of information—not an oration or filibuster. Leo kept his mouth shut, waiting for Trump or McGahn to speak.

"Federalist Society," Trump said, seeing Leo. "I love you guys."

Leo waited through an awkward silence. Trump just stood there with McGahn. More silence. Against his better judgment, Leo spoke.

"So. I understand you want to talk about judges."

"I want to have this list."

"That's never been done before."

"Does that mean we shouldn't do it?"

Leo decided to let that question hang for a moment. He was curious about Trump's motives.

"Why do you want to do it?"

"People don't know who I am," Trump said. "They don't know what I think about these issues."

True enough, Leo thought. The two discussed the risks: each name could and likely would become fodder for opposition research and embarrassments could surface; feelings could be hurt if names did not appear on the list; some conservatives could be displeased if certain names did not appear. Leo said previous Republican presidents—specifically both Bushes—gave the process of selecting a nominee short shift, leading, in his opinion, to poor choices.

At this Trump interjected.

"Is Souter as bad as everyone says he is?"

This may have been Trump baiting the hook. "Everyone" meant conservatives. For judicial conservatives, David Souter is the defining example of a nomination process that fell apart at the White House and produced a nominee with no track record and a justice so unmoored from originalism (as Leo and his ilk see it) as to be indistinguishable from a Clinton or Obama nominee. For judicial conservatives, Souter was synonymous with failure—an opportunity missed by a White House that didn't care about the court, originalism or conservative voters. When George W. Bush nominated Harriet Miers, conservatives revolted because they feared another untested nominee, like Souter was for George H. W. Bush, might, absent their angry intervention, be headed for the high court. From Leo's point of view, a rigorous process was one that ran through the Federalist Society and a lengthy judicial record meant a string of decisions grounded in originalism first and precedent second. Leo wanted judges to have a long record of originalist muscle memory—where the questions of law are by second nature run through the gauntlet of original powers given the federal government in the Constitution, not, as Leo would describe it, the aggregated powers and imagined rights the court dispensed to various pleaders and grievance-merchants during the 20th century. Leo doesn't necessarily oppose modernity in terms of civil rights, gay rights, environmental or labor regulation. He merely wants the courts to interpret the Constitution's approach to these questions based on laws passed by a state or Congress. The impetus must come from the state or federal legislature, not the court. If there is ambiguity, Leo does not want it filled with what he and other judicial conservatives call judicial fiat. Leo wants the court to be a cautious custodian of American law, not an innovator. For these reasons, Trump's question about Souter captivated Leo, which may have been its purpose.

"Actually, he's worse," Leo said, noting that Souter's judicial record was almost entirely on the New Hampshire Supreme Court and therefore gave little indication of how he would approach the U.S. Constitution. To Leo's thinking the selection process in any White House must begin with candidates with established records on the federal bench. Trump nodded, but Leo was careful to keep the points brief.

"Is Roberts as bad as Souter?"

That startled Leo a bit. Conservatives had found fault with Roberts but did not generally associate him with Souter.

"Why do you ask?"

"Because of Obamacare," Trump said.

"Do you not agree with the decision?"

"No."

"Why not?"

"Because he made it up."

As Leo said to me: "That was my epiphany. That told me what I needed to know. This was a guy who at his core gets it."

As with Souter, Trump wanted to know how Roberts was nominated, what the process was and what might be done differently. As much as Leo thought he was measuring Trump it was he, Trump, measuring and, to a degree, reeling in Leo.

"So the list," Trump said. "Who do you think should be on the list?"

Leo came prepared and allowed Trump to reel him right in.

"I happen to have a list here," Leo said, reaching into his jacket pocket. "Would you like to see it?"

"They're all judges," Trump said, after going over the single-spaced list of names and current judicial positions, some from state supreme courts.

"This is 10," Trump said. "I really wanted a dozen."

"Well, you have 10."

"Can't we do a dozen?"

Leo looked at McGahn. The two agreed to talk later. Trump walked away. Meeting over.

Leo thought 10 names were plenty for any candidate list. Because it had never been done before, there were no expectations. Ten would more than suffice. Plus, Leo knew enough about the 10 suggested names to be relatively sure nothing would go wrong if their backgrounds were carefully checked. He felt good about 10. He didn't want to go beyond that. But Trump, as is typical, was fixated. He often gets fixated and rare is the instance when he can be talked out of that fixation. In this case, he was fixated on the number 12. He wanted 12 names. That was Trump's number and all other considerations were secondary. Leo spent several days researching more judges to add to the list. Leo kept thinking, it's not even a binding list. It's just illustrative. Who cares if there are 10 names or 11 or 12? Trump cared. He would not accept anything less. Finally, Leo came up with an 11th name. He called McGahn.

"I've got good news and bad news. The good news is we have the list done. The bad news is it's 11, it's not 12."

"You're kidding me. He's not going to like that."

"Well, he's got 11. If you want to add a 12th, go ahead. But this is what I have for you."

Amazingly, Gorsuch was not on this first list. Gorsuch was not well enough known to Leo's team and thus not understood to be a reliably conservative judge with a devotion to originalism. This matters not only in terms of Leo's understanding of how many supposed originalists he knew who were already on the federal bench—he came with six names—but in the infancy of the notion that he should be prepared for a candidate who might want such a list and how that preparation might influence, might enhance, the vetting process if that candidate won the presidency. Leo was being asked to be better prepared and in return was offered the judicial Holy Grail in exchange—effective veto power over the next nominee.

Talk about "The Art of the Deal."

But Leo prevailed. The original list contained his 11 names and was released on May 18. The list included: Thomas Hardiman, 3rd Circuit Court of Appeals; Don Willett, Texas Supreme Court; Raymond Kethledge, 6th Circuit Court of Appeals; Thomas Rex Lee, Utah Supreme Court; Joan Larsen, Michigan Supreme Court; Steven Colloton, 8th

Circuit Court of Appeals; Raymond Gruender, 8th Circuit Court of Appeals; David Stras, Minnesota Supreme Court; Allison Eid, Colorado Supreme Court; Diane Sykes, 7th Circuit Court of Appeals; and Bill Pryor, 11th Circuit Court of Appeals.

The list was greeted, like so much of the Trump campaign, as an oddity. It landed amid dozens of other events and commotions, many of them seemingly vital and unanswered questions: Would House Speaker Ryan endorse? Would Trump seek Ryan's removal as chairman of the Republican National Convention? Would the Bush family endorse Trump? Which prominent Republicans would boycott Trump's nominating convention? How would Trump form his transition team? And when would Trump secure the magic number of 1,237 delegates to guarantee the nomination? As this book is dedicated to studying the important and not the sensational, let me say I missed the full importance of the Supreme Court list when it was unveiled. I did find it original and newsy. But I did not comprehend its importance then or how its importance evolved as the campaign continued.

"I take no credit for the list," McConnell told me. "It was important because of the nature of the nominee. If it had been any other nominee, a more conventional nominee, I don't think it would have been necessary. But with this guy, everybody, you know, wanted to know is this guy really a Republican? It was comforting."

To understand the list's evolution is to understand how Trump and his team came to understand the power of the Supreme Court as a rallying cry to base supporters and a reassuring gesture to undecided or wavering Republicans. I can think of no other issue that Trump made his own that better accomplished these difficult tasks. Republicans uncertain about Trump ultimately gave him their vote because of the Scalia vacancy and how he would fill any future vacancy. Even among Republicans repulsed by Trump, the high court kept them Okay Trump instead of Never Trump.

"What I could not predict," McConnell told me, "was by the fall both candidates were so deeply unpopular this could be best described as a 'hold your nose' election. We discovered after the election Trump got 9 out of 10 Republican votes, just like Mitt Romney did. And the single biggest issue to bring them home was the Supreme Court. The list was tied to justify voting for him. I can't tell you I was smart enough to figure that out when I made the call [on the Scalia vacancy] initially. But, clearly, in the end, it was hugely helpful to getting him elected."

The potency of the Supreme Court and its future showed up vividly in Election Day exit polls. Among all voters, 21 percent said it was "the most important factor." Among those who said that, 56 percent backed Trump. The court was important because it was an institutional representation of law, justice and culture. For conservatives, Trump's ability to influence the court was a proxy for their opposition to gay marriage, abortion, Black Lives Matter and what they perceived as a general hostility to police and the judicial system. The contrast here with Clinton voters was stark. Of the voters who said that the U.S. justice system treats "all fairly," 73 percent voted for Trump, while of those who said it treats "blacks unfairly," 72 percent voted for Clinton.

The Supreme Court issue also helped Trump supporters overcome reservations about honesty, trustworthiness, qualifications and temperament—exit polls show that even among Trump supporters he ran well behind Clinton on these qualities. When Republicans would mentally jot down all their reservations about Trump, the Supreme Court was one issue that kept pulling them back, kept balancing that ledger. It is an underappreciated truth in Trump's campaign that in addition to its anti-elite appeal and its rejection of bipartisan globalism, it was also decidedly antagonistic to the cultural direction the nation had taken in the past 20 years. Whether the question was about abortion, gay rights, transgender bathrooms or flag burning (remember its brief revival during the transition?), the future of the Supreme Court served as a placeholder for deep-seated cultural grievances among white evangelicals, Republicans generally and a good number of white Catholic Democrats in states like Pennsylvania, Wisconsin and Michigan. These voters knew the country was changing and were uncomfortable with the pace and trajectory. Not only did Trump offer paeans to patriotism and nostalgia, he offered voters a tool by which to slow modernity—a center-right majority on the high court. As high as the Supreme Court numbers were in exit polls, I am confident the actual percentage is at least four points and possibly six points higher. Trump supporters disdained exit polls and avoided them nationwide—one of the reasons early exit poll data was so depressing for Team Trump and why, in the end, it was revealed to be inconsistent with actual voting preferences.

The Supreme Court list reached its maximum level of political potency when Trump boosted the list to 21 names and declared that, if elected, he would choose Scalia's replacement from this binding and comprehensive list. The list was not really 21. It got to 21 because Trump, McGahn and Leo decided to add Utah Republican Sen. Mike Lee. That was a nod to Lee's own attentiveness to the court and judicial issues, but only a nod. It was pure politics. Adding Lee to the list cemented Cruz's eventual endorsement. Added to the list were: Gorsuch; Margaret Ryan, U.S. Court of Appeals for the Armed Forces; Edward Mansfield, Iowa Supreme Court; Keith Blackwell, Georgia Supreme Court; Charles Canady, Florida Supreme Court; Timothy Tymkovich, chief justice of the 10th Court of Appeals; Amul Thapar, Eastern District of Kentucky; Frederico Moreno, Southern District of Florida; and Robert Young, chief justice of the Michigan Supreme Court. Trump released it September 23 and, again, it attracted little attention, but its importance would grow over time. Trump's reliance on Leo gave him a list that satisfied any conservative with a passing interest in the high court and positively hypnotized those who cared deeply about originalism, Scalia's successor and having a Trumpian rather than Clintonian court.

Two days after Trump won he called Leo and summoned him to Trump Tower. Leo entered Trump's personal office on the 26th floor, soon to be joined by Bannon, Priebus, McGahn, Ivanka, Jared and Sessions. It was there Trump decided to cut the list from 21 to six and begin the vetting process. The six were: Gorsuch, Pryor, Hardiman, Kethledge, Sykes and Thapar. Trump formed a vetting committee of: Priebus, Bannon, McGahn, Sessions and Mark Paoletta, counsel to Pence. In the middle of the conversation Trump looked up and said he would like to get to know Maureen, Scalia's widow. Leo said he could put them in touch. Trump asked if he had Maureen's number— knowing the answer. Leo wrote it down on a sticky note found amid the clutter of Trump's desk. Trump stuck it absentmindedly on a pile. Before the meeting adjourned, Trump offered Sessions the job of attorney general—a nomination he would not announce for eight days.

That same week, McConnell called McGahn.

"I said, 'Don, we have a chance here now that the Democrats have lowered the threshold to 51 votes to have a huge, positive impact on the

3rd branch.'" McConnell said. "I told McGahn, 'If you can get them up here quickly I will give first priority to circuit court judges.' And he did."

Before Trump's Supreme Court subcommittee began its work, Leo conducted phone interviews with the six finalists. He keeps the hand-written notes in a soft-cover binder in his Washington office. Leo then relayed his impressions to the search committee. In early January, it was time for face-to-face interviews. All six were brought to Trump Tower and appeared before the committee. That vetting process winnowed the list to three: Gorsuch, Hardiman and Pryor. It was now time for Trump to interview each finalist. Those interviews occurred in Trump's penthouse apartment. Everyone was sneaked into the Tower by car, entering through a special side entrance and moved to the apartment on a designated elevator. Trump interviewed Hardiman first. Then Pryor. Gorsuch last. When it was over, Trump left the impression Gorsuch was the choice.

"Right out of central casting," Trump said.

The transition team debated when to make the announcement. Three days were considered: January 18, for a big preinauguration splash; January 23, to set the first week off with a bang; or January 31. The third option emerged because there was simply too much else going on. It turned out to be a wise decision. By the time Gorsuch was presented to the nation, Trump needed something to go right, something to just *look* right. His angry outburst at CIA headquarters about his inauguration crowd and the bungled debut of his first travel ban contributed to a sense of a presidency already off the rails and full of ego, impetuosity, temper tantrums and fleeting coherence.

The fight over Gorsuch's nomination, once it began, had very little to do with Gorsuch, Trump or even McConnell. Why? Because his confirmation was a foregone conclusion. Democrats could and did object, but they knew McConnell would move the nomination to the floor under the protection of a simple majority vote. McConnell had the votes.

Trump spoke of his satisfaction with the Gorsuch confirmation on May 1, 2017, with my CBS colleague John Dickerson, then-moderator of *Face the Nation*. "The best moment? Well, I think the Supreme Court Justice—I've always heard for my life, that if you're president and you put on a Supreme Court Justice, that's about as big as it gets," Mr. Trump told Dickerson during a behind-the-scenes interview at his Saturday rally in Harrisburg, Pennsylvania. "And when you think about it, every five-to-four decision that we win for the next 40 years—because hopefully Justice Gorsuch is going to be there for a long time . . . he's only 49 years old—is something you did. So that's a real legacy in a certain way, very important."

That moment—the Gorsuch confirmation—was, in a certain way, a gift Trump inherited. The presidency and ownership of the Gorsuch selection process was, of course, all Trump's. But the means by which the Senate was so easily able to confirm Gorsuch, once nominated, arose from a fight many years before. It was, it turns out, a gift unintentionally provided to him by Senate Democrats and their approach to a federal appeals court nominee few Americans remember. His name was Miguel Angel Estrada Casteñeda and he stands now, I would submit, as the most important American never to serve on the District Court of Appeals for the D.C. Circuit.

That court is to the American judiciary what AAA baseball is to the Major Leagues. Justices confirmed to this court become short-listed for the Supreme Court. That's because it is viewed as the most rigorous of all federal appeals courts, the place where the toughest cases are adjudicated before they are appealed to the Supreme Court. It is also the court where disputes over federal law, congressional intent and federal rule-making are most frequently heard—often with no lower court review. Three of the current Supreme Court Justices served on the court, as did former Chief Justices Fred Vinson and Warren Burger and Associate Justices Wiley Rutledge and Scalia.

Bush 43 nominated Estrada to this court on May 9, 2001. Estrada was born in Honduras and joined his mother in America at age 17, after she divorced his father. He was graduated magna cum laude and Phi Beta Kappa from Columbia University in 1983 and magna cum laude from Harvard Law School in 1986. At Harvard, Estrada was editor of the *Law Review*. He clerked for Associate Justice Anthony Kennedy in 1988, Kennedy's first year on the high court. Estrada worked as assistant solicitor general for George H. W. Bush, thereby making the professional acquaintance of future Chief Justice Roberts. After his nomination, Estrada received the American Bar Association's highest recommendation—Well Qualified. He was a conservative Hispanic jurist heading to the on-deck circle of the Supreme Court. Confirmation would mean Bush or a future Republican would be well positioned to nominate the first Hispanic to the highest court in the land, a history-shattering moment Bush coveted and Democrats feared.

Senate Democrats demanded Estrada's writing during his time in the solicitor general's office, a request a bipartisan group of former solicitors general opposed on the grounds it would diminish the office's ability to function in the future. A leaked memo summarizing liberal opposition to Estrada mentioned the political implications of a conservative "Latino" landing on the Supreme Court. Racism was denied but Democrats used unprecedented tactics to nullify Estrada's nomination. They required seven cloture votes—which require a 60-vote threshold—to advance Estrada. It was the first time a filibuster had been used to stall a judicial nominee who had a majority of Senate support. Each cloture vote registered 55 votes to end debate and move Estrada's nomination to a final confirmation vote. It was also the first filibuster ever deployed against a circuit court nominee. After 28 exhausting months of partisan strife and no resolution in sight, Estrada withdrew his nomination on September 4, 2003. It is a tragic footnote of this history that Estrada's wife, Laury Gordon Estrada, died on November 28, 2004, just over a year after the confirmation battle ended. The cause was an accidental overdose of alcohol and sleeping pills. Estrada's wife miscarried during the nasty confirmation struggle and had been traumatized by the process from then until her death.

There are many fascinating twists and turns in the Estrada story, but for our purposes its most important legacy is how Estrada's defeat led Republicans to abandon the Senate filibuster in Supreme Court confirmations. It did not happen immediately; other bit players had their time on the stage, but Estrada is why the majority party can and will confirm a Supreme Court nominee with a simple majority vote. Deploying the filibuster against a federal judicial nominee is a decidedly new tactic that started with Estrada.

It cannot be lost in the history of partisan tug-of-war over the Supreme Court that the most politically damaged nominee ever to win confirmation, Clarence Thomas, became an associate justice via a confirmation vote of 52–48 (with 11 Democrats joining 41 Republicans to confirm and two Republicans joining 46 Democrats to reject). Clearly, Thomas would never have survived a filibuster. But not one Democratic lion of the Senate then—not Edward Kennedy, not Robert Byrd, not George Mitchell, not Patrick Leahy, not Al Gore, not Alan Cranston, not Paul Simon and certainly not Biden—used the filibuster. In that era, Senate custom was to respect the will of the electorate and defer to the president. If nominees were qualified and possessed character sufficient for the post, the Senate was inclined to confirm or at least conduct a debate and vote without the specter of a filibuster. Scrutiny of qualification and character increased in line with the gravity of the appointment. But deference to the presidency governed.

Thomas could have been defeated by a Democratic filibuster but was not. Why? Because. It. Just. Didn't. Happen. That's why Biden, late in 2017, issued a public apology for Thomas's confirmation. It was not just a #MeToo mea culpa. It was a recognition that Biden did not use the filibuster to defeat a nominee who today probably would not survive a rigorous #MeToo vetting. Whether Anita Hill's allegations against Thomas were all true, mostly true or partially true obscures the deeper reality—if they were raised now, in an early vet, Thomas would never be nominated. Never. Biden apologized for deferring to Senate history. Whether it's worth apologizing for, our partisan politics, the same ones that over time glued Republicans more ardently to Trump, may not be capable of answering.

As we remember Thomas's nomination and the tool Democrats did not use—the filibuster—it should be clear that its use against Estrada constituted a new line crossed, a new partisan maneuver to reverse the history of deference and use every procedural tool available to the opposition party to thwart a president. That reversal of habit, custom, history and precedent bore consequences that brought Democrats, whether they wish to admit it or not, to their powerlessness to stop Gorsuch or any of Trump's subsequent federal bench nominees who came up for a confirmation vote. Just as McConnell made clear he would never allow a confirmation hearing for Merrick Garland, he would see Gorsuch confirmed with a simple majority. With Gorsuch, no filibuster would apply. The process had no mystery. Democratic opposition was genuine but practically meaningless. Trump and McConnell had the power. With McGahn's help, both had, unwittingly and with only the vaguest of intentions, sealed it that February afternoon when Scalia died.

The story does not end with Gorsuch. Trump's presidency is historic in that he nominated and saw confirmed 12 judges to federal appeals courts in his first year in office. In February 2018, seven more nominations were pending. Twelve confirmed circuit judges is the highest number ever for the first year of a presidency. Obama had three, G. W. Bush six, Clinton three, George H. W. Bush five, Reagan eight, Carter 10, Nixon and Kennedy both 11. By mid-June of 2018, Trump had 21 circuit court judges and 20 district court judges confirmed. Trump's judicial legacy may be among the most long-lasting and least anticipated of his candidacy and presidency. It is as much a welcome surprise to McConnell as it is anyone else, and considering McConnell's lifelong focus on the courts as the truest fulcrum of American power, may well explain his docility to other parts of the Trump agenda—trade and immigration to name just two—he finds objectionable.

"Being majority leader is a little like being the groundskeeper at a cemetery," McConnell said. "Everybody is under you, but no one is listening. The one thing you can do is schedule. We had a record number of circuit court vacancies."

Those jurists will influence appeals court decisions for decades. Four of the state supreme court judges on Trump's original list of potential U.S. Supreme Court nominees are now circuit court judges. Their average age is 50. One judge from the second list, Amul Thapar, 48, is also a circuit judge. They are, in the long arc of jousting over the judiciary, Estrada's legacy. So long as Senate Republicans maintain their majority, Trump can reshape the federal bench. The only way Democrats can block Trump and slow his and Leo's unambiguous effort to populate the federal courts with young, originalist jurists is to win a Senate majority. With that majority Democrats can delay confirmation hearings and deny confirmation on the floor—holding Trump nominees in endless limbo. Democrats know this and so does the Trump White House. Depending on where Trump's political fortunes are in the fall of 2018, Republicans may need the issue as much as Democrats. In base-mobilization elections, as midterms tend to be, the future of the federal bench may prove equally potent for both parties—making Trump's record and McConnell's audacious gamble among the most important in modern political history.

FIVE

Immigration

"I am establishing new vetting measures to keep radical Islamic terrorists out of the United States of America. We don't want 'em here. We want to ensure that we are not admitting into our country the very threats our soldiers are fighting overseas."

Trump was sitting inside the Pentagon, announcing his travel ban. It was 4:31 p.m. on January 27 and Trump's presidency was one week old. His presidency was about to mature rapidly as it confronted the costs of inexperience and haste. Trump had chosen the location carefully. He cast the "extreme vetting" executive order in proto-military terms. It was about immigration control, the foundation of national defense in Trump's thinking and phrasing.

"We only want to admit into our country those who will support our country and love, deeply, our people," Trump said. "We will never forget the lessons of 9/11 nor the heroes who lost their lives at the Pentagon. They were the best of us. We will honor them not only with our words but with our actions and that is what we are doing today."

With Trump's words I was reminded of a conversation I had with Ray Paradez, a 53-year-old church maintenance man who had driven four hours to an August 2016 Trump rally.

"I mean, I'm mad," Paradez said. "I've been mad. I'm one of the angry voters that they've been talking about for the last year."

One issue above all others vexed Paradez: immigration.

"I'm just angry that the Republicans, it's like they're milquetoast. Ryan [House Speaker Paul Ryan], a big amnesty hawk. It's pathetic. If you're here illegally, you shouldn't be sponging off the taxpayers, getting all kinds of benefits. You should follow the law. They're not supposed to be here. If they're caught, they're supposed to be deported. Not released and just go about their business and like they were before they were caught. I'm sick of it."

Trump's travel ban executive order was not precisely responsive to Paradez's gripes, but it was part of the larger set of immigration changes Trump set in motion, and they reflected the long-suppressed sentiments of millions of voters. That's why Trump's campaign immigration appeals worked. Critics called Trump a racist, but I had interviewed voters since the mid-1990s who were furious with what seemed to them a nonchalance bordering, literally, on indifference to the concept of America as a place so special as to require a grueling and lengthy legal immigration process. I first met these voters in my home state of California in 1994 when then-Gov. Pete Wilson backed Proposition 187 (which sought to deny non-emergency benefits to illegal immigrants and require state employees to report undocumented immigrants to federal officials). It passed with nearly 60 percent of the vote, with sizable support among whites and slightly more than 50 percent support among African American and Asian voters, according to the Field Poll. Fewer than 30 percent of Hispanic voters backed the initiative. Many analysts considered this the end of the Republican Party in California and the death of Wilson's political career because of Prop 187's perceived hostility to an emerging and demographically important constituency—Latinos. Many years later, Trump decided he would appeal to white voters outside of California aggravated by what they regarded as the business and political classes' tendency to look the other way when it came to illegal border crossing. Trump sensed, correctly, that millions of voters distinguished sharply between legal and illegal immigration and, more importantly, craved a candidate who would celebrate the former and angrily denounce the latter. They wanted resistance to what they perceived to be a bipartisan blurring of the political and legal definitions of legal and illegal immigration. Plenty of well-meaning voters and analysts do and will consider this tendency evidence of embedded racism. Trump did not. Neither did his supporters. Trump won. That truth ought to give the critics alleging racism some measure of pause—if not philosophically at least strategically.

Upon becoming president, Trump immediately latched onto immigration policy and symbolism—propounding a screeching and disorganized travel ban executive order. Politically, it was responsive. Legally, it was problematic. Trump's executive order would run into many obstacles, some of which Trump and his aides could have navigated more deftly. But this particular policy and others pursued in 2017 did not emerge from a vacuum or represent only the agenda of immigration hard-liners like Bannon and Miller—they also spoke to voter frustrations visible at almost every Trump rally.

After his brief remarks at the Pentagon, Trump carried out what would become a familiar ritual during his first year—moving from his podium to a small wooden table to sign an executive order, memorandum or bill. Afterward, he would hold up with evident pride his picket-fence black signature for all the world to see.

"And this," Trump said as he beheld the blue leather folder holding the short-lived Executive Order No. 13769, "is the protection of the nation from foreign terrorist entries into the United States. We all know what that means. Protection of the nation from foreign terrorist entry into the United States. That's big stuff."

Big stuff, indeed. The nation was about to start feeling much older, too, as the first glimpses of Trump's new immigration ideas, defiant attitude, disregard for careful planning and, in short order, belligerent defensiveness began to emerge.

Before Trump set this all in turbulent motion, the event had begun placidly and grandly within one of the Pentagon's most sacred spaces.

Vice President Mike Pence approached the presidential podium inside the Hall of Heroes, where the marble-lined walls at that time honored, by name, each of the 3,498 Americans who have received the Medal of Honor. The medal represents the highest national honor for bravery, valor and selflessness to unit and country. The Hall of Heroes is on the main concourse of the Pentagon, where Pence, according to the schedule released by the White House, was to accompany Trump for the ceremonial swearing in of James Norman Mattis as the 26th secretary of defense.

In a warrior culture where courage and duty are respected virtues, few places are more suffused with both than the Hall of Heroes. The names and stories stand apart. My CBS colleague and national security correspondent David Martin has interviewed nearly three dozen Medal of Honor recipients and learned of one common denominator: no one ever "wins" the Medal of Honor. What is required to receive it is Hell on Earth, the worst day of their lives—harrowing, desperate, bloody, lonely, riddled with death and, eventually, survivor's guilt. To a man, recipients have told Martin they would trade the medal instantly to retrieve all, or just one, of their fallen comrades from the clutches of death.

"We stand in a place of honor," Pence said with a heavy sigh. "Now, Mr. Secretary, your president has called you, to lead all of the armed forces of the United States. He and I have the highest faith in your judgment, your courage and your dedication to this nation."

Trump came to the Pentagon having just wrapped up a brief press conference and lunch with British Prime Minister Theresa May, the first head of state to meet Trump since Inauguration Day. Then–White House Chief Strategist Steve Bannon told me before May's arrival that heads of state were "stacked up like planes waiting to land," eager to meet Trump. Bannon said May's team—led by Foreign Secretary and former London Mayor Boris Johnson—was startled at the "nationalist and populist" direction of Trump and his new team. May was about to see those sensibilities in action. Bannon was also sure that May, having taken stock of Trump and his new approach to world politics, would return to London fortified and commence driving a harder bargain in soon-to-begin negotiations with the European Union over the terms of Britain's "Brexit." Bannon was right about the number of world leaders seeking face time with Trump. He was probably correct about the level of May's surprise at Trump's nationalist/populist zeal. But Bannon was dead wrong about the Trump effect on May's approach to Brexit. From the earliest days, Bannon overestimated his ability to read others and predict future events. He lost far more White House policy battles than he won. In fact, he was, on this day, about to witness his one and only undiluted policy achievement come to fruition.

While Trump was riding across the Potomac River to the Pentagon, Press Secretary Sean Spicer informed traveling White House reporters the president would sign two executive orders at the Mattis event—one on boosting military spending; the other, according to Spicer, on "extreme vetting." Trump's schedule—released that morning—indicated he would sign two executive orders. No explanation had been given about the orders' contents. Now reporters knew why. Extreme vetting could mean the "Muslim Ban" from Trump's campaign. It could mean something short of that. Whatever it meant, news was stirring. Events were about to spin wildly out of control in Washington, across America and in airports the world over.

Mattis was officially sworn in on Inauguration Day, having been confirmed 98–1 in the swiftest confirmation process of the entire Trump cabinet. He was the first retired general to serve as defense secretary since George C. Marshall, tapped by President Truman in 1950 as the United States was mired in the first dispiriting phase of the Korean War. Congress had to pass a special law allowing Mattis to serve. In 2008 Congress shortened the moratorium on veterans leading the Pentagon to seven years (it had been 10 since 1947). Mattis retired in 2013 and was not an active part of Trump's campaign. Though Trump loved to call Mattis by one of his two nicknames, "Mad Dog," the general much preferred his other nickname—"Warrior Monk." The monk part owed to the fact Mattis never married, was raised in a home without television and devoted his life to reading—particularly on the history, tactics and suffering of war.

"Welcome to the headquarters of your military, your always loyal military where America's awesome determination to defend herself is on full display," Mattis said in his soft, almost syrupy voice. "Those serving today have been tested and you can count on us all the way. Thank you for your confidence in me, Mr. President."

As Trump shook Mattis's hand, he whispered, "Total confidence."

"And that's total confidence, believe me," Trump said at the podium, proceeding to describe Mattis as "a man of total action. He likes action. He is the right man at the right time. The men and women of the United States military are the greatest force for justice and peace and goodness that have ever walked the face of this earth."

Trump signed an executive memorandum on rebuilding the military and looked on at the assembled crowd of dignitaries, including former Republican Sen. William Cohen of Maine, defense secretary under President Bill Clinton. Cohen was there as a show of respect to Mattis and the Pentagon—not Trump and certainly not the executive order to come that was about to take Cohen, Mattis and much of the wet-behind-the-ears Trump administration by surprise.

The travel ban executive order suspended for 90 days immigrant and nonimmigrant entry to any traveler who began his or her journey in seven named countries or transited through those countries. It listed exemptions for those traveling to the United Nations or carrying North Atlantic Treaty Organization or diplomatic visas. The seven covered countries were Iraq, Syria, Iran, Sudan, Somalia, Libya and Yemen.

Trump signed the order at 4:43 p.m., closed the blue folder and handed it to Mattis, who stood just over his left shoulder. Trump's presidency was one week, four hours and 42 minutes old. The White House did not know what to call the order. Critics alternatively labeled it a travel ban and a Muslim ban. Initially, the White House rejected both, but Trump eventually embraced "travel ban." By whatever name, as it evolved the order triggered confusion in airports around the world, protests at airports in America and immediate legal appeals as pro bono attorneys materialized to represent affected travelers.

Implementation was supposed to be immediate. But immigration officials did not know whom to stop and for how long. The White House labored to explain what the "big stuff" order was all about. Many of the initial answers were later withdrawn. Many simple questions elicited dumbfounding silence. Did the travel restrictions apply to members of the U.S. military? Yes, we think so, came the answer. Did it apply to Iraqi pilots traveling to America to train with U.S. instructors as part of the fight against ISIS? Yes. Did the restrictions apply to refugees? Yes. What about representatives of nongovernmental organizations? Yes, we think so. What about travelers with "lawful permanent resident status" (green card holders)? Yes, they were restricted, too.

Many of these answers were amended or wilted under political, procedural or legal pressure. The original muscularity of the first order atrophied, almost by the hour, with each question, each new real-world scenario, each instance in which a traveling human being bumped up against a one-size-fits-all (wait . . . wasn't that an Obama thing?) set of travel restrictions.

Among the government officials who knew nothing about Trump's signing the executive order was Acting Attorney General Sally Yates. In an exquisite example of Trumpian hostility to Obama-era holdovers, Yates was driving to Reagan National Airport for a flight to Atlanta to see her husband when she first received a call from her chief of staff that Trump had signed a new travel order. The first definitive account of the order's contents were found by Yates on the *New York Times* website. This is true. It is amazing. And true. It must be recorded as such. Yates described the experience on June 27, 2017, at the Aspen Ideas Festival:

"I was in the car on the way to the airport. I had just finished a meeting on the Mike Flynn situation and I was in the car. I got a call from my principal deputy. It's about 5 o'clock or so and Matt calls me and says 'You're not going to believe this, but I was just on the *New York Times* website. And it looks like the president has instituted some sort of travel ban.' That's how we found out about it at the Department of Justice. Read about it on the internet."

Yates boarded her flight to Atlanta. There was WiFi, and because the commercial airliner had arranged it, the acting attorney general of the United States was able to look for a copy of the executive order online. Please understand. This would be the executive order it would be Yates's obligation to enforce, the executive order she had not been briefed on, her deputy had not been advised of and that was about to set off confusion, lawsuits and protests the world over.

"Over the course of that weekend it was a whole lot of trying to figure out what the heck is this thing and to whom does it apply. At that time, we were getting conflicting signals, but when the music stopped the White House told us, 'Yes. It applied to LPRs, lawful permanent residents, people with green cards. They would not be allowed to come back into the country even though they had legal status here. It applied to people with visas."

Yates said she knew legal challenges had already been filed; she had to assemble, if she could, a legal team armed with a defense of the order's contents. "Until we could get a handle on what this was and whether we thought it was lawful, my instructions were you can defend on procedural grounds . . . but we're not going to take a position on the constitutionality until we have a chance to actually figure out whether we think this is constitutional."

Late that Saturday afternoon, Trump signed another executive order—this one applying new ethics standards to White House officials—and told the reporters nearby that all was well.

"It's not a Muslim ban," Trump said. "But we are totally prepared. It's working out very nicely. You see it at the airports. You see it all over. It's working out very nicely and we're going to have a very strict ban and we're going to have extreme vetting which we should have had in this country for many years." What worked "nicely," I later came to learn from interviews on this subject, was the new signal Trump had sent domestically and internationally, namely that the immigration drawbridge was being pulled up and when it was lowered a new set of sentries would enforce newly restrictive rules. Whatever was to become of the first executive order, this signal, in Trump's mind as well as Bannon's, was worth every moment of chaos, confusion and bureaucratic heartburn.

A short time later, a Trump official told reporters on a conference call that the story wasn't people being detained at the airports. The only story that would matter, this unnamed official said, was if people who should be detained—meaning terrorists—were *not* detained for questioning or deported. It may sound like a throwaway line or hastily drafted talking point, but it is crucial to understanding the underlying mind-set of the executive order and those who drafted it. The assumption was if you were coming from the seven named countries or transiting through those countries—even if you had a green card or visa or had been screened and admitted through the refugee program—there was, a priori, something suspicious and possibly terroristic about you.

To underscore this point, the unnamed official asked reporters would it have been better, as an example, to have had the order implemented the day after the San Bernardino shooter entered the United States or the day before? It was a curious example to cite. There were two assailants in the December 2015 attack in San Bernardino that killed 14 and injured 22: Syed Rizwan Farook was born in the United States of Pakistani heritage and his wife, Tashfeen Malik, was a lawful permanent resident born in Pakistan. The list of seven nations covered by the executive order *did not include Pakistan.* Moreover, under no circumstances would the executive order have affected Farook, as he was a U.S. citizen.

Within days, the administration, under massive legal and political pressure, lifted restrictions imposed on lawful permanent residents. Again, even if the administration had kept those restrictions and a traveler with a profile similar to Tashfeen Malik's sought entry, the executive order would have had no consequence because Pakistan, Malik's country of birth, was not covered. In those pressure-packed moments when the White House could not defend what it had done, it had reached for the scariest scenario imaginable—even though in the San Bernardino case it was utterly invalid. This left the administration open to charges it sought justification through demonization.

The same unnamed officials amplified Trump's all-is-well description of what was happening in airports across the globe. "When you consider the scope of the action and complexity of the action and the intricacy of what was done, it was astonishing, in that context, how relatively little disruption occurred and how professional and efficient Customs and Border Protection has been and how well it's been handled at every level of government." This comment came in close proximity to a question about an immigration official at JFK Airport in New York reported to have told a detained traveler, "Call Mr. Trump to find out why you can't get in."

By that first Saturday night, the White House was becoming a bit unnerved. Protests and legal complaints were multiplying. Answers remained elusive. Tempers were fraying among travelers and immigration professionals charged with carrying out the new mandate. The first sign of legal jeopardy came when U.S. District Judge Ann Donnelly in New York, based on a petition filed by the American Civil Liberties Union, issued an emergency order that blocked implementation of the travel restrictions. The court order was limited but focused on the most conspicuous legal flaws in the order. Judge Donnelly barred U.S. immigration personnel from deporting anyone who arrived in the United States with a valid visa from the named countries and anyone approved for entry as a refugee. Protests raged at airports in New York, Chicago, San Francisco, Los Angeles and San Diego.

Amid this legal tumult, Priebus, Spicer and Conway were in a quintessential and distinctly non-Trumpian cocoon—the Alfalfa Dinner D.C. held inside a swanky hotel. Trump was invited to the A-list Washington dinner, full of monied interests, philanthropists, high-flying lobbyists, corporate chieftains and government officials. According to *The Washington Post,* as many as five of the eight wealthiest men in the world (Michael Bloomberg, Jeff Bezos, Bill Gates, Larry Ellison and Warren Buffett) attended. This was less an event for the 1 percent as for the 1 percent of the 1 percent. In a sign of bipartisan and elitist bonhomie, Priebus, Conway and Spicer were given exalted positions at the head table on the dais. Crudely, the travel ban intruded. Priebus was called away from the festivities. "We had secure phones at Alfalfa," Priebus said, referring to lines placed at the Capital Hilton, a frequent visiting spot for presidents because of its security arrangements and communications. "I tried to start dealing with it on a secure line." Talk about a glitzy fiasco. The next night, Sunday, two federal judges in Boston issued a seven-day stay—"temporary restraining order" in legal parlance—because the travel order appeared to violate the due process and equal protection clause of the Constitution. Judges Allison Burroughs and Judith Gail Dein barred U.S. immigration officials from detaining or deporting any legal entrant under the refugee program, lawful permanent residents and any traveler from a named country with valid entry documentation.

Editorial pages and pundits described Trump as a tyrant and a disorganized one at that. But again, the travel ban Trump signed was *the least* restrictive of the eight offered for review. The other seven had more countries and more restrictions.

"There were about eight different options on that travel ban and a lot of them would have been more restrictive," Priebus told me. Settling on the original travel ban, viewed from this perspective, was seen by some top White House officials as a small victory. This particular concept of "victory" was common in Trump's White House. Steering Trump toward the least damaging option was an ongoing struggle. It was not uncommon to encounter a frazzled Trump official or advisor who, after a particularly hectic and zigzagging week, would say: "You should have seen what we stopped from happening! It was much worse!" On the first set of travel restrictions, Bannon and Miller drove the process.

There was legal coordination, but only the bare minimum, conducted through the Justice Department. The checklist for approval—typically two to three pages in most White House operations—was far shorter. The key lawyer at the Department of Homeland Security was Dean Hamilton, who, like Bannon and Miller, was an immigration hardliner. Hamilton would later emerge in 2018 as a key advocate for Trump's "zero tolerance" policy and the subsequent family separation controversy. As for the travel ban, Homeland Security lawyers were more involved than the White House, though the final version was cleared by the Justice Department Office of Legal Counsel.

Trump, according to those directly involved, spent a couple of hours reviewing options, with Bannon and Miller driving the process to a rapid conclusion. To many, the less restrictive option seemed the best political and policy choice, in part because the named countries had been flagged by the previous administration.

The Obama administration, as Trump officials accurately reminded reporters, had identified all seven originally named countries as terror hotspots and therefore worthy of some manner of travel restriction. But Obama never issued an order affecting all travelers and possibly touching U.S. military in transit, military personnel working with the United States, nongovernmental organization employees, refugees and green card holders. By all appearances, the Trump order had implicated these groups and possibly more. No one really knew who would be snared in the dragnet, only that it was to be cast with far-reaching and possibly fear-inducing impact. The underlying assumption was described as this: terrorists were constantly transiting, menacing America by the hour, and every second lost exposed the nation to peril.

The validity of the assumption would struggle to stand the test of time.

Also on Sunday, the Department of Homeland Security issued a statement defending the executive order in the context of inconvenience, not constitutionality. "The president's Executive Order affects a minor portion of international travelers and is a first step towards reestablishing control over America's borders and national security." The statement characterized airport inconveniences as mild and statistically insignificant, affecting "less than 1 percent of the more than

325,000 international air travelers." It was an unequivocal declaration of the new Trump approach to who may or may not enter the United States. "No foreign national in a foreign land, without ties to the United States, has any unfettered right to demand entry into the United States or to demand immigration benefits in the United States."

What was so striking about this issue and subsequent litigation was not how many times or ways Trump amended his policy to align it with the Constitution but how, in its initial drafting and subsequent early defenses of that policy, the Trump White House emphasized points outside of the Constitution. Equal protection and due process are not about ratios of convenience and inconvenience. If you are a lawful permanent resident, a visa holder without a criminal complaint against you or even a refugee cleared for entry, you enjoy and are unconditionally afforded constitutional protections. Full stop. "Equality under the law" means precisely that. And the reference to a "foreign national" seeking an "unfettered right to demand entry into the United States" cast aspersions, to put it mildly, on their foreignness, and overlooked their established legal status under American law—which a green card holder possesses, as does a visa holder and even a refugee. Trump's approach was a stark rejection of this legal construct and a base-mobilizing political love-note to a darker, post-9/11 nativism that elevated "safety" over all other legal norms.

Immigration has become a deeply passionate and confused issue in post-9/11 America. Questions of "differentness" are not merely cultural or preferential but central to a sense of safety and American sovereignty. Plenty of Trump critics can deny and denounce this attitude. But that Trump won offers compelling evidence that millions, possibly tens of millions, of registered voters consider this topic of primal importance. What is immigration policy's goal? Is it to serve employment needs in border states and for the agricultural industry? Is it to serve some universal cultural norm? Is it to serve America's national security and nothing else? Trump asked the last question and he asked it without hesitation or guilt. Millions responded in the affirmative, as millions did in California in 1994 when Proposition 187 posed the question slightly differently. California might be appalled to consider this, but its 1994 approach to the issue of non-emergency aid to illegal immigrants at least partially informed Trump's hostility to non-legal immigrant populations many years later. California may have moved on, but many voters in the interior of our country did not. Uniquely, Trump sensed this and acted aggressively.

Trump's first executive order failed to distinguish, as Trump did successfully during the campaign, between those with legal and illegal status. If an immigrant had received a green card, been conferred refugee status or transited in and out of the country through cooperation with the U.S. military, that immigrant would not "demand entry or benefits." In fact, that immigrant would be applying for that status and the U.S. government would grant it according to its rules and regulations, which, as any legal immigrant will attest, can be time-consuming and costly and cumbersome. Immigrants who entered under these conditions scarcely felt as if the U.S. government was bowing to their demands. The first Trump order, in other words, sought to block the orderly and legal processing of immigrants who received green cards or visas or who had been granted refugee status.

On that Sunday, Trump issued a statement that sought protection (amazingly, considering the political prehistory) under Obama-era guidelines. "My policy," the Trump statement said, "is similar to what President Obama did in 2011 when he banned visas for refugees from Iraq for six months. The seven countries named in the Executive Order are the same countries previously identified by the Obama administration as sources of terror. To be clear, this is not a Muslim ban, as the media is falsely reporting. This is not about religion—this is about terror and keeping our country safe." It must be said that banning the issuance of new visas is fundamentally different from subjecting existing visa holders to deportation or layered interrogation.

Remember, over this turbulent weekend Yates and other Justice Department officials were trying to determine if lawful permanent residents were covered under the new travel restrictions. Yates was told, in no uncertain terms, that they were—as were travelers with valid visas. This deepened Yates's nervousness about potential violations of the Constitution.

Shortly before 7 Sunday night, a top White House domestic policy advisor conducted a conference call with reporters. It was said that immigration officials had been told, though the executive order did not say it, that lawful permanent residents had an exemption and could be

cleared for entry. This became part of the evolving White House defense for an order it was beginning to realize could not withstand legal
scrutiny. The argument was not about what the executive order said but
what the White House, not the Justice Department or Department of
Homeland Security, said to immigration officials about its implementation. Again, this reinforced the notion that the executive order was
subject to changes on the fly and that the White House was fully empowered to quietly rewrite an executive order through subdirectives,
updated guidance and other seat-of-the-pants improvisation. It made
a mockery of the White House's fulsome defense of the process leading up to the order's tumultuous rollout and, to put it mildly, uneven
implementation.

"Internally we have been clear about this from the beginning and
we have waived people through," the top official said, referring to
green card holders and citing statistics from that time showing that
170 travelers with green cards had, under the duress of uncertainty
about their rights under lawful permanent resident status, applied
for and received a waiver. "The executive order has a waiver authority
and it is our position that that waiver authority has always covered
lawful permanent residents and the secretary of Homeland Security
shares that view." That is not what the executive order said and it
is not how its implementation was communicated to the Justice Department that had to defend it—as written—in court. References to
what the White House thought the order meant and what its internal
belief system was or what the view of the Homeland Security secretary meant little to the underlying legal objections and questions. The
order was being challenged in court as written—not as haphazardly
implemented.

The official then tried to say the green card issue had been resolved
with no unanswered questions.

"It is the policy of the executive order and the policy of the administration that possessing an active green card is definitionally in the
interest of the United States to readmit you and therefore, by definition,
if you have a green card it is in the national interest of the United States
to readmit you."

Reporters then asked the official if green card holders had to seek
special permission before traveling or at least alert a federal agency of

their travel intentions to avoid complications of additional screening or delays. He hesitated.

"[Department of Homeland Security] has been given detailed guidance but additional layers of detail will be issued tonight," came the reply. "I want to withhold temporarily the answer in terms of the exact procedure of the act of receiving the waiver itself . . . so it's stated with absolute clarity since I know that if even by the smallest measure if I say anything that's a little off we'll have to change that."

This confirmed the order was being reworked in real time and subject to internal reworking going forward, prima facie evidence of a bollixed process and legal clumsiness.

After more detailed questions, Spicer jumped on the line and lashed out at reporters. "What would you rather have? A terrorist attack? Would you rather wait until they killed somebody?"

The following Monday morning, just after 7, Trump tweeted: "Only 109 people out of 325,000 were detained and held for questioning. Big problems at airports were caused by Delta computer outage. . . ." And an hour later: "If the ban were announced with a one week notice, the 'bad' would rush into our country during that week. A lot of bad 'dudes' out there!"

That same day Yates was informed the department would have to decide, by Tuesday, if the order was constitutional. Newly minted Trump-appointed lawyers joined Yates, an Obama administration holdover, and career lawyers for the discussion. She described the conversation at the Aspen Ideas Festival. "We went around the table with me asking them, 'Tell me why you think this is lawful. How are we going to defend this?' At the end of that, I was not comfortable that it was, in fact, lawful or constitutional and kept the senior Trump appointee back to tell him that I was very uneasy with where we were, and that I wasn't sure what I was going to do."

After further deliberation, Yates decided she could not lawfully enforce the order because she could not send department lawyers into court asserting the travel restrictions had nothing to do with religion, but only about enhancing national security.

"I did not believe that to be a defense that was grounded in truth. And I couldn't send Department of Justice lawyers in to defend something based on a defense that I did not believe was grounded in truth, which then left the dilemma of, okay, do you just resign then or do you direct the department not to defend the travel ban? I went back and forth on that. But, sort of the bottom line on that was that I didn't feel like I would be doing my job if I just essentially said 'I'm outta here. You guys figure this out.' That would have protected my personal integrity, but I didn't believe it would have protected the integrity of the Department of Justice."

Late that Monday, Yates issued a directive not to defend the travel restrictions.

"Not surprisingly, I got a letter about 9 o'clock that night firing me. So that was that."

The next day Spicer accused Yates of "betrayal."

"There's a difference when she as the acting attorney general is not only responsible, but required to execute lawful orders and defiantly says no. As someone who was chosen to lead a department, she was rightfully removed," Spicer said at the White House briefing. "Ironically it went through their offices—the Department of Justice's Office of Legal Compliance. So the idea that it went through the entire process of which they were part of and then she chooses not to execute actually is bewildering as well as defiant." The irony wasn't that Spicer misnamed the relevant Justice Department office—Legal Counsel, not Legal Compliance—it was that two days before that office had issued a statement specifically admitting that Yates and the department's senior management were not consulted on the executive order.

Spicer went on. "If you have a legally executed order and the attorney general says 'I'm not going to execute it,' that is clearly a betrayal."

The Yates firing also gave the nation its first true inkling of how Trump interpreted loyalty and punished those who did not meet his standards. Before quoting Spicer's explanation of that credo, remember the following: Yates was not consulted, had not seen the executive order while it was being drafted and was not read-in on its contents before it was signed; the Office of Legal Counsel did not consult her or senior Justice Department lawyers and it offered no defense of the policy implications or the means by which the executive order could or would be implemented; the implementation of the order was being changed almost by the hour, thus undermining the legal validity of the order as drafted. Yates operated as acting attorney general in this real-life atmosphere. She chose not to have Justice Department lawyers appear in court to defend a policy she did not believe was legally defensible, based on the contested language of the ban. That constituted, in Spicer's words, "betrayal." He extended the thesis to the entire Trump administration.

> That kind of comes with the job. If you do not believe in the president's agenda, and I think every one of the cabinet members—every one of the appointees—understands that they serve at the pleasure of the president. And I think we talked a lot about this during the transition. This isn't about joining the government to execute your ideas or your initiatives. The president was very clear during the campaign, whether it was economic security or national security, that he has an agenda that he articulated to the American people. And that it is his job to lay that vision out and the people that he appoints or nominates and announces as staff members, or cabinet-level members or agency heads, their job is to fulfill that. And if they don't like it, then they shouldn't take the job. But it is the president's agenda we are fulfilling here.

Looking back, many senior officials regard the botched executive order as a "training wheels moment."

Along with Trump's impatience, which drove a bad policy process into the public sphere, the president's Twitter habits became a part of the story—another glimpse into the exhausting mania to come. The tweets also spawned the first efforts to temper his Twitter habits. The advice was simple and sincere: communicate more presidentially and less emotionally; keep the tweets accurate and even-keeled; use them to drive policy and politics forward, not derail momentum, create distractions or confuse the public. It was a futile effort.

Gingrich also tried and failed to temper Trump's tweets. "I went by and I saw him one day and I said in the Oval Office, 'Ten percent less Trump would be 100 percent more effective.' And he looked at me for a half second and said, 'Are you talking about my tweets?' I said, 'Yeah. I like about 80 percent of them.' And he said, 'No. Gotta be 95 percent.' And I said, 'No It's 80.' We're negotiating over what percent of his tweets I like."

Gingrich found that part of Trump maddening and genuine, by which he meant genuinely maddening.

"Part of it is genius. Sixty percent to 65 percent of the time he is dominating the news at no cost by getting awake at 5 in the morning and tweeting. And part of it is just stupid. Because he is at a margin where he can't let anybody edit him."

Gingrich then quoted poet Rainer Maria Rilke, something Trump would never do but something Gingrich delights in doing to make the mundane more interesting: "There is a line from Rilke, 'If you take away my demons will the angels leave also?' Trump is caught in this." (For accuracy's sake, the verbatim quote is: "Don't take my devils away, because my angels may flee too.") Priebus fretted too, but came around. "It turns out his tweeting and raw reactions to current events are exactly what the American people voted for."

On February 3, U.S. District Judge James Robart imposed a national ban on implementation of the order. The administration appealed to the 9th Circuit Court of Appeals, which rejected all attempts to reinstate the travel restrictions. At a February 16 press conference, the only lengthy one of his first year in office, Trump for the first time called the executive order a travel ban and admitted it would have to be revised.

"As far as the new order, the new order is going to be very much tailored to what I consider to be a very bad decision, but we can tailor the order to that decision and get just about everything," Trump said. "Let me tell you about the travel ban. We had a very smooth rollout of the travel ban, but we had a bad court, got a bad decision. We're gonna put in a new executive order next week some time. The rollout was perfect."

Then Trump pulled the curtain back on the deliberations behind the first order, giving credit to (or placing blame on) Kelly at Homeland Security (as a footnote, Kelly was in a Coast Guard plane when Trump signed it and was not aware it was coming at the time).

"Now, what I wanted to do was put out the exact same executive order but said one thing, and I said this to my people, give them a one-month period of time," Trump said. "But General Kelly, now Secretary Kelly, said if you do that, all these people will come in in the month, the bad ones. You do agree there are bad people out there, right? That not everybody's like you? You have some bad people out there. So, Kelly said, you can't do that and he was right. As soon as he said it I said, Wow, never thought of it. I said how about one week, he said no good. You got to do it immediately, because if you do it immediately, they don't have time to come in; now nobody ever reports that, but that's why we did it quickly. Now, if I would've done it in a month everything would have been perfect. The problem is that we would've wasted a lot of time and maybe a lot of lives because a lot of bad people would have come into our country. Now in the meantime, we're vetting very, very strongly. Very, very strongly. But we need help, and we need help by getting that executive order passed."

God almighty. There is so much to unpack there.

Trump suggested he wanted to wait and roll out the executive order gradually to improve implementation. Nothing the White House said in the immediate aftermath of the executive order's signing suggested debate or consideration of this kind. Trump then said if there had been a month to fully prepare the system for the travel ban, it "would have been perfect." Trump and his acolytes had been telling the world for days it had been perfect. Perfect is always in the eye of the beholder and the beholder, as the country was first learning through this process, was always Trump. As for the terrorists prevented from coming in, the travel ban was blocked throughout its short life—meaning nothing was genuinely being done to block terrorists of the kind the White House said were being blocked, detained or vetted. Moreover, by January 31, the administration had lifted the ban on 900 refugees "in transit," so those coming whom the order in theory would have stopped because they had possible terroristic intent entered the country anyway.

On March 6, the administration announced Trump signed a new executive order and said that it would be implemented on March 16—again demolishing most of the excuses used to defend the first order. Trump did not explain the order. Tillerson, Kelly and Sessions did, reading prepared statements but taking no questions at the Department of Homeland Security, Kelly's turf.

"To our allies and partners around the world," Tillerson said plaintively, describing this new set of restrictions as temporary, "please

understand. This order is part of our ongoing efforts to eliminate vul-
nerabilities that radical Islamic terrorists can and will exploit for de-
structive ends." Tillerson then explained Iraq had been removed from
the list due to "close cooperation" from the Iraqi government and because it was "an important ally in the fight to defeat ISIS."

Tillerson then mentioned something that should have been assumed but because of the first go-round needed emphasis. "Now. We
spent the morning briefing the Congress and the press. And we will
continue to talk to key stakeholders this afternoon."

Sessions came to the mics to describe one national security aspect
of the new order. "Many people seeking to support or commit terrorist acts will try to enter through our refugee program. In fact, today,
more than 300 people, according to the FBI, who came here as refugees
are under an FBI investigation today for potential terrorism-related activities. The executive is empowered, under the Constitution and by
Congress, to make national security judgments and to enforce our immigration policies in order to safeguard the American public. Terrorism is clearly a danger for America."

Sessions was dead-on about Trump's immigration authority, except when it violated due process or equal protection, as the first order, according to federal judges, clearly did. But Sessions intentionally
distorted the statistic about refugees and terrorism investigations. He
made it sound as if 300 refugees had committed acts of terrorism or
had at least been indicted or arrested. Not true. They were under investigation for "potential terrorism-related activities." By FBI guidelines, that indicated they could have been subject to something called
"assessments." This is the lowest of three levels of investigation. "Assessments" do not require "any particular factual predication," meaning factual declaration. In any given year, the FBI conducts 7,000 to
10,000 preliminary or full investigations—both higher than assessments. The Trump administration refused to answer questions about
what kind of investigations were being conducted involving the 300
refugees Sessions mentioned. If they were part of the 7,000 to 10,000
full or preliminary probes, that would be 3 percent to 4 percent—but
even the Trump Justice Department would not confirm that with
hard data. What we do know is that no refugee admitted to the United
States had been responsible for a terror-related or terror-implicated

death since 9/11. Moreover, the United States has admitted more than 3 million refugees since 1975 and only 20 have been convicted of a terror crime. The exact number of people killed by refugees from 1975 to 2015 is three.

Kelly made some matters clearer than they had been. "It is important to note that nothing in this executive order affects existing lawful permanent residents or persons with current authorization to enter our homeland. I have spent much of the day today on the phone with members of Congress, the leadership, explaining the ins and outs of this EO [executive order]. So, there should be no surprises."

This second order faced legal challenges as well and was significantly amended by a presidential proclamation Trump signed on September 24 with an implementation date of October 18.

It read in part:

> I have determined to restrict and limit the entry of nationals of 7 countries found to be 'inadequate' with respect to the baseline described in subsection C of this section: Chad, Iran, Libya, North Korea, Syria, Venezuela and Yemen. These restrictions distinguish between the entry of immigrants and nonimmigrants. Persons admitted on immigrant visas become lawful permanent residents of the United States. Such persons may present national security or public-safety concerns that may be distinct from those admitted as nonimmigrants. The United States affords lawful permanent residents more enduring rights than it does to nonimmigrants. Lawful permanent residents are more difficult to remove than nonimmigrants even after national security concerns arise, which heightens the costs and dangers of errors associated with admitting such individuals. And although immigrants generally receive more extensive vetting than nonimmigrants, such vetting is less reliable when the country from which someone seeks to emigrate exhibits significant gaps in its identity-management or information-sharing policies, or presents risks to the national security of the United States. For all but one of those 7 countries, therefore, I am restricting the entry of all immigrants.

It also added Somalia because of its government's "inability to effectively and consistently cooperate, combined with the terrorist threat that emanates from its territory, present special circumstances that warrant restrictions and limitations on the entry of its nationals into the United States." Iraq was again singled out for "additional scrutiny" due to "inadequate identity-management protocols, information-sharing practices, and risk factors."

The third version was the most comprehensive, far-reaching and legally sturdy. It was also permanent, not temporary. The addition of non-Muslim countries and the underlying analysis of each country's traveler databases, information-sharing and intelligence cooperation gave Trump firmer legal footing to assert the travel ban was based on identifiable security risks, not religious or regional bias. The Supreme Court affirmed it on December 4 and it took full effect December 8. On June 26, 2018, the Supreme Court, in a 5–4 decision, upheld the travel ban, saying its provisions fell "squarely within the scope of Presidential authority."

From the point of view of Trump lawyers, the travel bans hewed closely to constitutional powers given the president to protect the nation and direct border control. Trump was pushing those powers to be sure—but within the confines, the lawyers argued, of existing law in the modern context of non-nation-state terrorism. Trump wasn't erecting what Franklin Roosevelt and the U.S. military called "concentration camps" for 110,000 to 120,000 people, 62 percent of whom were American citizens, of Japanese descent detained after Pearl Harbor. Those camps were created under an executive order and upheld as a legal act at a time of war (which had been declared by Congress, unlike the current amorphous and still-undeclared war on terror).

Trump did not lock anyone up, he merely imposed travel restrictions on countries with inadequate screening procedures, lousy databases or a history of fomenting or exporting terrorism (these arguments evolved, as did the language of the executive orders, becoming more consistent with U.S. law in each iteration). Throughout, the administration argued against itself by claiming that every variation was legal even as it rewrote the text and eliminated legally questionable components.

There were two ISIS-inspired terrorist attacks under Trump's watch in 2017—both involving suspects radicalized while they lived legally in the United States; one, Sayfullo Saipov, entered on a diversity visa lottery, and the other, Akayed Ullah, on a family immigrant visa. Saipov has been charged with killing eight and injuring 11 after driving a truck down the Hudson River Park's bike path on Halloween. Ullah was charged with wounding five after setting off a pipe bomb inside the Port Authority Bus Terminal on December 12. Both were lawful permanent residents—meaning after legally entering the country their immigration status was upgraded in accordance with strict standards of residency, employment and legal conduct.

Nothing about Trump's immigration policies would have prevented Saipov's or Ullah's entry. In reaction, Trump denounced the visa lottery system and so-called chain migration—which immigration advocates describe as family reunification. Regardless, the impulse behind the first flawed and failed travel ban can be found here—overhype the danger, judge by the group and seek to set new immigration boundaries most likely to demonize those who either are Muslim or, like New York city terror suspects Saipov and Ullah, sound as if they are Muslim. There is no evidence either Saipov or Ullah arrived in the United States intending to commit acts of violence. That both received lawful permanent residence status proves they abided by all U.S. laws and patiently proceeded through the legal process of enhancing their status—following U.S. law instead of overstaying their visas or diversity lottery status (as millions of immigrants do). Were the minds of Saipov and Ullah infected here, in America? That is a chilling unknown. The simple truth, though, is that nothing Trump did or said about immigration policy likely would have deterred either accused terrorist or affected whatever it was that poisoned his mind.

Another striking truth about Trump's immigration policy was it did one thing consistently and aggressively: enforce the law. Nothing more. Nothing less. Yes. The law. Outside of the travel ban, Trump did nothing to change or alter existing federal law on immigration. That may sound shocking but it is true. Trump did not deport more undocumented immigrants in 2017—the number (226,000) was actually down by 6 percent from 2016. But the administration arrested just under 110,000 people, a 42 percent increase over the year before. Trump also deployed more immigration court judges to speed up deportation proceedings for those arrested. The administration also increased sweeps in search of alleged criminal gangs or drug smugglers and, unlike in previous administrations, if others were found to be undocumented in the process, they were subject to deportation. Trump made the very act of undocumented entry a crime sufficient for deportation. Thomas Homan, Trump's former head of Immigration and Customs Enforcement, said it plainly on June 13, 2017: "If you're in this country illegally and you committed a crime by being in this country, you should be uncomfortable, you should look over your shoulder. You need to be worried. No population is off the table." That harshly interpreted existing law. Trump enforced that very harsh interpretation. The law was there to be enforced. Trump merely intensified its enforcement.

What about the wall? The idea was so inefficient, expensive and impractical that the Republican Congress resisted giving Trump the billions he sought. And yet the concept of a significant physical barrier on the southern border—some semantics are at play here—is federal law. George W. Bush signed it in October of 2006. It was called the Secure Fence Act and authorized Congress to fund (which it never did) a double-layered fence along 700 miles of border separating the United States and Mexico. It was an election year and both parties wanted a show vote on border security. The vote was not about devoting money to construction of a physical barrier, it merely authorized an allocation of funds at a later date. Democrats correctly assumed Bush would never build it and so the vote was a safe alternative at the time to harsher measures bubbling in the Republican-led House to classify any undocumented immigrant a felon. The choice was simple. That's why Sens. Hillary Clinton, Barack Obama, and Chuck Schumer, as well as 23 other Democrats, went along.

In 2015 Trump took the idea of the wall to extremes, turning that show vote into a symbol of Washington's lying tendencies and his own half-joking seriousness on border security. The wall symbolized many things to many Trump voters. I know. I met hundreds of them and had lively conversations about what the wall meant: strength, sovereignty, safety and, to some, exclusion. Trump told supporters absurd stories about how high the wall would be (20 feet, 30 feet, 40 feet, maybe more!) and they would laugh. Who will pay for it? "Mexico!!!" They would laugh even harder. Trump's goofy exaggeration enchanted. His crowd knew what he meant—by God, he is going to build some kind of wall and that's what we want! Trump supporters did not care how high or what it was made of. What they wanted was the damn thing built and who knew, maybe Trump could do it.

Immigration differentiated Trump more than many political analysts realized at the time. It touched economics and culture, identity and patriotism. It also looked and sounded racist or, at minimum, nativist. Here Trump was a true political alchemist. He turned a topic most political elites in both parties considered tarnished and turned it into gold. That was a campaign success. On the question of governing, Trump achieved not nearly as much. As 2017 ended, most of Trump's agenda (with the exception of immigration arrests) remained unfinished, ill-defined and unconstructed.

On the political side, Trump defenders said this is precisely what Trump promised during the campaign and what voters like Ray Paradez thunderously cheered. It was, they argued, the verdict of the people and the underlying construct of federal law—which gives the president wide discretion on immigration—that justified the travel ban legally and politically. It was the political side of this argument that never failed Trump with his base of supporters. They considered it a promise kept and cheered his continued legal battling, barely noticing the alterations in the executive order along the way. For them, Trump told the world to take a hike because anyone who might be a terrorist or might think like a terrorist or might even want to associate with one—well, hell, they were not welcome in America anymore. Tough shit. Trump was boss. And he said screw you. For Trump supporters, this was one of those larger truths, and no room was set aside for constitutional subtleties such as equal protection or due process—even though the legal gyrations and final product took account of both.

"He always wins," Gingrich said, describing Trump's approach to the travel ban and setbacks in general. "Because the times he didn't win didn't count. Great salesmen never notice the 'Nos.' Because the 'Nos' wear you out. But if you can hang in, it's amazing what you can accomplish."

This was not the only immigration achievement of Trump's first year. Sessions, his attorney general, did more to advance that agenda than any other cabinet secretary and did so by drilling down on the very issues Trump supporter Paradez raised with me in the summer of 2016. Sessions attacked sanctuary cities—jurisdictions that intentionally forbid the sharing of information about the immigration status of someone picked up in a police investigation—from every conceivable legal angle. He sued California over three separate laws that erected barriers between local law enforcement and cooperation with federal immigration agents. In Texas, he sued to protect a law there that required information-sharing on immigration violations between local jurisdictions and the feds. He also made it more difficult for sanctuary cities to obtain Justice Department grants. On the issue of undocumented individuals facing deportation, Sessions determined the problem was insufficient numbers of immigration judges on the southern border to handle deportation orders (under law, such orders must go through a hearing process). Sessions dispatched more than 100 judges to Homeland Security detention facilities nationwide, resulting in 2,800 more verdicts than would have been achieved had the judges not been on site. Sessions also sent a signal about the importance of immigration enforcement to every U.S. Attorney's Office by assigning to each of the 94 offices a "border security coordinator." By April of 2017, illegal border crossings had fallen by 70 percent to their lowest statistical level in 17 years. By mid-2018 those numbers had risen again and Trump, as a result, grew frustrated with the limits of Justice Department intervention and with the GOP-led Congress's indifference to his calls to legislatively accelerate deportations.

The lesson of this process is not that the president—Trump or any other—has the constitutional authority to originate immigration policy or define the terms of its implementation; that has always been true. What matters in 21st-century America is that Trump is an early 20th-century exponent of that power. He wants an emphatically American definition of immigration law—far more language-specific in terms of implementation and symbolism than any president's since *the late 19th century*. Perhaps dimly, Trump understood that all presidents, by virtue of the Constitution, exercise wide authority over immigration. He acted. This book does not argue that he acted, in every instance, lawfully or unlawfully. It does argue that he acted in response to the American democracy as the duly elected president and pushed the enforcement envelope as far as he believed the law would allow. This approach provoked numerous legal challenges, some of which Trump won, some of which remained pending in late July 2018.

Trump may have pursued this aim imperfectly, but it could well be argued that he put the question "Is it time to have another immigration policy?" squarely before the voters and, having received the answer through his election, pursued its political and legal application to the fullest. What might matter most to Trump supporters and opponents is that while Attorney General Sessions moved the Trump agenda forward on many immigration fronts, Trump lost valuable political capital outside of his political base during the protracted travel ban fight. Yes, Trump sent a decidedly anti-immigrant signal and found rapturous endorsement among his followers. But all available polling evidence suggests he did not expand his reach or improve his ability to persuade. In fact, polling evidence suggests exactly the opposite. One litmus test will be the 2018 midterm elections. But in the 2018 legislative year, it was clear that Trump had an immigration megaphone but little else. Even a majority Republican Congress was indifferent, suggesting the GOP was too weak to reject Trump but strong enough to ignore him until the next verdict of the people—the midterms—had been rendered. This was GOP opposition by paralysis, another unique aspect of the Trump phenomenon. This occurred, in part, because Trump mishandled the "big stuff" travel ban moment and undercut his own larger legislative goals through haste and belligerence. Early defense of the travel ban trafficked in terrorism-fed fear-mongering and clung to dubious but scary-sounding statistics. Exaggerated claims of danger tended to reaffirm critics who contended that beneath the travel ban lay religious bias and racial animosity.

SIX

Jeff Sessions

It was mid-December 2017 and Ty Cobb, a distant relative of the Ty Cobb of Baseball Hall of Fame legend and, in his own right, a highly regarded Washington attorney who has bankrolled Democrats, was struggling to explain the unique burdens of working for Trump.

Cobb was the White House lawyer assigned to Special Counsel Robert Mueller's Russia investigation. Like so many prominent first-year members of Trump's team, Cobb was jettisoned in 2018. He joined the legal team in late July 2017, after Trump fired his longtime attorney Marc Kasowitz. Cobb took the job after other D.C. lawyers turned Trump down. Some didn't like the case. Others didn't like Trump. Still others were afraid of the association with a Trump White House. Cobb considered it a call to service and put up with all manner of Trump abuse in service not so much to him but to the office and institution of the presidency.

Cobb is a Buddhist who has traveled the world to many significant shrines of the faith. Cobb is also a Deadhead, his sojourns to Grateful Dead concerts, when the band was still touring, nearly as frequent as to Buddhist temples. He sports a gray 19th-century mustache waxed to perfection so the curls circle just beneath his chubby red cheeks. Cobb is not a Trumper. He's not a Never-Trumper. He's a lawyer with a client—the 11th billionaire Cobb has represented. That 11th billionaire also happened to be the 45th president of the United States.

"You don't want to own it," Cobb told me, referring to the "crazy" Trump White House. "You would like people to understand the lines you have self-imposed and the obligations. The mere fact that you have a position doesn't mean you are a true believer. You have certain rights and obligations that go with that position. As I keep telling the president twice a week, 'My obligation is to the institution, sir.' He hates that."

Cobb viewed himself as a servant of the law, the White House and the presidency. He struggled against the Trumpian pull to be a loyalist above all. Within the White House Cobb counseled cooperation with Mueller. He produced thousands of pages of White House documents and arranged all interviews with key White House and Trump campaign personnel. Cobb believed then and believes now that Trump is innocent—no conspiracy with the Russians and no attempt to obstruct justice. His advice to the president was persistent and simple: you are innocent; act like it. Longtime friends of Trump came to regard Cobb as a peacenik playing games with Mueller and his cabal of legal ball-busters. One person who held this general opinion was John Dowd, who was one of Trump's personal lawyers. In fact, it was a clash between Dowd and Cobb that sits at the center of one of the great untold stories of Trump's angry relationship to the special counsel investigation—the death of an early January 2018 interview with Trump.

Cobb had set the table for a Trump interview with Mueller on January 27. "There was such momentum," Cobb told me. "They [special counsel's office] were caving. I was telling Dowd, 'You have to keep meeting with them every day. You got to make them want it.'" By the end of December, according to Cobb, Mueller's team had all the documents it requested and had conducted 80 percent of the interviews it sought. By mid-January, after another session with McGahn, the interview work was nearly done . . . the biggest catch being Trump. The main areas of inquiry were the Flynn and Comey firings and related questions about possible obstruction of justice. Then Cobb did something he had never done since joining the White House as Trump's lawyer on Mueller matters—he granted an extended, on-the-record and on-camera interview. He did it with me. It was for my podcast "The Take-out." We taped the night of January 18. During the show, Cobb made international news, saying that Trump was "very eager to sit down and explain whatever is responsive" to Mueller and his team, so long as the interview was not "a perjury trap." He also said, "there was no reason for [the Russia investigation] not to conclude soon," which Cobb on my show defined as "four to six weeks." That public appearance and Cobb's lobbying for a Trump interview with Mueller unnerved Dowd. "He was freaked out," Cobb said. "That's the day Dowd put his foot on the brake. I was trying to make clear we were getting close. Dowd was talking to the president without telling us. Dowd just got scared." Dowd always opposed a Trump interview with Mueller. In this moment, he prevailed. The interview fell apart and other issues arose for Mueller's team later in 2018, many turning on Trump fixer Michael Cohen and other revelations linked to Russian lobbying and transactions touching on those in the Trump orbit. Dowd left the Trump legal team before Cobb departed. Giuliani replaced him, for better or worse, and played a much more high-visibility role as Trump's legal mouthpiece.

Cobb, in many respects, was a prism through which to view Attorney General Jeff Sessions—once a figure of rectitude and respect within Trump's inner circle but later one of derision and lily-livered infamy. Sessions's struggles on the Trump loyalty trail began at his Senate confirmation hearing. Sessions arrived as one of the first cabinet picks named by Trump during the transition and as his first and most loyal supporter in the Senate. Sessions was also, viewed from a certain angle, one of Trump's "forgotten people."

Republican Senate colleagues considered Sessions too conservative and too nationalistic for his own good—and the party's. Sessions staked out positions against illegal *and* legal immigration. Almost no Republicans opposed legal immigration, but Sessions argued that legal immigration suppressed wages for lesser-educated, native-born workers. That these workers tended to be disproportionately white may or may not have been a coincidence. What mattered was that worldview seamlessly matched Trump's. In the Senate, Sessions also opposed free trade, welfare, criminal justice reform, gay and transgender rights and abortion. On these issues, Sessions did not merely strike poses; he authored amendments and gummed up pieces of legislation with his hard-core conservativism. That did not, necessarily, make Sessions a GOP pariah. To the contrary, Sessions was pleasant and cordial. His word was good. He was likable and liked.

But Sessions did not play ball and did not join in bipartisan deal-making or featherbedding. He was a genial crank, a loner in the GOP cloakroom and an island of rocky ideological isolation. Trump's campaign gave Sessions relevance he'd never known before and elevated his Senate staff into the upper reaches of Trump's tiny policy and management circle. Sessions became somebody with Trump and his day, January 10, 2017, before colleagues on the Senate Judiciary Committee was to be the jumping-off point to the best, most fulfilling job of his career. Sessions prepared diligently for the hearing and was well-versed in Justice Department budgets, policies and practices. He prepared for questions on immigration, civil rights, federal sentencing, voting rights, gay rights and restoring the rights of felons to vote. More than halfway through the hearing, he was feeling good. His top aides, sitting only feet away, considered the hearing a smash success and had begun to turn their attention to post-confirmation matters. Then came the question that would turn Sessions, Trump and their aspirations and expectations upside down.

"If there is any evidence that anyone affiliated with the Trump campaign communicated with the Russian government in the course of this campaign, what will you do?"

That question came from former Minnesota Sen. Al Franken, a Democrat in good standing at the time (before he resigned amid allegations of sexual harassment).

Sessions hesitated momentarily.

"I didn't have—did not have communications with the Russians."

That is not the entire exchange, and that matters in the context of lying to Congress—a federal crime that as of this writing Sessions has not been charged with. The context is relevant to the still-convoluted tale of Sessions's involvement in the Trump campaign as it relates to Russian officials. Sessions also came to represent the early partisan narratives surrounding the Russia investigation. If you were already suspicious of or hostile to Trump, Sessions looked and sounded guilty. If you were supportive of Trump and skeptical of the Russia collusion story, Sessions looked and sounded cautious and lawful—and picked on by Trump political antagonists.

That part of the story will play out in 2018 and Sessions's standing as a loyalist and/or toady will be the subject of countless historical and political cross-examinations.

Like so much about Trump's first year, it's hard to separate the substantive from the silly. There were parts of both in Sessions's rise, fall and perpetual purgatory. His story is a microcosm also of the bizarrely careless Trump campaign, the pliability of loyalty and the harrowing price of perceived weakness. Woven through the Sessions story are Trump's own battles with the Justice Department hierarchy and the FBI and his Twitter bulldozing of norms dealing with the president's allowing federal investigations to proceed without interference and commentary. Sessions's story is also about Trump's misunderstanding of pop icon politics in Alabama and his bungling of the Roy Moore mess. Trump lost a Senate seat and tarnished the Republican National Committee in the process. The ruin left in Alabama after Trump plucked Sessions from the backbenches and hoisted him to attorney general hardly seems worth the cost. The plotlines are seemingly endless. *Sessions* could be a Netflix miniseries. It could run for several seasons on the first year of Trump's presidency alone. By my lights, we wouldn't even get to Roy Moore's Alabama until season three.

Sessions was a Trump surrogate. But Trump's campaign didn't manage surrogates any more than it managed Trump. Surrogates could do what they wanted when they wanted. No supervision. Sessions was the first *and only* GOP senator to endorse Trump. He provided the campaign with its top speechwriter, Sessions's aide Stephen Miller, and the eventual leader of the transition, Sessions's chief of staff Rick Dearborn. Sessions's loyalty to Trump predated Mike Pence's and was nearly as dog-like devotional. But Trump turned on Sessions, humiliating him in public and forcing him to ponder resignation . . . all before May of 2017. Sessions also played a key role in Trump's decision to fire FBI Director James Comey, part of a staggering series of events chronicled in the chapter "10 Days in May."

Where to begin with the Sessions story, which is, of course, a Trump story? Which is *the* pivotal moment? Is it the February 28, 2016, rally where Trump packed Madison City Schools Stadium in

Madison, Alabama, with 32,000 supporters, and where Sessions endorsed him? Is it the Washington meeting Sessions convened a few weeks later for Trump to curry favor with top conservatives, the one that would lead to the pivotal Supreme Court list? Is it when Sessions rode with Trump in his campaign SUV as Trump phoned Pence to make him his running mate? Is it the meeting in Trump's private office in Trump Tower two days after the election when the process for selecting Neil Gorsuch as a Supreme Court nominee was launched and when Sessions was offered the attorney general slot? Is it the day Sessions, now attorney general, stunned and angered Trump by recusing himself from all investigations related to Russia, Trump, the White House and the campaign?

It's all of those. But more than any other it's Sessions and Franken in the Russell Caucus Room, jousting not over what Sessions knew or didn't know about Russians, but what he would do if, as attorney general, he came across incriminating evidence about the Trump campaign and Russians. That's the context of Franken's question and it's at the heart of why Sessions's answer and subsequent actions infuriated Trump. It provides the most tantalizing clue about what Sessions thought may come from the Russia investigation.

Here is Franken's question: "CNN just published a story alleging that the intelligence community provided documents to the president-elect last week that included information that, quote, 'Russian operatives claimed to have compromising personal and financial information about Mr. Trump.' These documents also allegedly say, quote, 'There was a continuing exchange of information during the campaign between Trump's surrogates and intermediaries for the Russian government.'"

Franken continued: "Now, again, I'm telling you this as it's coming out, so you know. But if it's true, it's obviously extremely serious, and if there is any evidence that anyone affiliated with the Trump campaign communicated with the Russian government in the course of this campaign, what will you do?"

Sessions replied: "Senator Franken, I'm not aware of any of those activities. I have been called a surrogate at a time or two in that campaign and I didn't have—did not have communications with the Russians and I'm unable to comment on it."

At the moment, neither Sessions nor his team of advisors thought the exchange was terribly meaningful. The question was kind of convoluted and drawn from breaking news they neither prepared for nor could anticipate. Top advisors to Sessions told me months later it all felt inconsequential. Looking back, they said they do not question their judgment at the time; only their inability to judge the surrounding politics and the questions this seemingly innocuous encounter raised.

In retrospect, Sessions failed the basic test of politics and law. In both instances, training instructs you to focus on the question asked and nothing else. In law, you divulge as little as possible. In politics, you take the question in your direction, not the direction its premise leads. The simple answer from Sessions could have been (and in retrospect Sessions wishes it had been): "Senator Franken, you present a hypothetical. I don't generally answer hypothetical questions. But public curiosity about this topic is high and therefore justifies this limited response. If I am confirmed as attorney general and evidence is presented to me or the Justice Department indicating problematic communications between a foreign government and either presidential campaign, you have my word the evidence will be investigated."

For whatever reason, Sessions did not answer Franken's question but attempted to answer three others—whether he knew about compromising information on Trump, whether he was a campaign surrogate and if he communicated with Russians. This approach proved to be Sessions's undoing. Pretending he was not a surrogate was absurd. Sessions campaigned aggressively for Trump. His closest advisors formed the policy backbone of the campaign. Every Republican senator knew that and Sessions's joking dismissal of his central role in Trump's campaign waved a red flag of deception, one that made his next statement even more suspect. Denying any contacts with Russians was foolish and false.

It was foolish because no senator on the Foreign Relations Committee, of which Sessions was a member, would not meet with Russian diplomats or emissaries for Russian diplomats. To admit that would not be a scandal. But to deny it *might* sound curiously evasive. As was later revealed, Sessions had at least three meetings with Russian Ambassador Sergey Kislyak—one at Trump's first big foreign policy speech in Washington in April of 2016, another in July at the Republican National

Convention in Cleveland and a third at his Senate office in September. According to *The Washington Post,* U.S. intelligence intercepts of Kislyak revealed he and Sessions had "substantive" conversations about Trump's approach to Russia and prospects for improved relations. The intercepts were based on Kislyak's representations to Moscow about progress he was making with Sessions as a Trump surrogate, according to the *Post.* In all three instances, Sessions was already a full-blown Trump surrogate and known throughout the ambassadorial ranks as the only senator with regular access to Trump and someone who was populating the small and influential ranks of Trump's inner circle. Pretending none of this was true deeply undercut Sessions's reputation for truthfulness among GOP colleagues. It also betrayed an ugly inability to comprehend the realm he was about to enter—Hey, dummy, all of this is surveilled! Don't you know that??!??! If it was a bid to establish his loyalty to Trump, it didn't get him very far.

There's another layer of context and it is deeply important in this regard. Sessions knew what it was like to be grilled by the Judiciary Committee. He had experienced it. Sessions faced withering questions in May of 1986 as a Reagan-nominated judge for a federal district court in Alabama. Democrats badgered Sessions with questions about civil rights and scrutinized written testimony from a deputy of Sessions's in the U.S. Attorney's Office in Mobile that accused Sessions of referring to the National Association for the Advancement of Colored People (NAACP) as "un-American." The deputy, Thomas Figures, an African American, also testified Sessions admonished him to watch how he spoke to "white folks." He also testified that Sessions applied "un-American" to the Southern Christian Leadership Conference, Operation PUSH and the National Council of Churches—all affiliated with civil rights advocacy and routinely accused during the civil rights struggle in the Deep South of being leftist or communist agitators.

Sessions told the committee he "may have said something about the NAACP being un-American or communist, but [I] meant no harm by it." Sessions was 39 at the time, just beginning his political career. His fumbling answers increased Democratic opposition and deepened Republican anxiety. The Republican-controlled Judiciary Committee rejected his nomination on a vote of 10–8 (with liberal Republican Sens. Arlen Specter of Pennsylvania and Charles McCurdy "Mac" Mathias Jr.

of Maryland joining all eight committee Democrats). Sessions became
the first Reagan judicial nominee to die in committee and only the second federal judicial nominee in 48 years not to win confirmation. Had
Senate Democrats confirmed Sessions, he would have been a federal
judge for life, unavailable to Trump as surrogate, attorney general or
eventual whipping boy. In unpredictable and sometimes galling con-
tours, history is made of such things. The point is Sessions knew what a
confirmation hearing was like—or certainly should have remembered.
That makes his rookie mistake with Franken even harder to comprehend. Unless it wasn't a mistake but a bid to prove loyalty or an effort
to conceal.

Whatever it was (and by now Mueller may have told the nation),
Sessions's conduct set in motion a torrent of events that cascaded
through the first year of Trump's presidency. When it was disclosed
Sessions had met with Kislyak, the explanation (undermined by subsequent intelligence intercept evidence) was that Sessions took those
meetings as a senator, not as Trump surrogate. You can't do that when
you're a campaign's only surrogate. You can't do that when one of the
meetings is at Trump's biggest foreign policy speech and you're there as
part of the cheer team. If the meetings were benign, why didn't he tell
Franken and the committee when asked?

Moreover, why didn't Sessions correct the record in the immediate
aftermath of the hearing, as he knew well that witnesses were routinely
granted that courtesy? It looked like Sessions might have been trying
to deceive the committee. Why? No one knew. Few could understand.
Democrats wanted him to resign. Republicans wanted him to recuse
himself from the Russia investigation. On the question of recusal, ethics lawyers inside the Justice Department recommended it. McGahn,
White House counsel, called Sessions to feel him out on the question of
recusal, but sources insist he was trying to learn Sessions's intentions,
not instruct him on how to proceed.

Cobb relayed the context of the call, saying Sessions told McGahn,
"All the ethics people here at the Justice Department are telling me I
have to do this. And McGahn says, 'fine.'" As for Trump's attitude,
Cobb told me the president was frequently confused about the extent
and limits of his power. "He would never order anybody not to do this
[recuse]. He would say, 'What can we do to see if we can talk Jeff out

of this? You know, I don't want him to do this. Is it mandatory? Can we figure out what's going on? And what are the consequences for the department? What does it mean that he is recused? Educate me.'"

Sessions did recuse himself, stepping to the podium late in the afternoon of March 2 at the Justice Department press room. Sessions looked fidgety and spoke haltingly. He had been attorney general for 22 days. His forehead was shiny, his gray hair thin and slick against his scalp, his cheeks flush.

"Let me be clear. I never had meetings with Russian operatives or Russian intermediaries about the Trump campaign. And the idea I was part of a 'continuing exchange of information during the campaign between Trump surrogates and intermediaries for the Russian government' is totally false. That is the question Senator Franken asked me at the hearing and that's what got my attention. It was just breaking news. And that is the question I responded to. My reply to the question of Senator Franken was honest and correct as I understood it at the time. I will write the Judiciary Committee soon . . . to explain this testimony."

McGahn got wind of Sessions's intent and tried to stop his recusal, doubting he was in real legal jeopardy and knowing Trump's style was to respond to political heat with more of it. But McGahn's call didn't get through.

"At my confirmation hearing, I promised that I would do this," Sessions said as he raised a white sheet of paper in his left hand and placed it in his right. The paper snapped audibly as Sessions squinted through wire-rimmed glasses perched at the edge of his nose. "If a specific matter arose where I believed my impartiality might reasonably be questioned, I would 'consult with the department ethics officials regarding the most appropriate way to proceed.' . . . I have been here just three weeks today. A lot has been happening. . . . We evaluated the rules of ethics and recusal. I have considered the issues at stake. . . . I asked for their candid and honest opinion about what I should do about investigations, certain investigations. And my staff recommended recusal. . . . I believe those recommendations are right and just. Therefore, I have recused myself in the matters that deal with the Trump campaign."

Sessions was then asked about the September meeting in his office with Kislyak, the third meeting of the campaign year he had with the ambassador. After describing how the meeting was scheduled (a diversionary tactic), Sessions said "we listened to the ambassador and what his concerns might be." Total dodge. A second reporter followed up, asking what happened in the discussion with Kislyak. Sessions took his glasses off with his right hand and looked down at the floor. "I don't remember a lot of it, but I do remember saying I'd gone to Russia with a church group in 1991, and he said he was not a believer himself. We talked a little about terrorism and somehow the subject of Ukraine came up. It got to be a little bit of a testy conversation." He was asked if they discussed politics. "I don't recall, but most of these ambassadors are pretty gossipy. I don't recall any specific political discussions."

Sessions was then asked a two-part question. His answer or non-answer was a testament to administration-wide obfuscation on basic details of interactions with Russian officials.

"Did you consult with the White House about your decision? And just to follow on the last question with hindsight, do you believe that this is a coincidence that the Russians asked you for a meeting? Did you believe you were targeted because it came at the height of Russia's interference? And at the same time, then-candidate Trump was giving an interview to RT saying that he didn't believe that there was anything to the reported interference." This was about RT (formerly Russia Today), a Moscow-owned and operated network that provides pro-Russia news content and commentary to cable and internet audiences outside of Russia. Trump's willingness to sit down with RT struck some as needlessly cozy and oddly coincidental to Russian efforts, undetected at the time, to meddle in the election.

Sessions shook his head.

"I don't recall and don't have a sense of any connection whatsoever about that. I'm not sure I even knew what—when we set up the meeting what was going to be going on in the world at the time, so I can't speak for what the Russian ambassador may have had in his mind."

Sessions was asked again if he cleared his recusal with the White House. It was noted hours earlier Trump and Spicer said he shouldn't. Sessions fell into his most halting and hesitant cadence, stopping and starting to describe the gap between his sense of propriety and the White House's.

"I did share with the White House counsel, or my staff has, that I intended to recuse myself this afternoon. Um. But. Um. I. Um. I feel like. 'Cause they didn't. They don't know the rules, the ethics rules. Uh. Most people don't. Uh. And, um. But when you evaluate the rules, I feel like that uh, uh, I, uh, I should not be involved in investigating a campaign I had a role in."

Without Sessions, the Russia investigation fell to Deputy Attorney General Rod Rosenstein, whom Trump nominated on January 31, 2017. Rosenstein is a Republican, appointed U.S. attorney for the District of Maryland by George W. Bush in 2005. Before that he was an investigator and lawyer for Independent Counsel Ken Starr's Whitewater investigation. Rosenstein's legal work won bipartisan praise. He pulled no punches as a prosecutor and did not shy away from Democratic wrongdoing in the heavily Democratic state of Maryland. He was a solid legal conservative versed in and committed to legal process and norms (all of the above would be later questioned by Trump and a handful of House Republican echoists).

In the aftermath of Sessions's recusal, Rosenstein faced the specter of monitoring a potentially unwieldy federal investigation into Trump's campaign and Russian officials—a task that could devour the department and might prove his political undoing. Rosenstein had no time to process his options. Within days, Trump tweeted that Obama had wiretapped Trump Tower (for posterity let it be recorded here that Trump's original tweet misspelled "wiretap" as "wiretapp"). FBI Director James Comey asked the Justice Department to refute the allegation. To reread this makes one wonder if it *actually happened*. Did a U.S. president accuse his predecessor of illegally surveilling his private offices (Trump's noxious tweet used the 1970s vernacular of "wiretap" when he meant surveillance via any variety of interceptors).

It happened—the accusation, I mean. The alleged surveillance did not. The allegation never had a basis in provable fact or rational suspicion. Trump leveled the charge anyway. This happened. In America. And we've almost forgotten about it. Not because it wasn't egregious and ghastly, but because it has been overtaken by other Trump tweets ordering this investigation or that (something presidents are not supposed to do), decrying Sessions as weak and condemning Justice Department professionals for failing to reopen closed cases. With Trump's Twitter rants, the road to judicial perdition just kept going, hauling the nation's understanding of and adherence to depoliticized law enforcement who knows where. Trump argued throughout he was merely punching back and trying to draw attention to shady Democratic deals and circumstances at least as odious as those alleged against his campaign or political allies. By mid-June of 2018, a Justice Department Inspector General report, which would have been the venue to vindicate any of Trump's wild assertions, faulted FBI personnel but did not vindicate Trump. The president said it did anyway—a perfect illustration of his attempt to shape history and the truth with negligible respect for or belief in either.

Trump made it appear he was contemptuous of the law and he didn't care. There were times in his first year when even friends like Roger Stone compared Trump to Nixon. Whether Trump becomes our next Nixon is, at one level, irrelevant. Impeached. Resigned. Reelected. Oddly, each appears possible. What will last is the recorded history of a president who spoke more maliciously about federal law enforcement—accusing it of harboring malevolent political tendencies—than any of his predecessors. That some of Trump's supporters believe he may be right is also telling, not only in terms of their allegiance but to the shadow cast by a president playing political hardball with the Justice Department.

In the hinterlands of America, where Trump focused his attention, the interpretations and verdicts were decidedly different.

The day Mueller was appointed, my CBS colleague, Dean Reynolds, traveled to Dixon, Illinois, and met Trump supporters at Bill and Dick's Barber Shop. There he met Guy Ball, a voice of Trump's ardent flyover followers.

"Everybody is looking for something to dig at," Ball said. "It's a witch hunt. That's what he tweeted this morning. They keep saying the Russians interfered in our elections. How did they interfere? I mean, I never hear that talked about on TV."

Ball then described why he loved Trump as candidate and stood with him as president.

"I liked the way he recognized that there is a country out here," Ball said. "It consists from coast to coast. Not coast and coast. And he targeted that area. These are people who have concerns. These are people who have needs and they're being ignored."

Trump owed his 2017 and 2018 durability in the polls to voters like Ball. They remained with Trump through the first year. As for the torrent of criticism and negative publicity, another voter Reynolds met in Dixon, Steve Huber, said it missed the point. "I almost tune off the news anymore," Huber said as he browsed for books inside Books on First. "It's all about how he's behaving, not what he's really doing to help our country."

Trump supporters overlooked a lot—even as they accused the media of overlooking Trump's accomplishments. Naturally, most voters overlook day-to-day developments, especially when Trump threats and noisy tweets are so numerous. That tendency does not, however, mean some of what Trump said about the federal judicial system was not problematic. It must be recorded Trump tried to influence federal investigations by asking, on Twitter no less, they be launched or reopened. It must be noted Trump denounced federal court rulings, and the legitimacy of the judges who authored them, simply because he found them disagreeable. It might be reasonably observed these caustic attitudes about a national judiciary would make a bungling banana republic dictator (think Raúl Juliá in *Moon over Parador*) blush.

When Sessions recused himself, Trump could only turn to Comey. Turn to him he did, allegedly using whatever means he could to elicit loyalty and convey the trouble the Russia investigation was causing. And we must remember this. The Comey that Trump would eventually fire was the Comey that Trump lionized during the campaign—praising him for the handling of the Clinton email investigation. "The FBI, after discovering new emails, is reopening their investigation into Hillary Clinton," Trump said to cheers in Manchester, New Hampshire, on October 28, 2016. This was hours after Comey, in a letter to congressional Republicans, announced the move. "I have great respect for the FBI for righting this wrong." Three days later Trump addressed a roaring crowd in Grand Rapids, Michigan, and specifically praised Comey. "It took a lot of guts. I really disagreed with him. I was not his fan, but I tell you what: what he did, he brought back his reputation. He brought it back. He's got to hang tough because there's a lot of people want him to do the wrong thing. What he did was the right thing."

Because the sequence of events in Trump world (all events, not just the *breaking news* variety) is so hard to remember, here is a small tick-tock of Giuliani, the FBI, the Clinton email developments and Comey in the crucial closing days of the 2016 campaign:

October 3—Agents in the FBI New York field office investigating Anthony Weiner, estranged husband to top Clinton advisor Huma Abedin, recover a laptop Weiner shared with Abedin that contains emails from Clinton. They do not inform Comey or seek a warrant to read the emails. Instead, the agents search metadata, essentially "to" and "from" communications that reveal sender and receiver and the time of these communications. Metadata does not reveal the contents of the communication.

October 7–14—FBI agents inform Giuliani of "new" information on the Clinton email investigation, according to Giuliani's subsequent public description of events.

October 25—While on *Fox & Friends,* Giuliani is asked if Trump has something planned for the homestretch of the campaign other than rallies. "Yes," Giuliani says. "We've got a couple of surprises left."

October 26—Again on Fox, this time with presenter Martha Mac-Callum, Giuliani says, "We've got a couple things up our sleeve that should turn things around."

October 27—The New York FBI field office informs Comey of Clinton emails on the Abedin-Weiner computer and requests Comey re-open the Clinton investigation to evaluate this "new" evidence.

October 28—Comey sends a letter to Congress suggesting this new information may have relevance to the Clinton email investigation as it might suggest new wrongdoing. Republicans leak the letter to reporters. The letter appears to violate FBI protocol prohibiting actions 60 days before an election that could influence the outcome. The same day Giuliani appears on conservative Lars Larson's radio show. On the show, Giuliani discloses he is in contact with former and current FBI agents he would not identify who, he said, had been providing information about Clinton investigation developments. (This raised the prospect of a violation of the Hatch Act, a federal law that prohibits FBI agents and other federal employees from taking actions—targeted leaks to the media being one of them—that could be construed as partisan or seeking to influence political debate.)

October 29—Giuliani tries to clarify his Lars Larson interview on CNN by saying he had only been speaking with "former" FBI agents, calling his reference to current FBI agents erroneous.

October 30—Comey tells Congress his investigators have been reviewing the emails "around the clock" since learning of them three days before. The review was carried out under a warrant later found to be defective because there was no known basis to suspect the emails were new or evidence of a crime.

November 4—Giuliani appears on *Fox & Friends* and discusses the Comey letter about Clinton, Abedin and Weiner. "I can't even repeat the language I heard from the former FBI agents," Giuliani said. "I had expected this for the last, honestly, to tell you the truth, I thought it was going to be about three or four weeks ago." Democratic Reps. Elijah Cummings of Maryland and John Conyers of Michigan request a Justice Department Inspector General investigation of Giuliani on the basis of his *Fox & Friends* interviews. "It is absolutely unacceptable for the FBI to leak unsubstantiated—and in some cases false—information about one presidential candidate to the benefit of the other candidate. Leaking this information to former FBI officials as a conduit to the Trump campaign is equally intolerable." A mid-June 2018 report by the Justice Department's Inspector General David Horowitz, for which Giuliani said he was interviewed, found no evidence of a crime.

It must also be noted that in late 2017 and through early 2018 Trump and a small number of his House Republican allies turned against Rosenstein, implying he might be part of an effort to undermine Trump through the Russia investigation. It was a strange turn against a prosecutor who handled a case Trump desperately tried to revive in 2017.

Under Trump's persistent Twitter prodding the Justice Department in late 2017 reopened an investigation into Clinton's alleged role in the sale of Canadian firm Uranium One to Russia's state-owned atomic energy company in 2010. During the campaign, Trump and Giuliani routinely referred to the sale as a hijacking of precious U.S. uranium reserves and implied it was done as payback for contributions to the Clinton Foundation. "Remember that Hillary Clinton gave Russia 20 percent of American uranium and, you know, she was paid a fortune," Trump said at a rally on October 24, 2016. "You know, they got a tremendous amount of money." What Trump ignored was the original investigation resulted in guilty pleas in Russia and the United States for money laundering and that those pleas were secured through an investigation supervised by none other than Rosenstein and Andrew McCabe, whom Trump tapped to replace Comey.

The new 2017 Justice Department investigation commenced after hectoring from Trump on Twitter, including this missive on October 19: "Uranium deal to Russia with Clinton help and Obama Administration knowledge is the biggest story that the Fake Media doesn't want to follow." The sale was approved by the Committee on Foreign Investment in the United States, also known as CFIUS. The nine-member committee did not include Clinton. The State Department did have a seat on the board. CFIUS must unanimously approve sales of minerals, technology or other assets with potential national security implications. The Uranium One deal was approved unanimously and the members who so voted have said subsequently they would take the same decision.

When Rosentstein appointed Mueller on May 17 it set off a crisis of heart-stopping drama inside Trump's West Wing.

Priebus was in his office late that afternoon when McGahn rushed in with two thunderbolts—a special counsel had been appointed and Sessions had resigned. Priebus was more or less expecting the special counsel—it's where things had been heading for days. But he was not expecting Sessions to resign. That was the bigger crisis.

"Where is he?" Priebus asked, meaning Sessions. McGahn did not know but thought he was still in the West Wing, having just left the Oval Office.

Priebus rushed into the hall and looked frantically for Sessions who simply could not—not now, at least—become the former attorney general. Sessions wasn't in the Oval or the hallway nearby. Priebus dashed toward the suite of communications offices on the other side of the hallway from the Roosevelt Room, wondering if Sessions was talking to White House press staff about how to announce his resignation.

On the way, Priebus bumped into Pence, who said he had seen Sessions head for West Executive Avenue, the small road that separates the West Wing from the Eisenhower Executive Office Building and where top White House staff park. It is also where SUVs carrying cabinet secretaries drop them off for White House visits. The route to West Exec (as it is known to White House staffers) was down the stairs by the Cabinet Room. Priebus tore down those stairs and past the lower level of West Wing offices, past the White House cafeteria (known as the White House Mess) and bolted through the double doors to find Sessions inside his idling black Suburban.

"You cannot resign," Priebus said. "You cannot resign. This cannot happen. Can you come inside and talk about it?" The fear of headlines announcing a special counsel and the resignation of Sessions was almost more than the system, even the Trump hyped-up system, could bear.

Sessions said he couldn't take Trump's abuse and wanted out. He was reluctant to make this move but thought it was the right thing to do. Sessions looked a little flushed and his voice was halting. Priebus begged him to get out of the Suburban and come back inside the West Wing. He had to get Sessions to un-resign. Quickly.

Sessions returned to Priebus's office and agreed to rescind his resignation. Trump accepted the reversal, but the fiasco deepened his sense of disappointment. Sessions returned to the Justice Department weaker in Trump's eyes than before. He was angry enough to resign but too soft to carry it out. That Sessions reversed himself to help Trump scarcely mattered.

Priebus quieted one storm so the White House could face another—Mueller. Priebus knew no president could face that investigation without an attorney general—even a recused one. If Sessions had resigned, the nominee to replace him would have been extremely hard to confirm and if he or she was confirmed the political price to be paid in terms of distraction, clout and time would have been staggering. A confirmation fight would have also damaged Trump's domestic agenda and would have risked Republican defections. Another consideration was the effect a Sessions resignation would have on Trump's conservative base. The risks were enormous. That's why Priebus ran around in such a panic. He had to find Sessions and turn him around. While Priebus did this there were a few amazing moments when Trump had no attorney general and Sessions had no future. Then Priebus performed another strenuous maneuver—not the first and not the last.

A short time later, Sessions did something nearly as unthinkable. He typed up a resignation letter and signed it. Conspicuously, he left it undated. Without the knowledge of Priebus or McGahn, Sessions gave the letter to Trump—telling him he could fill out the date whenever he wanted. Sessions resigned subject to Trump's whims, with which he, Sessions, had long since had enough.

Priebus blew his stack. He told Sessions that letter had to be retrieved because it represented a permanent "collar" around the neck of Sessions and the Department of Justice. The letter gave up the department's independence—because every conversation with Sessions, as long as Trump retained possession of that letter, would be colored by the possibility he could be sacked. Sessions agreed but said by way of defense he was sick of wondering when or if Trump would fire him. Sessions also said it made the decision for Trump, giving him a letter he could execute whenever he wanted, thus creating for himself more job security, not less. You see, Sessions had by this time figured out Trump really didn't like to fire people. Priebus spent the next two weeks lobbying Trump to give up the letter—which he eventually did. In the meantime, though, Trump kept it nearby.

Trump blamed Sessions for his woes but he was often his worst enemy. Few events made that more evident than a late-night December 2 tweet. It read as follows: "I had to fire General Flynn because he lied to the Vice President and the FBI. He has pled guilty to those lies. It is a shame because his actions during the transition were lawful. There was nothing to hide." If Trump, as the tweet clearly implied, knew at the time of the investigation that Flynn lied to the FBI, then Trump's suggestion or request or intimation to Comey (whatever it was) that he would like the FBI to back off the Flynn investigation looks like an effort to obstruct justice.

The White House fingered Trump personal lawyer John Dowd, saying he misconstrued what Trump wanted to say and garbled the sequence of events in the tweet. That was the explanation. Oh, really? If it was to be believed, it was the first and only time in the Trump presidency when a tweet on Trump's personal @realDonaldTrump account was attributed to another author. We can only assume it coincidental that it was the only legally compromising tweet. If all this was true, the ultimate remedy was simple enough. All the White House had to do was declare publicly when Trump learned Flynn lied to the FBI. It refused. Repeatedly. So did Dowd. After raising the possibility of obstruction of justice through his own Twitter account, Trump took no steps to clear his name, clarify the sequence of events or explain how his attorney could have confused such a simple and potentially damaging point of law.

As Jonathan Turley, a law professor at George Washington University, wrote in *USA Today*: "Trump personal lawyer John Dowd is facing the worst possible fate of a Beltway barrister. He is about to become a noun, verb and adjective. A 'Dowd' may soon be the operative term for a legal action that is so self-destructive and stupid as to compromise not only a client but yourself. More specifically, it could be simply the shorthand for 'death by tweet.' The three words 'and the FBI' could constitute an admission against interest for the president in the investigation of possible obstruction of justice."

To be intentionally blunt and redundant: in the waning days of Trump's first year it was his tweet about his fired national security advisor that raised the freshest questions about what Trump knew when, what he did about it and whether those actions could constitute obstruction of justice. Sessions did not do that. Comey did not do that. Mueller did not do that. Trump did.

It is possible all of this is benign. It is possible Trump did not know when he fired Flynn that Flynn had lied to the FBI. It's possible the FBI kept that information confidential. It's also possible, as McGahn and others contend, that then-Acting Attorney General Sally Yates did not make it clear that Flynn's answers to the FBI about Russian contacts were, in fact, part of a criminal investigation. It's possible Dowd blew it. But even if all of that is true, the tweet exposed Trump to legitimate, probing inquiries about obstruction of justice. None of this can be blamed on partisanship, a witch hunt, a hoax or a ruse. It can only be blamed on Trump.

And we are not even through the first half of season one of *Sessions*.

What Trump regarded as cowardice Sessions saw as honor. He blundered in his confirmation hearing. He knew that mistake, no ·matter how honest in his own mind, compromised his authority in the eyes of Justice Department ethics lawyers, the Senate and, possibly, the country. To regain that trust and give the Justice Department a chance to succeed on all other initiatives he intended to pursue, Sessions decided he had to recuse himself. He made the call without telling Trump and he never stopped suffering. Not because he did something wrong. Because he did something Trump didn't like, something that smelled "weak," something that broke the Trump code of loyalty. Critics may call it Trump's *omertà*. But until there's a charge of criminality, there is no reason to believe Sessions had something to be silent about.

It was regarded as a minor development at the time, but Trump's criticism of Sessions triggered the one and only crisis of confidence among pro-Trump conservatives. It all began in Norfolk, Virginia, on July 22, when Trump told Priebus he should obtain Sessions's resignation. They were flying to commission the USS *Gerald R. Ford* aircraft carrier—a "100,000-ton message to the world," in Trump's words. Trump told him emphatically "no slow-walking this. I want the letter." Trump knew Priebus wanted to keep Sessions and thought that delaying Trump might be the best way—it had been in the past. Trump kept on Priebus all that Saturday. Priebus said he would work on it but warned that the move would be explosive and detrimental. Trump was placated and backed off.

But on July 24 at 8:49 a.m. Trump tweeted that Sessions was "beleaguered." The full tweet read: "So why aren't the Committees and investigators, and of course, our beleaguered A.G., looking into Crooked Hillarys crimes & Russia relations." Sessions was beleaguered because Trump wanted to fire him, had twice had his resignation and was trying to redirect his Justice Department's actions dealing with Clinton. It is amazing and appalling. And pitifully true. By this time, Senate Republicans had picked up from various West Wing sources that Sessions was hanging by a thread. They came out in his defense. More importantly, so did conservative organizations.

Trump was playing with fire he did not understand. Pro-Trump conservatives were pro-Sessions conservatives first. They were with Sessions before Trump had a reality TV show. Sessions had been with them on immigration, abortion, gay rights, civil rights, budget and taxes. Sessions was often a lonely voice on such issues, garnering few votes for amendments of impeccable ideological purity. Pro-Sessions conservatives admired his determination and willingness to lose on behalf of their ideas.

When Trump attacked Sessions, he was attacking this history and their cause. Within days, conservatives, egged on behind the scenes by Sessions advisors, pulled together and authored a scathing letter warning Trump not to fire Sessions. It also demanded Trump stop belittling him. In not so many words, Trump was given a choice—carry on his self-destructive alpha male flailing or keep Sessions and keep quiet.

On July 28, more than 100 conservative activists penned a letter to Trump under the heading "We Support Jeff Sessions." It read in part: "Jeff Sessions has been a loyal, highly visible and early supporter of President Trump and his policy agenda. To lose his leadership would be disastrous for the president's policy agenda. Though the president's displeasure with the investigation may be understandable, a move to replace Jeff Sessions as attorney general would not be. No one in the Trump administration has shown more commitment to the president's principles than Sessions—he continues to be a loyal ally of the president and of the people who elected him." Trump backed down, sending word through back channels he wouldn't fire Sessions.

"It was not a mistake to make him attorney general," Bossie told me. "His mistake is he was weak when it came to recusing himself for attorney general over something he should not have recused himself for. He should have taken the heat. He should have said this does not rise to the level and this thing doesn't get out of control. That was his mistake. That diminished him to the president, it weakened him to the president. When you don't have the confidence of the president you should know you should take a hike, and he didn't. He wasn't willing to do that."

Lewandowski considers Trump's treatment of Sessions a case study in loyalty—Trumpian loyalty.

> Part of the problem is the president is exceptionally loyal. Jeff was the first and only U.S. senator to endorse him. Not kind of. The first and only U.S. senator to endorse him. Chose candidate Trump over his Senate colleague, Ted Cruz, who wanted that endorsement more than anything. Jeff was there

when we made the offer to Mike Pence. He was in the car
when the offer was made to Mike Pence to be Vice President
of the United States! What the president looked at—who has
been loyal to me? Who can get through Senate confirmation? I think what the president is most disappointed with
in Senator Sessions is if Jeff would have said if you nominate
me I am going to have to recuse myself if there is an investigation, I think the president would have gone a different
path and rightfully so. What Trump wanted in an attorney
general is what Barack Obama had in both of his attorneys
general. Eric Holder was held in contempt of Congress multiple times. Guess what he said? "Go fuck yourself. I'm not
going to prosecute myself." In his entire business career, the
president has surrounded himself with tough, attorney killers. He hires killers.

Trump expected Sessions to be a killer. Trump abused Sessions
because he thought his character was defective; he had it exactly
backwards.

Speaking of exactly backwards, let's consider the dominoes that fell
after Trump appointed Sessions attorney general. Incoming presidents
frequently appoint members of Congress to cabinet positions. That creates a vacancy filled by a special election. It is exceedingly rare for a
new president to lose a seat in the House or Senate in special elections
created by one of his cabinet picks. When it does happen, it reflects
animosity toward the sitting president and a voter urge to swiftly push
back against the new agenda.

Alabama should have been the easiest situation imaginable. Trump
carried the state by just under 28 points. Sessions was wildly popular,
having won reelection unopposed in 2014. Simple playbook: the governor would appoint a new Republican senator, that senator would stand
for a GOP primary (if necessary) and then breeze to a general election
victory. How could Alabama, home to Trump's first stadium rally, be
any trouble?

But unexpected forces conspired against this neat little plan. Some
of them were out of Trump's control. Some were set in motion by
Trump's near-catastrophic brush with allegations of sexual misconduct

and abuse during the campaign. Others were triggered by Trump's own cult of outsiderdom.

So much mythology has grown up around the Alabama race. Let's stick to the basic facts.

Alabama's Republican Gov. Robert Bentley was drowning in a sex scandal and deeply tainted when on February 9, the day after Sessions was confirmed, he appointed his replacement, Alabama Attorney General Luther Strange. By the time of this appointment, Strange was already an announced candidate for Sessions's seat in the next election. Bentley interviewed 20 Alabamians to replace Sessions and Strange was one of them; so was former Alabama State Supreme Court Justice Roy Moore. Strange made the list of six finalists; Moore did not. Strange's appointment carried the whiff of Bentley's sex scandal and raised an uncomfortable question: did Strange's request, made shortly before Election Day, to delay ongoing State House impeachment hearings against Bentley factor into his winning the Senate sweepstakes? Strange denied any linkage. Importantly for Strange, he won the immediate praise of Karl Rove and the National Rifle Association as a worthy successor to Sessions.

Nevertheless, Moore was a cult figure among hard-core Alabama conservatives. He was a political figure that, like Trump, defied convention and thumbed his nose at anyone who disagreed with him—even and especially in the Republican Party. As conservative as Strange was, Moore was more fanatical on issues of immigration, abortion, gay rights, civil rights and the centrality of God in the American experience. Moore was by any definition an authoritarian Christian; he was thrown off the bench for ignoring a judicial order to remove a statue of the Ten Commandments. Moore demonstrated no interest in American pluralism, even the more constrained interpretations embraced by Alabama conservatives. Moore wanted to evict Muslims from Congress, criminalize homosexuality and Christianize federal law. And he ran against Strange and beat him twice, making him the GOP nominee and the future horror show for Trump, Republicans and Christianity.

Moore was hit by numerous credible allegations of sexual misconduct that he frequently denied by hiding behind his wife, lawyers or other campaign operatives. Senate Republicans refused to support Moore but the Republican National Committee, at Trump's prodding, reversed course and sent money and staff to help Moore defeat Democratic challenger Doug Jones. National Democrats steered clear of the race, but grassroots activists mobilized African Americans, suburban women and young voters to propel Jones to the kind of Clinton-coalition victory Hillary was betting on in Michigan, Wisconsin, Pennsylvania, Florida and North Carolina. That it didn't materialize for her but did for Jones made him the unlikeliest Democratic bounce-back story of 2017.

The crazy coda to season one of *Sessions* is he's still attorney general, Mueller is still prosecuting but Alabama does not have two Republicans in the U.S. Senate for the first time since 1994.

SEVEN

10 Days in May

It began as a distant, late-night rumble on the web, a single story about possible inaccuracies in a once-lionized FBI director's congressional testimony. Hours later came an unexpectedly noncommittal White House comment on said director. Then the earth seemed to shake and the foundations beneath the White House groaned.

I will never forget sitting in the CBS White House booth in the press room and hearing, through the closed glass door of my telephone booth–sized office, Reuters White House Correspondent Steve Holland, a friend and superb journalist, bark in the hallway to no one in particular: "Something's *happening*!" I got up as other correspondents burst out of their offices and into the tiny hallway that leads to the James S. Brady Briefing Room. I had only taken a step when I heard and saw on my BlackBerry (yes, I still had one) that Trump had fired FBI Director James Comey. What?!?!?! I hustled to our live-shot position on the North Lawn. There would be a Special Report on CBS News. In New York, Scott Pelley, then the anchor of the *Evening News*, moved to the studio.

At 5:47 p.m. Eastern, we went on the air as Pelley announced the startling news:

"This is a CBS News Special Report. President Trump has just fired the director of the FBI, James Comey. It is an unusual move. It hasn't happened since the administration of Bill Clinton. Comey, of course, has been leading the investigation of whether Russia was involved in the U.S. election in terms of influencing the election and also whether any associates of Donald Trump were colluding with the Russians to influence the election. Comey was appointed to a 10-year term by President Obama. About three years of that term have gone by. So he would have had another seven years to go. Major Garrett is at the White House for us this afternoon. Major, what can you tell us?"

I stood on the North Lawn knowing only that Comey had been fired. The backstory, or what amounted to the first White House attempt to explain the historic firing, would come in time. In that moment, I had to communicate to the nation the signals apparent only hours earlier that this breaking news event might be coming. I confess it was clear only in retrospect.

"Well, Scott, Sean Spicer, the White House press secretary, has confirmed to me the president did take this action, firing the FBI director. And the first inkling, Scott, that we got that James Comey's tenure as FBI director was in some degree of jeopardy came at today's White House briefing when Sean Spicer was asked if the president still had full confidence in the FBI director. Sean Spicer deferred on that question. He was reminded he had said, emphatically, many weeks before, that Comey had the president's confidence. Spicer specifically did not use those words in relation to Comey's stature at the FBI as of today. It is also worth pointing out that it is the FBI that has been conducting a counterintelligence investigation relating to questions raised about the possible activity of Russians and the Trump campaign and it is that investigation that has yet to reach any conclusions about whether that collusion did or did not exist even though this White House has asserted many times there's no evidence of that. That investigation is ongoing and continues to be somewhat of an irritant to this White House, which wants to shut down any more inquiries along that line. But the FBI has been sturdily keeping that investigation open and therefore that question unresolved."

Moments later, my producer, Jackie Alemany, sprinted to my position on the North Lawn with Trump's statement and a memorandum from Attorney General Sessions and Deputy Attorney General Rod Rosenstein outlining the reasons for Comey's ouster. I had less than three minutes to read the statement and the memorandum before Pelley, as our special coverage continued, came back to me for a live update.

"We also have Major Garrett back on the White House lawn and he has the official statement from the White House. Major, what are they saying?"

"Two statements," I began. "One from the press secretary Sean Spicer. One from the president himself to the now-former FBI Director James Comey. The statement from Sean Spicer said the president accepted the recommendation of Deputy Attorney General Rod Rosenstein and Attorney General Jeff Sessions to terminate James Comey, in a letter the White House [at this point I hoist the pages in my hand to show the live TV audience, the top page clearly showing Trump's signature] just released from the president to James Comey, dated today. In it the president says, 'While I greatly appreciate you informing me,' this is to James Comey, 'on three separate occasions that I am not under investigation, I nevertheless concur with the judgment of the Department of Justice that you are not able to effectively lead the Bureau. It is essential,' President Trump writes in this letter, 'that we find new leadership for the FBI that restores public trust and confidence in its vital law enforcement mission.' The letter says Comey has been terminated effective immediately. Scott.'"

Pelley seized on the newsiest part of the statement I had just read.

"Major, would you, for clarification, read that first line again?"

I knew Pelley wanted me to make sure the audience understood the gravity of Trump's declaration and how it was being communicated through his letter to Comey.

"Yes. This is from the president of the United States to the FBI director," I said as I held the statement in my hand, reading carefully and adding emphasis. " 'While I greatly appreciate you informing me,' Comey informing the president, 'on three separate occasions,' I am quoting directly, the president says, 'that I am not under investigation,' I, meaning President Trump, this letter says, 'I nevertheless concur with the judgment of the Department of Justice that you,' Comey, 'are not able to effectively lead the Bureau.'"

Pelley then gave the audience the best road map to follow the hurtling events, an imperative in live breaking news.

"And what the president would have been referring to, Major, in terms of him being under investigation would have been something to do with the FBI's investigation of whether Russia had interfered with the U.S. election that made him president?"

I picked up on Pelley's question.

"And if there was any activity that could be construed or legally prosecuted as amounting to collusion. Now, when the president says he is not under investigation that is one aspect, but that doesn't suggest nor does it assert that no one around him or associated with his campaign isn't."

"Major Garrett, thanks very much."

Pelley wrapped up my end of the live coverage. I dashed back inside the White House and prepared my report for the *CBS Evening News* in less than 30 minutes.

So began 10 days that convulsed the nation and the world as no other 10 had in the tumultuous first year of the Trump presidency. The firing of Comey was just the beginning of the mind-bending bizarreness of it all. First came conflicting White House explanations for Comey's ouster. Then came Trump telling the world he did it in part because of the Russia investigation. On top of that was an Oval Office meeting with top Russian officials manipulated in real time by state-owned Russian media while Trump smiled amid the high-stakes diplomatic punking. Then came talk that Trump demanded Comey's loyalty. And Trump said something about secret tapes. Another story about Trump telling the Russians Comey was a "nut job" and spilling sensitive information from a U.S. ally. North Korea tested a ballistic missile. Amid this came a massive global hack and data breach, possibly carried out by North Korea. The White House interviewed new FBI directors. One of the interviewees turned out to be the former FBI director who would become the special counsel to take over the Russia investigation Comey had been supervising. Near the end of all this, Trump began to privately lash out at senior staff and a siege mentality gripped the West Wing.

Throughout 2017 Trump believed the Russia investigation was not about crimes but about his victory. He saw it as revenge for winning: a collaborative effort of Obama-era loyalists in the intelligence community, Justice Department and (during the transition) White House who colluded—yes, that's the only time Trump would use that word—to create the appearance of cooperation between Trump and Russians. Whatever contacts occurred, Trump believed they were innocuous or Democratic traps to lure Trump officials into potentially compromising situations for later use. Trump believed the investigation was a Democratic tool wielded against him. If there was cause against him, Trump, in those 10 days in May, aided it considerably. He looked and sounded evasive and answers that did not stand up to later revelations or Trump's subsequent revisions compromised his credibility. Trump was his own worst enemy.

After 16 months covering the Trump campaign and 18 months of covering his presidency, I still don't know the bottom line of the Russia story. I know Washington has been knotted up over the story and I have chased many a false rumor about a pending indictment that never came. Trump's anger about the Russia probe was and remains genuine. Former White House lawyer Ty Cobb and others on the legal team spent hours each week pleading calm—with limited success. This is the context for Trump's outbursts. I use the word "context" because, as even Trump's loyalists admit privately, precedentially or presidentially there really was no excuse for much of what transpired in those days in May . . . or for some of the things that would follow. Trump continued to criticize Comey and bash top FBI officials throughout 2017, a pattern that first emerged during those 10 days.

In June of 2018 he was in some measure vindicated by a Justice Department Inspector General investigation that faulted Comey for "extraordinary and insubordinate" behavior that "violated long-standing Department practice and protocol" in publicly announcing no charges against Hillary Clinton in the FBI email-server investigation but nevertheless describing her actions as "extremely careless." The IG report, authored by Michael Horowitz, also found Obama-era Attorney General Loretta Lynch exercised "an error in judgment" by failing to cut short her extended meeting with former President Bill Clinton aboard Lynch's plane on June 27, 2016, in Phoenix. Horowitz also drew attention to text messages exchanged between FBI Deputy Assistant

Director Peter Strzok and Lisa Page, special counsel to the deputy FBI director. "These messages reflected political opinions in support of former Secretary Clinton and against her then political opponent, Donald Trump," the report said. "Some of these text messages and instant messages mixed political commentary with discussions about the [Clinton] investigation, and raised concerns that political bias may have impacted investigative decisions."

Taken together, these revelations did not undercut the legal basis for the Russia investigation, as Trump asserted, but did suggest he was, as his supporters believed throughout, onto something when it came to the conduct of Comey, Lynch and other FBI higher-ups. In classic Trump fashion, the president fired the FBI director, mounted an aggressive, convoluted and at times contradictory defense of that firing and heaped sensational charge atop sensational charge, creating a firestorm of innuendo. The Horowitz report gave those charges and noise a patina of "I told you so" legitimacy. To Trump's supporters in Congress it cast doubt on the origins of the Mueller investigation itself—an assessment not widely shared outside the most ardent ranks of Trump enthusiasts.

Before we jump into the 10 days in May narrative, an important point must be made. In those fraught and frantic 10 days, much was said by Trump and his advisors about those touched by or involved in Comey's firing—Deputy Attorney General Rod Rosenstein and Comey's deputy, Andrew McCabe. To reread those utterances is to see the White House portray Rosenstein and McCabe far more favorably than it would in 2018. So much happened in those dizzying 10 days that I have, for posterity and as a minor public service, re-created them through a time line that reflects my work and that of dozens of CBS News colleagues and other investigative reporters in Washington. It is a ticktock of a time when the clock seemed to simultaneously speed up and stand still. It was a time that left many of us, myself included, physically exhausted and mentally traumatized. The phrase "Is this happening?" was never far away. Neither was the chilling, inescapable answer. "Yes. Yes. It is."

MAY 8—DISTANT WARNING

At 10:38 p.m. ProPublica published an article headlined: "James Comey's Testimony on Huma Abedin Forwarding Emails Was Inaccurate." The story, written by Peter Elkind, noted that FBI Director James Comey testified the week before about his "incredibly painful" decision to publicly divulge some Hillary Clinton emails that were found on Anthony Weiner's laptop. The article mentioned Comey's description in that testimony that Huma Abedin, Weiner's wife and top Clinton advisor, had what he called a "regular practice" of forwarding "hundreds of thousands" of Clinton messages to Weiner. Elkind noted Comey had testified that "some" of those emails "contain classified information."

The key sentence of Elkind's piece, the one that was the first inkling the public had that Comey had testified incorrectly, came next: "The problem: Much of what Comey said about this was inaccurate. Now the FBI is trying to figure out what to do about it."

In the grand scheme of things, Comey's errors did not suggest a bombshell was coming. I filed it away as something to keep track of and see if lawmakers were so irked they would request formal revisions or recall Comey to clarify his garbled testimony. These were my mental notes. I had no inkling what would come next.

MAY 9—FIRING DAY

That morning, my CBS colleagues Andy Triay and Pat Milton confirmed what the FBI was willing to admit Comey got wrong, specifically that the number of emails Abedin forwarded to Weiner was smaller than Comey testified and that none was marked "classified." These inaccuracies, Triay and Milton reported, were known to the FBI days earlier but no effort had been made to publicly acknowledge them. Again, this seemed to me noteworthy but not earth-shattering.

That began to change at the daily White House briefing. Press Secretary Sean Spicer was asked if Trump still had confidence in Comey. This question arises whenever a top official has fallen out of favor and is the threshold question about their future. If the answer is yes, all is good. Anything short of yes and reporters know blood is in the water. Spicer spilled some blood. "I have no reason to believe—I haven't asked him [Trump]. So I don't—I have not asked the president since the last time we spoke about this."

At 5:42 p.m. the White House announced Trump "has accepted the recommendation of the Attorney General and the Deputy Attorney General regarding the dismissal of the director of the Federal Bureau of Investigation." Six minutes later the White House released a statement that read in part: "Today, President Donald J. Trump informed FBI Director James Comey that he has been terminated and removed from office. The FBI is one of our Nation's most cherished and respected institutions and today will mark a new beginning for our crown jewel of law enforcement." One minute later came the Sessions and Rosenstein memo.

Just before 8 p.m., Sessions emailed Justice Department staff, and fully backed a move that had set Washington on edge: "The President of the United States has exercised his lawful authority to remove James B. Comey as the Director of the Federal Bureau of Investigation. By operation of law and effective immediately, Deputy Director Andrew McCabe assumed the position of Acting Director of the FBI."

Within an hour Comey, who learned of his firing by seeing it on TV while touring an FBI field office in Los Angeles, had canceled a planned speech and headed for Los Angeles International Airport, his motorcade movement given mini-aerial-O.J.-in-the-Ford-Bronco treatment.

The day was manic and I had left the White House shortly before 9 p.m. Several reporters remained on the grounds, wondering if there would be more comment. About 10:30 p.m., reporters intercepted Spicer as he made his way back to the West Wing from a cable TV interview. Spicer came to a stop near the spot where the White House driveway intersects with a flagstone pathway that leads to TV interview positions. That walkway sits between large bushes on both sides. Spicer stood on the flagstones between the bushes and took questions. He was evasive and flustered. But he answered what he could, which wasn't much. Spicer told reporters: "The president made the decision today, and the letter was presented to the president today . . . my understanding was that he was made aware today." Spicer also confirmed Trump met with McCabe hours after deciding to fire Comey. It was later reported that Spicer at this time was "hiding" in the bushes. That became a parody and internet meme. The characterization was flat wrong and deeply unfair. Spicer did the opposite of hiding. He took questions and answered on behalf of the White House. Spicer said several questionable things as press secretary. He has had to live those statements down. But this episode should never be included in anything Spicer has to account for while press secretary. He did his job. Journalists who reported that he had been "hiding" did not.

MAY 10—THE CONFIDENCE GAME

The day broke with a *New York Times* story that drew parallels between Trump and Nixon: "Even a longstanding ally of Mr. Trump's, Roger J. Stone Jr., drew a connection as he defended the president. 'Somewhere Dick Nixon is smiling,' Mr. Stone, who worked for Nixon and is among the Trump associates facing FBI scrutiny, said in an interview.

On MSNBC's *Morning Joe,* Deputy Press Secretary Sarah Sanders was asked if the Comey firing had anything to do with the Russia investigation. Her answer: "Absolutely not." This was the first assertion of that kind from a White House official.

Shortly after 7 a.m. the world heard for the first time from Trump about the firing, on Twitter of course. "The Democrats have said some of the worst things about James Comey, including the fact that he should be fired, but now they play so sad!" said a 7:12 a.m. tweet. It was followed 16 minutes later by this: "Comey lost the confidence of almost everyone in Washington, Republican and Democrat alike. When things calm down, they will be thanking me!" Both tweets were treated like breaking news, part of a nonstop surge of breaking news in the coming days.

Just after 10 a.m., Russian Foreign Minister Sergey Lavrov arrived for his first visit to the White House of the Trump presidency. Russian Ambassador Sergey Kislyak also visited. Less than an hour later, the Russian Foreign Ministry released a photo of Trump and Lavrov in the Oval Office.

A short time later, Pence was on Capitol Hill and took a couple of questions from reporters. With words that should be remembered in the context of later Trump assaults on Rosenstein's character, Pence described Rosenstein as a man of "extraordinary independence and integrity" who has "a reputation in both political parties of great character."

At about 11:28 a.m., reporters were ushered into the Oval Office, expecting, as the schedule had indicated, to see Trump with Lavrov and Kislyak. Instead, they found Trump with Nixon-era advisor Henry Kissinger. Trump told reporters that Comey "wasn't doing a good job. Very simply. He was not doing a good job." This became another alert— Trump's first direct comment on the Comey firing. After reporters left the Oval Office, they asked White House staff why Lavrov and Kislyak were not with Trump and Kissinger was. Sheepish White House aides said they had no earthly idea.

A few moments later, the Russian propaganda agency TASS posted pictures of Trump with Lavrov in the Oval Office, the second example of Russian media stooges having been given preferential access to Trump, Lavrov and Kislyak at the expense of daily White House reporters and photographers. The White House offered no explanation.

Back on Capitol Hill, skepticism began to rise about the reasons for Comey's ouster. Sens. Mark Warner, Virginia Democrat, and Richard Burr, North Carolina Republican, invited Comey to testify before the Intelligence Committee they jointly chair. "We have heard the White House explanation of the facts, we've heard this reason that I don't believe passes the smell test," Warner told reporters.

At the White House briefing, Sanders said Comey was fired in part because of "an erosion of confidence" due to Comey's diverging from FBI protocol. "When you throw a stick of dynamite into the Department of Justice that's a big problem and not one that can be ignored. That's simply not something that's allowed in the justice system, nor should it be." Sanders also addressed mounting Democratic backlash. "It's, I think, the purest form of hypocrisy."

About 3:30 p.m. Trump tweeted his agreement with Sanders: "Dems have been complaining for months & months about Dir. Comey. Now that he has been fired they PRETEND to be aggrieved. Phony hypocrites!"

Just over three hours later, the White House, after taking repeated questions in public and private all day, distributed what it said was the time line of events leading up to Comey's firing. It read as follows: "The President, over the last several months, lost confidence in Director Comey. After watching Director Comey's testimony last Wednesday, the President was strongly inclined to remove him. On Monday, the President met with the Attorney General and the Deputy Attorney General and they discussed reasons for removing the Director. The next day, Tuesday May 9, the Deputy Attorney General sent his written recommendation to the Attorney General and the Attorney General sent his written recommendation to the President."

That version left many unanswered questions, such as the definition of "over the last several months" and if "strongly inclined to remove him" meant that was when Trump decided to fire Comey (meaning the thought process months before was largely hypothetical). It was also unclear if Trump's meeting with Sessions and Rosenstein was to discuss the possibility of firing Comey or to ask them for a reason or set of reasons to justify Comey's ouster. The days ahead would provide very little clarity. They would also provide some stark reversals.

Later that night, Comey emailed FBI employees: "I have long believed that a President can fire an FBI Director for any reason, or for no reason at all. I'm not going to spend time on the decision or the way it was executed. I hope you won't either. It is done, and I will be fine, although I will miss you and the mission deeply."

Just before midnight, *The Washington Post* published an article saying Rosenstein threatened to quit after being cast by the White House as the impetus for Comey's firing. Another news alert.

MAY 11—THIS RUSSIA THING

On *CBS This Morning*, Sanders for the first time said Trump had been considering firing Comey since he was elected. "He had a conversation on Monday with the attorney general and deputy attorney general and asked them for their thoughts, their feedback. They laid out a lot of the reasons you see reflected in that memo, but this was certainly something the president had been, again, considering since he had been elected back in November; there was a consistent erosion of confidence by the president in Director Comey's ability to do his job." Another news alert.

Shortly after 10 a.m., McCabe, the new interim FBI director, testified before the Senate Intelligence Committee. Burr thanked McCabe for "filling in on such short notice," as Comey was slated to appear. Burr then asked if McCabe was ever informed Comey told Trump he was not the target of an FBI investigation. McCabe said he could not comment. Later, Sen. Martin Heinrich, New Mexico Democrat, asked McCabe if it was true, as the White House had said, that Comey lost the confidence of rank-and-file FBI agents. "No. That is not accurate," McCabe said. "Comey enjoyed broad support within the FBI and still does to this day." Sen. Angus King, Maine Independent, then asked if the Russia investigation was, as the White House had said, one of the smallest things on the FBI's plate. "Sir, we consider it to be a highly significant investigation," McCabe said. Heinrich also asked McCabe about Trump's assertion that Comey told him three times he was not under investigation. Heinrich: "Is it your experience that people who are innocent of wrongdoing need to be reassured that they are NOT the target of an investigation?" McCabe answered: "No, sir."

At 11:30 a.m. NBC anchor Lester Holt began taping his interview with Trump, an interview that would add several more news alerts to the story. Just before 1 p.m., NBC aired the first excerpts of that interview.

> Holt: Monday you met with the deputy attorney general, Rod Rosenstein.
>
> Trump: Right.
>
> Holt: Did you ask for a recommendation?
>
> Trump: What I did is, I was going to fire Comey—my decision, it was not—
>
> Holt: You had made the decision before they came in the room?
>
> Trump: I was going to fire Comey. I—there's no good time to do it, by the way—
>
> Holt: Because in your letter you said "I accepted their recommendation," so you had already made the decision?
>
> Trump: Oh, I was gonna fire regardless of the recommendation.
>
> Holt: So there was—
>
> Trump: He [Rosenstein] made a recommendation. He's highly respected, very good guy, very smart guy. The Democrats like him, the Republicans like him. He made a recommendation but regardless of recommendation I was going to fire Comey.

Then Trump admitted Russia was at the heart of his decision on Comey.

> Trump: In fact, when I decided to just do it, I said to myself, you know, this Russia thing with Trump and Russia is a made-up story. It's an excuse by the Democrats for having lost an election that they should have won. . . . As far as I am concerned I want that thing to be absolutely done properly. . . . It should be over with. In my opinion, it should have been over a long time ago.

Trump then was asked about his assertion, in the letter announcing Comey's firing, that he was not under investigation.

> Holt: He [Comey] has given sworn testimony that there is an ongoing investigation into the Trump campaign and possible collusion with the Russian government. You were the centerpiece of the Trump campaign. So was he being truthful?
>
> Trump: I know that I am not under investigation. Me. Personally. I am not talking about campaigns. I'm not talking about anything else. I'm not under investigation.

For this narrative, I think it wise to pause and reach back to what Trump said about Comey right after his election in an interview with Leslie Stahl of *60 Minutes*. Stahl asked about Comey. "I respect him a lot," Trump said. "I respect the FBI a lot." In that same interview Stahl raised the issue of Comey's future.

"Are you going to ask for his resignation?"

Trump paused and drew a long breath.

"I think that I would rather not comment on that yet. I haven't made up my mind. There's been a lot of leaking, there's not a question about that, but I certainly would like to talk to him and see him. It's a tough time for him and I would like to talk to him before I answer a question like that."

"Sounds like you're not sure," Stahl said.

"Oh sure, I'm not sure. I want to see. He may have had very good reasons for doing what he did."

In the heat of the election and in endless written and spoken dissections since, Clinton has blamed Comey for her loss to Trump. As the election wound down, the Clinton email investigation did look like a net plus for Trump and Comey looked like an unwitting ally. At the same time, another Trump surrogate, former New York Mayor Rudy Giuliani, appeared to be doing all he could to enable, feed and stroke the FBI and, by all outward appearances, pressure Comey to act as he eventually did.

Back to our 10 days narrative. The day before, May 10, in an Oval Office meeting, Trump told Russian Foreign Minister Sergey Lavrov and Kislyak that Comey "was crazy, a real nut job. I faced great pressure because of Russia. That's taken off. I'm not under investigation."

At the daily briefing, Sanders denied explanations for the Comey firing had evolved. This denial came in the immediate aftermath of Trump having told NBC that the Comey firing was due, at least in part, to the Russia investigation. "Our story is consistent, the president is the only person that can fire the director of the FBI, he serves at the pleasure of the president, the president made the decision, it was the right decision. The people that are in the dark today are the Democrats." Sanders couldn't say on what dates Comey told Trump he wasn't under investigation. Sanders then admitted she was not fully informed the day before when she told reporters Trump had not already decided to fire Comey when he met with Sessions and Rosenstein. "I hadn't had a chance to have the conversation directly with the president to say— I'd had several conversations with him but I didn't ask that question directly—'Had you made that decision?' I went off of the information that I had when I answered your question." This would become a pattern for Sanders—saying she gave the information she had at a given time—for 2017 and into 2018, when she was forced to acknowledge giving inaccurate or incomplete information from the podium.

Since McCabe had just testified that Comey had not lost the confidence of rank-and-file FBI agents, I asked Sanders how she knew that. "I can speak to my own personal experience, I've heard from countless members of the FBI that are grateful and thankful for the president's decision." I asked her how many FBI agents she had spoken with. "Look, we're not going to get into a numbers game, I have heard from a large number of individuals that work at the FBI that said they were very happy with the president's decision."

About 4:30 p.m., seeing the sensation his NBC interview had become, Trump volleyed back on Twitter. "Russia must be laughing up their sleeves watching as the U.S. tears itself apart over a Democrat EXCUSE for losing the election."

Just before 9 p.m., another news alert came in the form of a *New York Times* story with the eye-grabbing headline: "In Private Dinner, Trump Demanded Loyalty. Comey Demurred." A short time later, Pat Milton, one of CBS's senior investigative producers, confirmed, via several FBI sources, that Comey recalled that Trump asked Comey if he would pledge his loyalty. Comey said he declined but instead told Trump he would always be honest. Later at the dinner, according to Milton's sources, Trump again told Comey he needed his loyalty. Again, Comey said he would be honest. Trump pressed him on whether it would be "honest loyalty." Comey said he responded by saying "Yes, you will have that." The dispute over what Trump said, what he meant and how Comey took its meaning would animate the debate over Trump's and Comey's credibility for months to come.

Comey provided his notes and testified about them under oath before Congress. Trump has denied Comey's recollections, but as of mid-July 2018, had not done so under oath. There are no known notes of Trump's recollections to verify his version of events (or tapes, for that matter). The dispute was part of the fog of Trump's war with the Russian investigation. What's clear is Comey came to believe Trump wanted his loyalty. What is also not in dispute is that Comey did not provide Trump the loyalty to which he thought he was entitled. Also not in dispute, Trump fired Comey on May 9.

Here's how that process went down, according to Cobb, who has re-created the memos and provided the White House witnesses to Mueller's team as part of its investigation. The key early wrinkle in the story was the White House Counsel's Office told Trump he did not have the power to fire Comey, possibly hoping that would nip the potentially reckless inclination in the bud. "There was a junior associate [in the Counsel's Office] who was looking at a variety of positions and what the conditions were for hiring and firing and on Comey it said you had to have cause," Cobb told me. "And it was wrong. And they subsequently learned differently. I don't know whether people didn't inform the president or intentionally didn't inform him but if they did intentionally misinform him, there's only one person who could make that decision—[White House Counsel Don] McGahn."

Trump learned from Miller, his top domestic policy advisor and speechwriter, that he could fire Comey without cause. In March, according to Cobb, Miller began building a case against Comey for Trump. "Stephen Miller is not a shy guy. And he's also somebody who not would ask anybody else to research something because he's the smartest guy in the room. So, he looked into it himself and concluded that you didn't need cause and he informed the president. It didn't prompt a blowup like 'My lawyers got it wrong!' Trump was like, 'Good to know. Thanks.'"

Miller joined Trump at his Bedminster, New Jersey, golf club the weekend before Comey's firing to begin work on the memo that would eventually find its way to Sessions and Rosenstein to justify Comey's firing.

"Miller comes up for that purpose," Cobb told me. "There is a lot of back and forth [in notes] between the president and Miller. They [Mueller's team] have all the handwriting. It's just Miller and the president."

Kushner supported firing Comey but Cobb insists he was not part of the Miller-Trump memo-drafting process. "He's there. For the weekend. It's raining. Jared's changing diapers. Jared is wholly uninvolved. There are no notes. There's nothing involving any evidence by Jared. Jared's not involved in this. He's told this is what they have concluded they are going to do. He's not animated or excited. He's cool with it. It's not something he opposed. He's like, 'I think that's the right move. Good luck.'" Others believe Kushner was more important to the decision, endorsing it throughout the weekend and giving Trump the feeling the politics and policy would work to his advantage. Kushner had substantial power to influence Trump during the first year—frequently with very few words. Kushner tended to hold back during large meetings and say little before or after—waiting for moments of time with Trump away from senior staff to render a verdict. It was often the final bit of reinforcement Trump sought. This may well have been his role in Comey's firing.

Gingrich, a frequent advisor and sounding board for Trump, has a saltier perspective from the outside. "I think Trump concluded Comey was a liar and totally unreliable and an ally of Hillary's. He just said, 'Fuck it. I don't need to have you around. I'm the president. You're not.' I think it's a simple as that. In the long run it may not be all that much of a negative."

MAY 12—PERFECT ACCURACY

Shortly before 8 a.m., Trump blasted Democrats and the news media. "Again, the story that there was collusion between the Russians & Trump campaign was fabricated by Dems as an excuse for losing the election." And: "The Fake Media is working overtime today!"

Noting the rising crescendo of criticism about conflicting public explanations offered by Spicer and Sanders, Trump tweeted somewhat defensively that "As a very active President with lots of things happening, it is not possible for my surrogates to stand at podium with perfect accuracy! . . ." And: "Maybe the best thing to do would be to cancel all future 'press briefings' and hand out written responses for the sake of accuracy???" Two more news alerts.

But those alerts, part of the hyperventilating nature of events, tweets and garbled explanations about Comey, would pale next to the tweet that rocked Washington as much as any event so far. At 8:27 a.m. Trump tweeted the following: "James Comey better hope that there are no 'tapes' of our conversations before he starts leaking to the press!"

About three hours later, Rep. Adam Schiff, Democrat of California and ranking Democrat on the Intelligence Committee, responded to the Comey-tape tweet. "Mr. President, if there are 'tapes' relevant to the Comey firing, it's because you made them and they should be provided to Congress." This sequence reinforced to reporters throughout Washington that Trump had truly ushered in a new form of political jousting—one that occurred strictly between key political actors, not minions, and entirely on Twitter.

A short time later, the White House Correspondents' Association, whose members cover the White House continuously, released a statement about the threat to future briefings.

> White House briefings and press conferences provide substantive and symbolic opportunities for journalists to pose questions to officials at the highest levels of the U.S. government. That exercise, conducted in full view of our republic's citizens, is clearly in line with the spirit of the First Amendment. Doing away with briefings would reduce accountability, transparency, and the opportunity for Americans to see that, in the U.S. system, no political figure is above being questioned.

About 3 p.m., Fox released its first excerpt of "Judge" Jeanine Pirro's interview with Trump. The newsiest part was a friendly exchange about what was going wrong with Trump's communications team.

> Q: Are you moving so quickly that your communications department can't keep up with you?
> Trump: Yes. That's true.

Q: So what do we do about that? [The use here of "we" betrayed the friendly, collaborative spirit of the interview.]

Trump: We don't have press conferences.

An hour later, Fox released more excerpts, this time focusing on the "loyalty" question and Trump's version of events.

Q: Did you ask that question?

Trump: No I didn't but I don't think it would be a bad question to ask. I think loyalty to the country, loyalty to the U.S. is important. You know, it depends on how you define loyalty, number one; number two, I don't know how it got out there because I didn't ask that question.

Q: What about the idea that in a tweet you said there might be tape recordings?

Trump: Well, that I can't talk about. I won't talk about that.

This raised another unusual aspect of Trump and the Russia investigation. Time and again, the explanation was incompetence or amnesia. In my experience around Trump and his team, incompetence was an acceptable explanation for absolutely nothing. Everything Trump does is great. His team is great. His people are the greatest. Achievements everywhere. And yet, numerous Russian-related revelations have been chalked up to ineptitude. The Trump world also suffered a plague of amnesia on one topic and one topic only—Russia. Trump forgot. Pence forgot. Flynn forgot. Sessions forgot. Kushner forgot. Eric Trump forgot. K. T. McFarland forgot. Hope Hicks forgot. Spicer forgot. Sanders forgot. Everybody forgot. How is it that Russia—and only Russia—infected top Trump personnel with the twin ailments of incompetence and amnesia? Legalisms aside, would you continue to employ, befriend or associate with someone or an organization chronically inept and forgetful? Probably not.

MAY 13—NORTH KOREA MISSILE

For the first time since the Comey saga began, the day passed without new developments. Trump flew to Lynchburg, Virginia, to deliver the commencement address at Liberty University, an evangelical college founded by former Moral Majority leader Jerry Falwell. On the flight down, Trump told reporters he was interviewing several candidates to replace Comey. "We can make a fast decision," Trump said.

Just before 7:30 p.m., another news alert, but this time it was not about Comey. U.S. Pacific Command said it detected and tracked a North Korean missile launch at approximately 10:30 a.m. Hawaii time. It said the missile landed in the Sea of Japan and was not consistent with the flight path of an intercontinental ballistic missile. Three hours later, the White House issued a statement that read in part: "With the missile impacting so close to Russian soil—in fact, closer to Russia than to Japan—the President cannot imagine that Russia is pleased."

MAY 14—MOTHER'S DAY

Trump spent the day at Trump National Golf Club in Sterling, Virginia. No news alerts. A brief respite.

MAY 15—CLASSIFIED INFORMATION

Just before 10:30 a.m., the White House surprised reporters by allowing them into a previously closed, meaning private, event with the president. It was the signing of an order directing the Justice Department to develop plans to reduce violence against law enforcement. Trump was surrounded by law enforcement personnel from across the country. The staging was not subtle. "Last year 118 officers died in the line of duty," Trump said. "And of those 66 were victims of malicious attacks. These attacks increased by nearly 40 percent from the year 2015. This must end. They've had it with what's going on and we're going to get it taken care of, we're going to get it taken care of quickly."

The daily briefing became a clash over Trump's "tapes" tweet. Four times Spicer refused to explain what Trump meant. "The president has no further comment on this," Spicer repeated somewhat robotically. NBC's Hallie Jackson asked about the effect the tweet might have on other White House staff.

> Q: Given that you've refused to confirm or deny any of this, how is any senior official supposed to be comfortable having a conversation privately with the president?

Spicer: As I've said, Hallie, the president's made it clear what his position is. I've answered the question over and over again the same way.

The next bombshell landed at 5:06 p.m. with a *Washington Post* news alert that Trump revealed highly classified information to Lavrov and Kislyak. Dozens of reporters scrambled to chase the story. About 90 minutes later, the White House released a statement attributed to National Security Advisor H. R. McMaster: "During President Trump's meeting with Foreign Minister Lavrov a broad range of subjects were discussed among which were common efforts and threats regarding counterterrorism. During that exchange the nature of specific threats were discussed, but they did not discuss sources, methods or military operations. The president and the foreign minister reviewed common threats from terrorist organizations to include threats to aviation."

In response, Senator Warner tweeted: "If true, this is a slap in the face to the intel community. Risking sources & methods is inexcusable, particularly with the Russians." That was swiftly followed by a release from House Speaker Paul Ryan's office: "We have no way to know what was said. But protecting our nation's secrets is paramount. The speaker hopes for a full explanation of the facts from the administration."

The sensational story positively floored the White House. The written statement had done nothing to calm the fury, and there was a sense inside the White House that anything could be leaked at any time about any subject. There was, of course, the need to clean up what Trump did in that private meeting. Trump had a tendency to talk more expansively about intelligence matters than his top advisors would have preferred. He did this in part because he was delighted and fascinated by being in on all the juicy details a president is relentlessly privy to. He liked to let people know how much he knew and had, to put it mildly, not mastered the art of suggesting without telling, of dropping hints that carried just enough signals but divulged nothing specific. If anything, Trump's entire bombastic, tabloid life had trained him to do exactly the opposite.

Top advisors did not believe Trump did anything fundamentally wrong with the Russians. They believe he just got carried away with details. What alarmed them most was not the president's conduct, but the near-instant conduit sensitive conversations, especially incautious ones, had to the news media. Alarm bells were ringing everywhere. There was a growing anxiety that intelligence operatives and Obama-era holdovers might be or were gathering damaging details and leaking them to undercut Trump. No specific charges or evidence ever surfaced to confirm this suspicion, but in those harrowing hours and days, the Trump inner circle did not know whom it could trust. That added, if it was possible, another level of anxiety.

The communications shop did not know what to say about the intelligence story because none of its members was involved in the Oval Office meeting and none had the clout to demand definitive answers. McMaster had to lay his personal credibility on the line. The sun was setting and the story was still blazing hot.

In a maneuver I had never seen at any previous White House, the national security advisor, via an announcement that came to the press room through the overhead speaker, indicated that he would address reporters outside the West Wing about 7 p.m. Like all the network correspondents, I had just finished my 6:30 p.m. evening news story and was now girding for McMaster to add a new layer to the drama, thus leading to rewrites and reworkings of the television stories for the Midwest and Pacific coast versions of the *CBS Evening News*. Print reporters scrambled from their laptops to what is known as the "stakeout" position just outside the north portico of the West Wing. There, a slightly sloping curved driveway leads to where reporters, TV videographers and still photographers stand or sit on their haunches awaiting news makers. We assembled in a tight semicircle behind a phalanx of TV cameras.

When the sun sets, the soft light on the Eisenhower Executive Office Building can be captivating. The blue sky above the gray edifice and the way shadows wrap around its many granite columns and balustrades had, in times past, been a source of calm for me after a long and tiring day. I remember waiting for McMaster and seeking some measure of peace amid the jostling reporters and mounting deadline pressure.

At 7:08 p.m. McMaster, grim and resolute, walked to the microphones. He glared into the cameras as he looked up from a prepared statement in his hands. "The story that came out tonight as reported is false. The president and the foreign minister reviewed a range of common threats to our two countries, including threats to civil aviation. At no time were intelligence sources or methods discussed. The president did not disclose any military operations that were not already publicly known. Two other senior officials who were present, including the secretary of state, remember the meeting the same way and have said so. And their on-the-record accounts should outweigh those of anonymous sources. I was in the room. It didn't happen." McMaster practically spat the last two lines. He took no questions, and turned away sharply, befitting the military bearing of an active-duty Army lieutenant general, which McMaster was while serving as national security advisor.

Moments later, Triay, my CBS colleague and producer who covers intelligence and federal law enforcement, reported that sources told him that Trump had said "something inappropriate" with Russian officials and that the intelligence was related to the fight against ISIS. Moreover, it had come from a country that would not want its intelligence discussed with the Russians. The sources said: "Details were discussed that should not have been discussed."

After McMaster returned to the White House, reporters descended on Spicer's and Sanders's offices, trying to extract more information. They found Spicer, Sanders and the entire communications team across the hall in the Roosevelt Room, which is located on the other side of the press staff offices and adjacent to the West Wing lobby. The hallway just outside the Roosevelt Room is an area where reporters are not allowed to congregate, in part because senior White House staff are sometimes required to leave their smartphones outside for high-level briefings. Reporters lurked in a tiny nook just outside the main press office, peering through an open door into that no-access hallway. They could see the door to the Roosevelt Room was ajar. Inside, loud voices could be heard. It sounded contentious and charged. Someone on the inside closed the door and it sounded as if the TV inside the Roosevelt Room had been turned to a high volume. Sanders emerged minutes later: "We do not have anything else to add. We put out multiple statements from Tillerson, [Deputy National Security Advisor Dina] Powell and McMaster. Tonight we're not answering any additional questions."

MAY 16—SOURCES AND METHODS

Before dawn the Russian Foreign Ministry in Moscow denied Trump gave up secret information. One of the lead reporters on the *Washington*

Post story told MSNBC that Trump did not reveal sources and methods, but exposed intelligence obtained through those sources and those methods. At 7:03 a.m. Trump tweeted this: "As President I wanted to share with Russia (at an openly scheduled W.H. meeting) which I have the absolute right to do, facts pertaining . . . to terrorism and airline flight safety. Humanitarian reasons, plus I want Russia to greatly step up their fight against ISIS & terrorism." On *CBS This Morning* shortly after 8 a.m., Greg Miller, the *Washington Post* reporter who broke the story, said the Trump tweet was "essentially confirming what we reported yesterday." Moments later, Trump turned his Twitter ire toward leaks. "I have been asking Director Comey & others, from the beginning of my administration, to find the LEAKERS in the intelligence community. . . ."

During a late-morning briefing on Trump's upcoming trip to Saudi Arabia, McMaster said this on the subject: "I think it's incumbent on all of us to bring in people with the right authority and the right mandate to take a look at how this leak occurred and how other breaches occurred as well."

Shortly after 1 p.m., Trump invited reporters into the Oval Office for a photo opportunity with Turkish President Recep Erdogan. During his opening remarks, Trump mispronounced Erdogan's last name. Later, Trump was asked what he "spoke to the Russians about." Trump: "Well, we had a very, very successful meeting with the foreign minister of Russia. Our fight is against ISIS. As General McMaster said. I thought he said and I know he feels that we had actually a great meeting with the foreign minister so we're going to have a lot of great success over the next coming years." Moments later, *The New York Times* published a story that Israel was the source of the intelligence Trump shared with Kislyak and Lavrov, a revelation Spicer refused to confirm or deny at the daily briefing, but that CBS later confirmed. Spicer used the briefing to rip White House leaks, calling them "dangerous."

As the events of the day piled up and strands of the story begin to come together, another news alert toppled the day with the publication, at 5:26 p.m., of a *New York Times* story that carried the headline: "Comey Memo Says Trump Asked Him to End Flynn Investigation." We did not realize at the time, but the future of the Trump-Comey story was going to turn on Comey's memos. CBS soon confirmed their existence. What Trump denied about those memos and the motives, alleged or construed, and the manner in which Comey took and distributed them, would become topics of parlor rooms and congressional debate for months. Within 10 minutes the White House issued a flat denial of the *Times* story. It read: "While the President has repeatedly expressed his view that General Flynn is a decent man who served and protected our country, the President has never asked Mr. Comey or anyone else to end any investigation, including any investigation involving General Flynn. This is not a truthful or accurate portrayal of the conversation between the President and Mr. Comey. The White House notes McCabe the week prior told Congress the White House had not interfered with any investigation." It is notable, considering all the subsequent criticism that came from the White House about Rosenstein and McCabe, that, in the heat of these battles during the 10 days in May, the White House singled out both for praise in terms of their professionalism, credibility and reputation.

Within minutes, the Senate Democratic leader, Charles Schumer, was on the Senate floor. "In a week full of revelation after revelation, on a day when we thought things could not get any worse they have. I was shaken by the report in *The New York Times* that alleged the president tried to shut down an active FBI investigation into a close political associate. And we are only one day removed from stunning allegations that the president may have divulged classified information to a known adversary. Concerns about our national security, the rule of law, the independence of our nation's highest law enforcement agencies are mounting. The country is being tested in unprecedented ways. I say to all of my colleagues in the Senate, history is watching."

There was another side to this stomach-churning week on Trump's Wild Ride. While many fretted about leaks, there was also deep soul-searching about Trump and his erratic tendencies. Even staunch Trump defenders, inside and out of the White House, had a hard time putting a positive spin on his reported conversations with Comey. One Trump loyalist admitted to me that no reasonable person would expect a president to talk that way to an FBI director. That loyalist said the most charitable interpretation was Trump had been clumsy but not criminal. Others were angry that no one appeared in charge of the White House message or decision-making. "How hard is it to have a message and fix a problem?" one source very close to the White House bellowed to me over the phone. "There is no chief of staff. There are four or five fiefdoms and no one is in charge of decisions or how to bring decisions to the president. He [Trump] knows it's a crisis and he's looking for answers." As was true in his campaign and now as president, the central issue in almost all of these dramatic stories was Trump's unpredictable and unschooled behavior—and how difficult it was to clean up.

"I think it's reaching the point where it's of Watergate size and scale, and a couple of other scandals we've seen," Sen. John McCain, Arizona Republican, told my CBS colleague Bob Schieffer, offering a coda to another crazy day in May.

MAY 17—MUELLER. FIGHT. FIGHT. FIGHT.

The morning began with considerable churning over what the Russians said they had and were prepared to share about the Lavrov and Kislyak encounter with Trump. About 7:30 a.m., the Associated Press tweeted that Putin was willing to give Congress records of Trump's conversation with Lavrov. In Moscow, our CBS Moscow producer, Sveta Berdnikova, reported that Putin made a joke about recordings but was serious about offering a transcript.

Shortly after noon, Trump, while delivering remarks at the commencement ceremony at the U.S. Coast Guard Academy, gave cadets some advice: "Over the course of your life, you will find that things are not always fair. You will find that things happen to you that you do not deserve and that are not always warranted. But you have to put your head down and fight, fight, fight. Never, ever, ever give up. Things will work out just fine. Look at the way I've been treated lately, especially by the media. No politician in history—and I say this with great surety—has been treated worse or more unfairly." Like so much with Trump, this section of the speech was his running commentary on the news cycle and a self-motivation pitch. Trump was talking to the cadets and himself. "Fight, fight, fight" was his credo and, he said, ought to be theirs. It stood as a compelling example of Trump's attitude inside a cauldron of pressure and negative publicity that he would live up to during the crises he subsequently set in motion or encountered.

On Capitol Hill, Trump's problem was not reporters but the top Republican and Democrat on the Senate Judiciary Committee. Chairman

Charles Grassley of Iowa and Democrat Dianne Feinstein of California sent a letter to the FBI and White House requesting all memos related to Comey's interactions with his superiors in the Trump and Obama administrations. Meanwhile, Sessions refused to comment on whether he saw any Comey memos, this as CBS confirmed Comey wrote many memos and was eager to testify publicly.

On Air Force One returning from the Coast Guard Academy, Spicer met with traveling reporters and was besieged with questions about what, exactly, Trump said to Comey and what he did or did not tell the Russians in the Oval Office. Spicer repeated the words "very clear" eight times to describe Trump's explanation. "The president wants to—is confident in the events as he has maintained."

At 6 p.m. the next news alert screamed across TV screens and smartphones: Rosenstein appointed former FBI Director Robert Mueller as special counsel to investigate all matters related to and arising out of the Russia investigation. "I have determined," Rosenstein said, "that a special counsel is necessary in order for the American people to have full confidence in the outcome." CBS confirmed through our Justice reporter, Paula Reid, that FBI investigators currently on the Russia investigation would likely stay on the case and that Mueller would have discretion over his team. At the White House, Trump released a statement: "As I have stated many times, a thorough investigation will confirm what we already know—there was no collusion between my campaign and any foreign entity. I look forward to this matter concluding quickly." The Mueller appointment elicited bipartisan praise.

The day had begun to wind down. Then another bulletin added a new layer of intrigue. At 9:21 p.m., *The New York Times* published a story with the headline: "Trump Team Knew Flynn Was Under Investigation Before He Came to White House." More reporters scrambled as the White House jumped into the fray, seeking to corral this revelation and offer some kind of explanation. It would take hours . . . until the next Trump tweet.

MAY 18—FLYNN FLAM

One of the first predawn news alerts arrived and it would become central to the eventual guilty plea secured from former National Security Advisor Michael Flynn. At 5:50 a.m., Reuters reported, "Michael Flynn and other advisors to Donald Trump's campaign were in contact with Russian officials and others with Kremlin ties in at least 18 calls and emails during the last seven months of the 2016 presidential race." Slightly more than two hours later, Trump tweeted in an attempt to shift the subject: "With all of the illegal acts that took place in the Clinton campaign & Obama Administration, there was never a special councel appointed!" Trump misspelled "counsel," something he corrected on Twitter at 10:08 a.m. after a testy meeting, one of many that week, with his communications team. Trump was enraged by the unrelenting scrutiny, negative press and inability of his press shop to redirect or silence bad stories.

The Flynn story continued to bubble on the Hill as the leaders of the Senate Intelligence Committee accused Flynn of failing to honor its subpoena.

The day took a shocking turn shortly after noon, when New York City police responded to a speeding vehicle that struck pedestrians in Times Square. At 12:36 p.m., Spicer tweeted that the president had been briefed on the Times Square situation. About this time, Trump headed into a planned luncheon with network news anchors and other TV news heavyweights. The encounter was strictly off-the-record, meaning no quotes or information from exchanges with Trump would be reportable. Shortly after 3 p.m. the White House, via then-Communications Director Hope Hicks, lifted the off-the-record lid ever so slightly and released this quote about Mueller's appointment: "I believe it hurts our country terribly," Trump said. "It shows we're a divided, mixed-up, not-unified country. And we have very important things to be doing right now, whether it's trade deals, whether it's military, whether it's stopping nuclear—all of the things that we discussed today. And I think this shows a very divided country. It also happens to be a pure excuse for the Democrats having lost an election that they should have easily won because of the Electoral College being slanted so much in their way. That's all this is."

Within minutes, senators who emerged from a closed-door briefing with Rosenstein came to a very different conclusion. Sen. Lindsey Graham, South Carolina Republican, told reporters the Russia investigation had shifted from a counterintelligence investigation to a criminal investigation. He praised the choice of Mueller. Sen. Claire McCaskill, Missouri Democrat, told reporters Rosenstein said he learned that Comey would be fired *before* Rosenstein wrote his memo. Sen. Chris Coons, Delaware Democrat, amplified McCaskill's report. "To be precise," Coons said to assembled reporters, "what he said was 'I learned that the president would fire James Comey on May 8th, I completed my memo on May 9th.' That's what he said in his opening statement. I wrote it down." Coons was asked if he believed this had become a criminal investigation. He chose his words carefully. "It is an investigation into whether or not criminal prosecution is appropriate," Coons said. "That also has a counterintelligence component."

Shortly after 4 p.m. Trump held a brief press conference in the East Room with Colombian President Juan Manuel Santos. In a rare move, Trump called on one of the sharpest reporters in the press corps, Peter Baker of *The New York Times*. Baker gamely tried to put the hectic week and its most pressing issues into perspective.

> Q: Mr. President. In the light of a very busy news week, a lot of people would like to get to the bottom of a couple of things, give you a chance to go on record here. Did you at any time urge former FBI Director James Comey in any way, shape, or form to close or to back down the investigation into Michael Flynn?
>
> Trump: No. No. Next question.
>
> Baker: As you look back over the past six months or year, have you had any recollection where you've wondered if anything you have done has been something that might be worthy of criminal charges in these investigations, or impeachment, as some on the left are implying?
>
> Trump: I think it's totally ridiculous. Everybody thinks so. And again, we have to get back to working our country properly so that we can take care of the problems that we have. We have plenty of problems. We've done a fantastic job. We have a tremendous group of people. Millions and millions of people out there that are looking at what you have just said, and said, "What are they doing?" Director Comey was very unpopular with most people. I actually thought when I made that decision—and I also got a very, very strong recommendation, as you know, from the deputy attorney general,

Rod Rosenstein. But when I made that decision, I actually thought that it would be a bipartisan decision, because you look at all of the people on the Democratic side—not only the Republican side—they were saying such terrible things about Director Comey.

Almost a day after the Flynn story was published, the White House issued a statement that denied Trump knew, during the transition, that Flynn was under investigation. As I have already established, Trump began to harbor deep misgivings about Flynn during the transition. The White House denial read in part: "Neither Michael Flynn nor his attorneys told Transition Counsel 'that he was under federal investigation for secretly working as a paid lobbyist for Turkey during the campaign.'" It should be noted that this denial spoke to what Flynn and his attorneys had told the transition counsel, not what Trump knew or had reason to suspect.

Whatever was known, it is worth taking a moment to remember that two Trump figures pled guilty to lying to the FBI in 2017. They were caught being untruthful about contacts with Russians. Were they hiding something? Was it *omertà* or panicked stupidity? Could two separate members of Trump's team—one a young, on-the-make wannabe foreign policy advisor name George Papadopoulos and the other, Flynn, a former head of the Defense Intelligence Agency—have been afflicted with the same panicked stupidity when the truth was benign?

Papadopoulos was a foreign policy advisor to Trump's campaign but occupied fringe status. He was photographed at a March 31, 2016, meeting with Trump in Washington, evidence that undercut statements after Papadopoulos's plea agreement that he neither met nor interacted with Trump. Papadopoulos was not a central figure in Trump world. He was in that picture and at the meeting because it, the meeting, had been haphazardly thrown together to show the world that Trump had at least *some* foreign policy/national security advisors. It was a clumsy photo op. But Papadopoulos was there, and that might have made him a juicy target for Russian intrigue and seduction. When Papadopoulos agreed to cooperate with Mueller's investigators, the world was left wondering what he knew and who it might implicate. Those questions have not been answered.

Flynn lied to the FBI about his contacts during the transition with Russian officials. Those conversations turned in part on the future of new economic sanctions Obama slapped on Moscow as punishment for election meddling, actions Obama could have taken much earlier in 2016 to flag the meddling and put Russia on notice *before the election*. Obama's lack of action reinforced Trump's suspicion that the Russia angle was exaggerated after Clinton lost. That is less important than the glaring fact that Flynn lied about his conversations with Russian officials. He, too, agreed to cooperate with Mueller's investigation. That so little else linking Russia and Trump world has come to light after these two plea agreements gives some credence to the theory that Flynn and Papadopoulos were just dopes playing out of their league— incompetents caught in lies because they were too frightened or dumb to tell the truth. They might be patsies in something more stupid than sinister. Or they might be keys to a complex and hard-to-prove scandal. Only Mueller appears to know.

MAY 19—ON THE ROAD TO SAUDI ARABIA

The day passed without incident or news alert. It was almost unbelievable. Washington was breathing somewhat calmly, in part because it knew Trump was preparing to leave for his first overseas trip. The White House and Congress tend to calm down when the president leaves the country. What's more, the Trump itinerary was already locked down and expectations were turning toward what he might accomplish on the world stage. The first stop was already a history-making decision. Trump was about to leave for Saudi Arabia. At 2:02 p.m., under sunny and calm blue skies, Trump, First Lady Melania, Jared Kushner, Ivanka Trump, and Priebus exited the White House and boarded Marine One for transit to Joint Base Andrews and then on to Air Force One for the long flight to Riyadh. On his walk to Marine One, Trump ignored shouted questions.

EIGHT

Saudi Arabia and the Middle East

The main cabin door of Air Force One swung open and one of Trump's senior Secret Service agents surveyed the scene and dared not take another step, lest he fall more than 20 feet to the tarmac of King Khalid airport below.

It was May 19, just less than four months into his presidency and Trump had just landed in Riyadh, Saudi Arabia, the last place anyone in America would have reasonably imagined the author of the "Muslim ban" would be touching down at this stage of his reign. Something was amiss and it wasn't upended expectations. While Air Force One powered down, Saudi laborers had feverishly unrolled a red carpet toward it, but the carpet did not align with the cabin door. The idea was that the movable stairs Trump and First Lady Melania were to descend would line up perfectly with the red carpet because the same red carpet with ornate gold trim on the edges also ran the length of the stairs. Inside the terminal, Saudi King Salman bin Abdulaziz Al Saud waited and increasingly frantic Saudi laborers and aides tried to come up with a plan. One thing was certain: Trump wasn't backing up Air Force One one inch.

An agent stood in the cabin door looking slightly befuddled, his arms outstretched and his hands clasping the inside of the cabin door, an American sentry in the desert kingdom. Reporters and Trump advisors spilled out of the back of the plane and shaded themselves under the wing on the port side. From the tarmac, the deep blue cone, baby blue trim and chrome belly of Air Force One looked as bright and polished as ever, even after flying nearly 7,000 miles. From the formal reception area where King Salman waited, however, Air Force One looked overwhelmed by the desert void behind it, its buffed metal lines melting into the pale and dusty horizon beyond.

The color scheme of Air Force One was chosen by President Kennedy, the product of cut-and-paste discussions on the floor of the Oval Office with legendary post–World War II industrial designer Raymond Loewy in 1962. The darker blue was thought by Kennedy to represent the future, the lighter blue tradition. The distinctive lettering on the side was inspired by the wide-spaced script on the original version of the Declaration of Independence. When designing Air Force One, Kennedy rejected a red color scheme and red uniforms for Air Force attendants because he didn't like the color and, more importantly, thought it reeked of imperial pretension. Imperial pretension. Inside America's flying White House Trump waited patiently for the signal that red-carpeted stairs, a king, a government of royals and a nation inching into a new future awaited his handshake.

Trump's arrival in Riyadh was engineered almost entirely by son-in-law and foreign policy novice Jared Kushner, the advisor Trump designated during the transition to handle his most sensitive foreign policy interactions. When nations stunned by Trump's victory clamored for an explanation of this new president's intentions, Kushner met them—provided they were important enough to U.S. interests and Trump's agenda. The Saudis sprang into action almost immediately, in the person of Prince Mohammed bin Salman, the ambitious young heir apparent to King Salman and the current face of Islamic reformation inside the kingdom.

Through intermediaries in the U.S., Mohammed bin Salman (MbS as he is universally known) conveyed to Kushner he considered Trump's election a potential turning point.

"They said he was up all night," Kushner told me in an interview in his White House office, referring to MbS watching the American Election Night returns. "He was very excited. He saw it as an opportunity for the country to restart with America."

The Saudis sent a delegation to meet Kushner at Trump Tower in November.

"I said the president has the following priorities: he wants to have a pushback against Iran's aggression; he wants to counter extremism; he wants to counter terror finance; and he wants to shift the military burden in the region. I said, 'So, if you guys can figure out a way to do that, that's great.' They came back to me with a proposal like two weeks later and said if you will make Trump's first overseas trip to Saudi Arabia, then this is what we will work on."

Work on it both sides did.

With Air Force One awaiting, King Salman, 81, walked gingerly with the help of a cane to the foot of the stairs. They never quite aligned so a throw rug was laid at the bottom of the stairs and draped over the misaligned royal red carpet. At 10:03 a.m. in Riyadh and 3:03 a.m. in Washington, Trump's foot landed on the rug bridging the tarmac and red carpet. At that moment, he made Saudi history and placed himself in a wholly different context in the Arab world. Trump became the first U.S. president to make the wealthy, autocratic kingdom his first visit outside of America (historically, Britain, Canada and Mexico have been so honored). Salman shook Trump's hand and as they walked to a royal tea inside the terminal, nine Saudi fighter jets, all purchased from U.S. defense contractors, performed a welcoming flyover, three planes each disgorging red, white and blue smoke to audibly and visually enhance the flattery and grandeur of Trump's arrival. The Saudi Royal family, custodians of Mecca and Medina, the two holiest sites in Islam, welcomed Trump to the kingdom as if he were a redeemer or deliverer. It would be the first of many opulent demonstrations for an American president captivated by gaudy adoration. Kingdoms know of such things.

"The highest they had done was four planes over," Kushner told me, referring to the aerial greeting. "They had nine planes [for Trump]. They had horses escorting, next to the limos. They gave the highest royal honors ever done. They rolled out the red carpet."

That night, Trump's limousine pulled up to another red carpet and phalanx of Saudi princes. King Salman was there to escort him inside the King Abdulaziz Center for World Culture in Dhahran. It was built by Saudi Aramco very near the site—known as the Prosperity Well—where oil in large enough quantities for export was first tapped in 1938. Before Trump exited, Saudi singers and performers began a chant of the *ardah*, a traditional dance of celebration after war that has now become a universal dance of tribute and celebration. Drums with brightly colored wool tassels were raised in the air by performers wearing black velvet jackets and *thawbs*. The percussion was rhythmic and deep, accompanying the hypnotic poetry repeated over and over: "We thank God things came that we wished for."

Trump was greeted again by Salman as the chanting and drumming continued. After handshakes, First Lady Melania stood some distance away as Trump moved with Salman toward the center courtyard. Melania then fell behind, as did Kushner and wife Ivanka. In the courtyard, Trump, 71, was positioned with Salman in one of two dancing lines of the ardah and handed a sword to be raised amid the swaying. Trump smiled and obliged. Trump was following in the dance steps of Presidents Obama and Bush but this ardah looked and sounded bigger, the chants raw, the drumbeats seemingly cathartic. Trump handed the sword back to his Saudi courtier and followed Salman inside, succeeded in the ardah line by Secretary of State Rex Tillerson, 65, and Commerce Secretary Wilbur Ross, 80, who joined in the hoisting and rocking, visibly swept up in the ardor. Feet away, Priebus and Bannon stood and marveled. Trump sword dancing in Saudi Arabia? Saudi princes singing that *Trump* was what they wished for?

It seems so long ago and in retrospect could be dismissed as a photographic trifle. A U.S. president and a Saudi king. It's happened before. Okay, this time they brought more jets and horses. It was anything but a trifle. It may have been the most important foreign policy event of Trump's first year. Not because it was unexpected, which it was, but because of its potential to realign the power grid in the Middle East and give the U.S. serious support in suppressing terrorist financing and indoctrination. "Potential." That's the potent word. There is a chance. Trump will grab it with both hands. So will the Saudis. History now awaits.

In the blur that was Trump's first year, it seems like the smallest of footnotes. Trump's first foreign trip. Oh yeah, he went to Saudi Arabia. Something about terrorism. Funny pictures of sword dancing. We sold some weapons or something, right? Then he checked the Israel box and flew to Rome to see the pope. The big three religions. Got it. Next.

It feels like that. Even to those who cover the White House. But some moments have the potential to cast a long, steady shadow. Trump in Saudi Arabia is precisely that kind of moment. It is way too early to make predictions, but there are those close to the president who believe Trump has already had an iconic moment as tide-turning and symbolically important as Ronald Reagan in 1987 at the Brandenburg Gate in then–West Germany: "Mr. Gorbachev, tear down this wall!"

What?

Trump couldn't have had a moment like that, could he? Did he? If he did, how did we miss it?

In truth, nothing was missed because nothing in the Middle East is ever clear in the moment or even a decade later. But sands are shifting in the region and Trump, by virtue of fortuitous timing and a strategic gamble, may be in position to nurture the most important transformation of Islam in a century—with side benefits that could reshape Middle East peace talks and, almost certainly, put the United States on a military collision course with Iran.

First back to Riyadh, MbS and Kushner.

"I would speak to MbS almost every day to plan it," Kushner said of talks during the transition about the Saudi pitch to bring 53 other Muslim or Islamic nations to Riyadh for a summit focused on combating terrorism and Iran, which the Saudi government consider inseparable. From Kushner's point of view, MbS came through. "Every single thing he promised me he delivered 150 percent on."

Why did the Saudis want him there at all?

The answer, humorously enough, revolves around one word.

Shit.

President Obama, in an interview with Jeffrey Goldberg in the April 2016 issue of *The Atlantic,* summarized the foreign policy approach of his second term: "Don't do stupid shit." That meant don't drive the United States deeper into the six-way Syrian civil war; do as little as possible to fight ISIS on the ground in Iraq; steadily draw down

U.S. troops in Afghanistan; and don't poke major powers in the eye—China over the South China Sea, Russia over Ukraine and Iran over terrorism throughout the region.

As Goldberg wrote: "The message Obama telegraphed in speeches and interviews was clear: He would not end up like the second President Bush—a president who became tragically overextended in the Middle East, whose decisions filled the wards of Walter Reed with grievously wounded soldiers, who was helpless to stop the obliteration of his reputation, even when he recalibrated his policies in his second term. Obama would say privately that the first task of an American president in the post-Bush international arena was 'Don't do stupid shit.'"

Another part of that article attracted wide attention and derision in Riyadh and Jerusalem. Goldberg wrote Obama "has questioned why the U.S. should maintain Israel's so-called qualitative military edge, which grants it access to more sophisticated weapons systems than America's Arab allies receive; but he has also questioned, often harshly, the role that America's Sunni Arab allies play in fomenting anti-American terrorism. He is clearly irritated that foreign policy orthodoxy compels him to treat Saudi Arabia as an ally. And of course he decided early on, in the face of great criticism, that he wanted to reach out to America's most ardent Middle East foe, Iran."

On November 12, 2015, in Fort Dodge, Iowa, Trump explained his plan to defeat ISIS: "I would bomb the shit out of them." Once in office, Trump vastly increased U.S. and coalition bombing runs in Iraq and Syria (regardless of risk) and gave field commanders free rein to use Special Forces as they saw fit to battle ISIS up close. Trump sent 59 Tomahawk cruise missiles into Syria to punish it for a chemical weapons attack, something Obama had considered but at the last minute rejected, prompting Adel al-Jubeir, the Saudi ambassador in Washington, to relay to Riyadh, according to Goldberg, that "Iran is the new great power of the Middle East and the U.S. is the old." By the end of his first year in office, Trump also agreed to send lethal defensive weapons to Ukraine to fight occupying Russians—something Obama rejected. Trump had also decertified the Iran nuclear deal that was Obama's singular Middle East obsession—negotiating a 10- to 15-year delay in Iran's ability to develop a nuclear weapon. Obama bet his entire Middle East strategy on the assumption that delaying Iran's pursuit of a nuclear weapon was the key to regional peace and the best way to give shifting Iranian political sentiments a chance to move the country from Shia Islamic theocracy to something more moderate, modern, possibly democratic and, on the whole, less hostile to the West. Obama's vision was a noninterventionist dream of U.S. persuasion remaking the Middle East and pacifying a once-implacable foe. It bore an aspirational resemblance to Bush the younger and Iraq. It is worth noting that Trump came to oppose both ideas.

Obama also told Goldberg this about future threats to the United States: "ISIS is not an existential threat to the United States. Climate change is a potential existential threat to the entire world if we don't do something about it."

As far as Trump was concerned, the stupid shit was *the Obama agenda*. Trump believed ISIS was a threat now and must be defeated in Iraq and Syria and chased wherever it lands next or in whatever new form it mutates into. On Iran, Trump is like King Salman and Israeli's hawkish Prime Minister Benjamin Netanyahu. All believe Iran is the menace of the Middle East and no issue takes precedence over reversing its export of terrorism and political adventurism. The Saudis and those Israelis aligned with Netanyahu (not all Israelis are) see Tehran as an existential threat. Trump's arrival shifted the kingdom's calculations. Trump offered the Saudis, protectors of the Sunni branch of Islam, an immediate alliance against Shia Iran and tacit support for whatever moves the kingdom decided would advance that strategic objective—including intensifying the proxy war with Iranian-backed Houthis in Yemen (regardless of the humanitarian cost), rattling the cage of Lebanon's Prime Minister Saad Hariri (by briefly taking him captive and in the process forcing him to acknowledge Hezbollah's influence over his government) and publicly accusing Qatar (home of Al Jazeera) of financing terrorism.

Kushner was candid about Saudi motivations and what Trump sees as an era of transactional foreign policy.

"They believe in the president. They want to be with the president. They don't take America for granted anymore. A lot of our objectives align with their objectives in the region right now. A lot of the radicalization started in Saudi Arabia so if you want to defeat it you need

Saudi Arabia working with you. They are the custodian of the two holy sites. They are leaders in the Muslim world."

During the summit, Salman addressed leaders from 54 other nations in ways the kingdom had not addressed terrorism since 9/11, despite years of U.S. pleading. The motivations might be complementary or coincidental to Trump. Regardless, Salman's words have the potential to change the direction of the Middle East by announcing the kingdom and like-minded governments, many of them monarchies, will no longer protect, finance or intellectually sustain terror groups (the Saudis, it has been documented, did all three).

Salman declared the summit the first step in a unified effort to "refute the frail claims of terrorists" and combat "this scourge that poses a danger to all humanity."

Salman then spoke on behalf of Islam: "One of the most important goals of Islamic Sharia is protecting life and there is no honor in protecting murder. . . . It considers killing an innocent soul tantamount of killing all humanity. These odious acts are attempts to exploit Islam as a cover for political purposes to flame hatred, extremism, hatred, terrorism and conflicts . . . we will be firm in finding anyone who financed terrorism in any way shape or form and bring them to justice."

From Kushner's perspective, that would be the Saudis hitting the 150 percent threshold. He paused to reflect on MbS and his push to return the kingdom to a moderate form of Islam with more rights for women and less theocratic oppression.

"It's not without speed bumps. He's got a lot of challenges. We're looking for it to be successful. If he [MbS] can lead the global fight against extremism, that's incredible. If he wants to push back against Iran's aggression, that's incredible. If he wants a more free and open society where women have equal rights and you don't discriminate against people for their race or religion, I mean, that's incredible. We should be trying to support him. He's taking on big, bold objectives. We have to give him the space to try to accomplish it. These places are not going to become Jeffersonian democracies overnight or maybe ever. Our job is to run America and not to define places where people have common interests with us and respect their cultures and let them see our values."

Trump's summit speech amplified Kushner's pragmatic but guarded optimism. It contained a line that White House officials believe may go down in history alongside Reagan's at the Brandenburg Gate. That may seem a leap until you understand that those around Trump believe terrorism and the Islamic extremism that fuels it are, in their words, the communist menace of our time. In this regard, Trump's foreign policy will prioritize efforts to check and defeat extremism over all other considerations, as decades of American presidents of both parties did during the Cold War. Trump will not and has not hesitated to embrace authoritarian regimes that battle extremism—even at appalling humanitarian costs (as in the Philippines, Turkey and Yemen, to name just three). Trump at times exhibits authoritarian tendencies, so there may be an intrinsic comfort factor. But if Islamic-inspired terrorism is the new communism, Trump appears willing to tolerate all manner of indelicacies to side with regimes that fight it on his terms. Some of that could be seen in his remarks.

"Above all we must be united in the one goal that transcends every other consideration. That goal is to meet history's great test—to conquer extremism and vanquish the forces of terrorism."

Trump then reminded the summit that, by some estimates, 95 percent of the victims of terrorism "are themselves Muslim."

"The nations of the Middle East will have to decide what kind of future they want for themselves, for their countries and for their children. It is a choice between two futures—and it is a choice Americans cannot make for you. A better future is only possible if your nations drive out the terrorists and extremists. DRIVE. THEM. OUT."

At this point, Trump raised his voice, and drew his words more slowly, wielding them not unlike a sword in an ardah dance. As above, every time Trump's speech used the phrase "drive them out," the official White House transcript capitalized every letter.

"DRIVE THEM OUT of your places of worship. DRIVE THEM OUT of your communities. DRIVE THEM OUT of your holy land AND DRIVE THEM OUT OF THIS EARTH."

For the Muslim- and Arab-majority nations in attendance, Trump offered a stark challenge and reassuring promise. The challenge—fight terrorism now or risk your future and American indifference that could migrate toward hostility. The promise—we will not overthrow you and we won't even fret over human rights violations, press free-doms or labor laws so long as you fight extremism. Trump spoke soothingly of gradual reforms and stability—precisely the approach authoritarians in the region prefer from America. Largely overlooked at the time, Trump's speech was undoubtedly the clearest distillation of his approach to foreign policy and his most systematic and public rejection of Obama (and Bush) Middle East policy.

"We had a very honest discussion which was terrorism was not just America's problem, this is all of our problem," Kushner told me, de-scribing his presummit conversations with MbS. "The King said in his speech there is no glory in death. What it did was galvanize a lot of the Muslim world around our objectives."

Some of those objectives were financial. The Saudis followed through on $110 billion in U.S. arms purchases, many in the pipeline and approved but not consummated during the Obama administra-tion, and up to $380 billion in business deals and infrastructure invest-ments over 10 years with U.S. multinational companies and investment houses. For Trump, foreign policy is in part transactional and he pri-oritizes deals that profit U.S. companies and, as he said at the time, "hundreds of billions of dollars of investments into the United States and jobs, jobs, jobs." Almost everywhere we traveled in the world dur-ing his first year, Trump would hawk U.S.-made arms. He wasn't the least bit shy about more widely distributing weapons of war, so long as American companies and workers gained. I had never seen an Amer-ican president so gleefully extol the technology of war and the jobs tied to the military-industrial complex. The four previous presidents I covered were hesitant to publicly discuss U.S. defense contractors. Not Trump. He has a love of weaponry and boyish admiration for the mili-tary. The United States has long been the world's top arms exporter and that quietly continued under Obama, though he did halt some sales to the Saudis to protest humanitarian casualties in Yemen.

In the first eight months of Trump's presidency, the Department of State achieved a record $75.9 billion in arms deals, besting the previous one-year record of $68.6 billion in 2012. Included were deals to Bahrain and Nigeria that Obama had blocked over human rights concerns. In April of 2018, Trump finalized an "Arms Transfer Initiative" designed to ease export restrictions and devote more government resources to selling U.S. arms abroad. Trump will send U.S.-made arms to the Middle East and other parts of the world to boost American jobs—this consideration now on par with human rights under the new policy. This will allow autocratic governments to enforce stability and set the pace of reform, should there be any, on their timetable and no one else's.

Kushner told me long after the summit he had confronted resistance inside the White House from the professional National Security Council staff and veterans at the Department of State. He was careful not to mention any names (and since turnover at the NSC and State has been so high the names are probably irrelevant now anyway). Kushner was and still is viewed skeptically by foreign policy experts, and debate continues about whether the Trump-Saudi antiterror summit was a turning point or a glutton's feast for defense contractors. The words about combating the ideology and financing behind terrorism have enormous . . . here's the word again . . . "potential" to change the region. It's far too early to know their staying power or ability to change minds or behavior. What Kushner told me is he had to overcome intense internal U.S. government resistance to having the summit at all. He described it as a test for him and the Saudis—and by that it can be described as a test of MbS.

"I had a lot of people here who did not want to do the trip, who said the Saudis will never come through," Kushner told me. "You will get there and it will just be a bunch of sand. They'll promise you things. They'll never do them. I said, 'Guys, they want to do this.' They [opponents in the U.S. government] said we should do an assessment on their [the Saudis'] ability to do it. And I said, 'Look, if you would have done an assessment of me on any objective I have set out to accomplish, you would have conclusively determined I didn't have the ability to do it.' I said they are giving us aspirational promises, let's give them the rope to try to achieve it or hang themselves. All right? So, people were very skeptical. I couldn't get people to come to the trip planning meetings. They said it's going to be a disaster. It's going to be on you. I had a lot of pushback on this."

Kushner paused to offer an assessment of how he sees his role on behalf of Trump and how he has come to believe his role may be more comfortably received in the Middle East and other parts of the world untouched by pluralism and democracy.

"A lot of these places around the world are family businesses. People know [what] my motivation in coming here was. I gave up a very good career. I came here because it was an amazing opportunity . . . they know when they talk to me I will give them honest feedback and I'm not trying to push my own agenda, I'm trying to push the president's agenda."

Part of that agenda can be found in Trump's decision to launch missiles into Syria after credible evidence emerged that the Assad regime, on April 4, 2017, again deployed chemical weapons against civilians. The nerve agent sarin was deployed from the air by Syrian jets on civilians in the northern province of Idlib. News coverage and social media posts showed men, women and children reeling, choking and foaming at the mouth before dying. Trump watched the graphic images on TV and saw more detailed analysis in intelligence briefings.

Trump asked for military options and gave the unmistakable impression he intended to strike. The question, of course, was how, where and by what means and at what cost. Trump went through three separate deliberations with Pentagon and national security officials, the last from a secure facility erected at Mar-a-Lago, where Trump was conducting a summit with Chinese President Xi Jinping. Before the first options briefing in the Situation Room, Trump met with Kelly, then Homeland Security secretary, Defense Secretary James Mattis and Joseph Dunford, chairman of the Joint Chiefs of Staff. Kelly's presence underscored Trump's reliance on his judgment even though the two had never met before the transition, when Kelly was interviewed to lead DHS. The meeting was to give Trump a sense of his range of options and risks before airing them out in the Situation Room with his national security team. It is notable that the only ones present for this pre-brief were from the military. No one from the Department of State or NSC was included. What early advice Trump took came entirely from the perspective of experienced and cautious warriors.

According to Priebus and Kelly, still Homeland Security secretary at the time but already trusted by Trump as a military advisor, the president took his time and asked the right questions. To both, Trump seemed uncharacteristically humble, soft-spoken, curious and measured. Both found it reassuring, considering the pace of things since

Inauguration Day. After the second meeting, Trump announced he wanted more time to weigh the options. Kelly manned the Situation Room inside the White House for the third meeting when Trump announced he would authorize a Tomahawk missile strike on the airbase from which the Syrian jets flew to unload the sarin gas on Idlib. There had been extensive discussions about the risks of even this relatively modest, one-time-only response. Trump gave the order.

Kelly recalled the next moments in the Situation Room as he watched Trump's very young and comparatively inexperienced communications staff react.

"They fell silent," Kelly told me. "The hush was startling. Someone asked, 'What do we do? Do we pick targets? What is there for us to do now?' I told them the plan is done and there is nothing for you to do about that. Here is what you can do. Plan for bad outcomes. Dead Russians in a hangar. Russians firing at the U.S. vessels that fired the cruise missiles. Dead civilians from an accidental targeting. Prepare for worst-case scenarios."

The missile strike came with none of those scenarios. Trump announced the Tomahawk strike in the middle of his dinner with Xi.

"It was a very important moment, in part because of the notion of saying casually to Xi I had to step out for a minute to hold a press briefing because we just fired 59 missiles into Syria," Gingrich told me. "The idea of calmly reminding him that there's only one country on the planet that can do this. And I've got the guts to do it. So be careful. Mattis said here are the tools I can give you so we're not risking any American lives."

Gingrich considers Mattis the most important voice on the Trump team. No one I have interviewed for this book disagrees. Mattis has commanded Trump's respect longer than any other cabinet secretary or White House official. Trump has never questioned Mattis's expertise or loyalty, never toyed with him on Twitter and never made even the slightest disparaging reference about him in private conversations. Mattis occupies a unique space in the Trump world because his clout is disproportionate to his visibility, volume and bearing. He's the anti-Trump and the fulcrum on which all national security policy turns.

"The success story is Mattis," Gingrich told me. "He's closer to Obama on policy than most Republicans, but most of what we're doing well starts with Mattis. The failure was Tillerson. I thought it was the choice he [Trump] needed. Tillerson never got it. He didn't know how to run the department and he didn't know the job of secretary of state is a staff job. It's a fairly big staff job, but it's still a staff job."

This is all a backdrop for the Riyadh visit. But there is one other vital component to the story. Family. The Saudi kingdom is populated by more than 15,000 princes and princesses. Saudi prehistory is the story of Islamic tribes and Bedouin families. Blood is the force of life, power, trust and alliance. In an unappreciated sense, Trump's own family fixation . . . not seen since John Kennedy and Robert Kennedy . . . makes perfect and seamless sense to the Saudis. When the foreign policy establishment scoffed at Trump's decision to invest son-in-law Kushner with the Middle East portfolio, the Saudis considered it the most natural and comfortable thing imaginable. They were inclined to deal with Kushner. Forget how many foreign policy degrees or monographs were under Kushner's name [none]. Kushner was family. He wouldn't cross Trump. He was Trump's voice in the room. No Department of State minders. No National Security Council micromanaging. Kushner was like a prince among princes. Son-in-law to the new president—experienced only in loyalty and conveying Trump's strategy. The Saudis were not insulted by Kushner. They were flattered. Flattery and hostility to Iran was a potent combination. In the lead-up to the Riyadh summit, the Saudis were hooked.

Here is a simple, neutral truth about Trump. He didn't choose Kushner to seduce the Saudis. He didn't imagine Kushner would be a prince among princes capable of setting the Riyadh summit in motion and currying enough favor with the Saudis to land billions in arms deals and investment, a public commitment to finance and house a counterterrorism center and a public declaration that terrorism was hollowing out a great religion. Trump trusted Kushner. What's the worst that could happen? Were the Saudis going to turn down a United States determined to confront Iran? Not likely. Trump knew what he wanted to do with Iran and Israel. The Saudis were on board. Kushner was a means to an end. He's no Henry Kissinger, though Kissinger is a frequent advisor. He isn't even Jeane Kirkpatrick. He might not even be Adlai Stevenson. He's the son-in-law. In Saudi Arabia, however, that might be up there with one of the things "that we wished for."

Kushner began working the Saudi account as soon as the transition began. Long before Trump settled on Tillerson as secretary of state, Kushner was working the Middle East portfolio. That started with Israel and flowed naturally and surprisingly to the Saudis. One of the oddest manifestations of Obama's foreign policy in the region was Israel and Saudi Arabia drifted closer together in mutual alarm at Obama's continued interaction with—they would argue dangerous deference to—Iran. While Israeli alarm over Iran's pursuit of nuclear weapons captured the headlines and deepened the rift with the Obama White House, Saudi anxiety rose steadily as Iran propped up the murderous Assad regime in Syria, used Hezbollah to exercise indirect control over the Lebanese government, financed Shia militias to dominate enclaves north of Baghdad and directed the Houthi military campaign against the Saudi-backed government in Yemen.

All this drove Israel and Saudi Arabia together in subtle ways long before Trump won the presidency. Both saw his ascendance as the last, best chance to confront Iran. That made Trump's Riyadh visit not only a singular event in the history of the kingdom but an astonishing nonevent in Israel—so much was it considered a nonthreatening and welcome event that Israel, for the first time ever, allowed Air Force One to fly directly from Riyadh to Tel Aviv even though Israel and Saudi Arabia, at least formally, are still sworn enemies with no diplomatic ties. Under no other set of strategic circumstances and at no other time in the nearly 70-year history of U.S.-Israeli relations would that have been true. None of this is dependent upon Trump. The Trump factor is the exploitation of the moment. It's a theme we will come back to later in the book.

"I called the night he was staying in Rome after he had been in Riyadh and Israel," Gingrich told me. "And he said every time he was in public for three days the Saudi king was next to him physically. And that they would chat. And I was thinking to myself what nobody around here really gets is this is a guy who is absorbing world leadership. His technique is not to have three bright guys at Brookings [Institution] give him a paper. His technique is, 'I think I will go chat with the Saudi king for three days.' He's done that very consistently."

Walter Russell Mead, a fellow at the conservative Hudson Institute and professor of foreign affairs at Bard College, is one of the few neutral academic observers of Trump's foreign policy. Like most, he is unnerved by contradictory Trump tweets and uncertain about Trump's "antiglobalist and mercantilist instincts." Mead still believes, like many Trump supporters, that the president is onto something he might not be able to articulate or even fully pursue, but it is something big and page-turning . . . the end of the post–World War II consensus. Mead wrote this November 29, 2017: "What gives Mr. Trump his opening is something many foreign policy experts have yet to grasp: that America's post–Cold War national strategy has run out of gas. For years foreign policy thinking was dominated by the idea that the end of the Cold War meant the 'end of history'—the inevitable triumph of the so-called liberal world order. In steering American foreign policy away from the inflated expectations and unrealistic objectives produced by the end of history mirage, the Trump administration is performing a much-needed service."

Trump's Saudi visit may have demolished—it certainly recast—the Obama-Bush image of America in the region. It rejected the sunny optimism of toppling governments and replacing them with American-style democracies. It elevated security and stability above all considerations, and Trump's words and actions signaled to Iran that Trump considered it on a streak of malevolence toward the United States and the West that he was determined to reverse. As Gingrich told me, recalling the military service in Iraq of Trump's closest military advisors: "Kelly, Mattis and McMaster all know personally that Iran killed Americans. They will push very methodically against the Iranians. There is zero love lost. Zero illusion."

Trump's long-term success in the region will, if achieved, only partly be related to his words or actions inside the kingdom. His sword swaying was symbolic. King Salman's sword work at the microphone was historic—possibly so much so that a generation or two from now it will be viewed as the turning point in the modern history of Saudi Arabia, 21st-century Islam and the U.S. battle against Islamist-inspired terrorism.

That's a tantalizing "possibly."

But let's not get ahead of ourselves. As the custodian of Mecca and Medina, King Salman and the Saudi government occupy a unique place in the history and future of Islam. Saudi Arabia has also been a hotbed of a warrior-like strain of Sunni Islam that in some respects has fed the terroristic impulses of Muslims since 1979. Wahhabist Islam is its name and the martial aspects of its interpretation of Islamic teachings justified armed vengeance against nonbelievers and Western targets of influence. The history is complex but suffice to say this strain of Islam influenced and informed the earliest generation of Islamist-inspired terrorists, from Black September to the historically political but increasingly militant Muslim Brotherhood in Egypt and eventually to Osama bin Laden's Al-Qaeda (15 of the 19 hijackers on 9/11 were Saudis), the Taliban and numerous offshoots and affiliated groups up to and including ISIS.

From 9/11 forward, every U.S. president and administration has begged the Saudis to denounce terrorism as an intolerable mutation of Islam. The appeals have been spectacularly unsuccessful. Throughout George Bush's two terms, the plaintive cry "Where are the moderate Imams?" became a pathetic cliché. They didn't exist. Or if they did they were so obscure they might as well have been in witness protection. When she was Bush's national security advisor, Condoleezza Rice would have her staff search constantly for any sign of Islamic criticism of terror attacks or terrorist tactics. One sermon from a backwater Jordanian imam with a handful of followers was immediately translated into English and shoved into a White House fax machine (yes . . . fax machine) and spit out to reporters as evidence Islam was redeemable. Islam, to generalize, did not cheer or advocate for terrorism. But it did not condemn. And by its silence Islam enabled. Frustration and a sense of helplessness led U.S. policy makers to change their rhetoric in hopes it would change Islamic behavior. The thought was if the United States stops calling it "Islamic terrorism" or "Islamist-inspired terrorism," perhaps the implied criticism will lose its sting and ability to inspire. Again, this is a complex tale with many variations and themes, but these calculations led to a linguistic diffidence in the West that stopped using Islamic modifiers to terrorism. This reached its zenith in the Obama-era CVE—the Countering Violent Extremism campaign. Anyone could be a violent extremist. Perverted forms of Islam had nothing, on their face, to do with jihadism, terrorism or mayhem—even as groups that committed atrocities in northern Africa, Asia and Europe proliferated and operated as franchisees of Al-Qaeda or its successors.

I don't need to tell you this appalled Trump and other Republicans running for the White House in 2016. Trump and others argued that the definition mattered, the specificity of the language meant as much if not more than the tactics, planes, bombs, troops and drones. To the Obama administration, Hillary Clinton and much of the foreign policy establishment, this was an ignorant and possibly dangerous hypersimplification. To Trump it was a warning shot to Islamist-inspired terrorists. You know why you are a terrorist. I'm going to tell you I know, too. Now we fight. That's the essence of Trump's counterterrorism policy. In not insignificant ways, Salman's speech agreed with its core philosophy.

When the Saudis stayed awake at night worrying about Iran and Obama and nuclear negotiations—which by Iranian demand never factored in Iran's terrorist activities or regional expansionism—they had little time, energy or political inclination to restore Islam or denounce terrorism. Trump and the Saudi moves are coincidental and complementary. They are not without connective tissue, but it would be wrong to credit Trump with master class timing or strategic insight. He despises Iran nearly as much as the Saudis and Israelis do. He has the benefit of good timing. Of such things great change can come.

Potentially.

NINE

Health Care Failure

"We're going to get this passed through the Senate. I feel so confident."

That was Trump in the Rose Garden on the afternoon of May 4, 2017, basking in victory with House Republicans arrayed around him on stage, up the stairs leading from the Garden to the Oval Office behind. There were so many House Republicans they could fit neither on stage nor behind Trump so they spilled out on the grass on both sides, some brushing up against the flower beds with crabapple trees, tulips, primrose and hyacinth separating the central lawn from the colonnade connecting the West Wing to the Residence.

Trump was in a chatty and celebratory mood and paused, for the first time in office, to marvel at the unexpected wonder of it all. It was, in its own way, an endearing and slightly vulnerable moment, one that betrayed perhaps more of the wear and tear of the health care struggle than Trump would have preferred.

"Coming from a different world and only being a politician for a short period of time—how am I doing? Am I doing okay? I'm president. Hey, I'm president. Can you believe it? Right?"

Rapt applause from House Republicans, still not sure how to take Trump's unexpected enthusiasm.

When the clapping died down, Trump continued. "I don't know, it's—I thought you needed a little bit more time. They always told me, more time. But we didn't. We have an amazing group of people standing behind me. They worked so hard and they worked so long. We don't have to talk about this unbelievable victory—wasn't it unbelievable? So we don't have to say it again. But it's going to be an unbelievable victory, actually, when we get it through the Senate."

Other than the confirmation of Gorsuch, Trump's young presidency was bereft of big accomplishments. This looked like one: House passage of a bill to repeal and replace the Affordable Care Act, also known as Obamacare. Trump was pumped up because this was a resurrection moment of sorts. The first draft of the bill had died on March 25 when House GOP leaders, lacking the votes, pulled it from consideration on the House floor. That was an enormous blow to Trump and a conspicuous failure of his White House and the unified GOP Congress that together, in theory, were going to deliver big results in short order.

"This is a great plan. I actually think it will get even better. And this is, make no mistake, this is a repeal and replace of Obamacare. Make no mistake about it. Make no mistake. And I think, most importantly, yes, premiums will be coming down. Yes, deductibles will be coming down."

It all seemed possible. Before it all crashed and burned. Trump had leaned hard into health care most of the first six months of his presidency but then largely abandoned it until taking up one component, the individual mandate, when he sought the large-scale tax cuts and federal tax code simplification that would be achieved in late December.

Trump's failure to repeal and replace the Affordable Care Act capped six months of legislative futility. It contributed to the downfall of Chief of Staff Reince Priebus and Health and Human Services Secretary Tom Price. It added to the uncertainty in the health insurance system. At the time, it generated some national anxiety about whether Trump and the Republican majority could govern. This concern was even more pronounced among House and Senate Republicans and became a major irritant with frontline Republican donors—that anxiety and irritation would play key roles later in the push to achieve tax reform.

On health care, the failure exposed something many analysts had long alleged but Republicans had long denied—repealing Obamacare was a winning political argument but lacked the fortification of a coherent alternative to Obamacare's benefits, taxes and cost structures. There was plenty of politics but not much policy. Trump inherited this mismatch and was, it would turn out, bedeviled by inadequate Republican preparation. He suffered as a result and that put him in uncharted territory—having to explain why Mr. Dealmaker couldn't strike a deal.

Trump did try to cut a deal on health care. He tried over and over and over. He called congressmen and senators to listen and cajole, lobby and plead. Repeatedly in Oval Office meetings, Trump's attention would drift away from health care minutiae (Medicare reimbursement rates, Medicaid coverage totals, premium subsidies, waivers, fees and eligibility) and he would simply ask the assembled lawmakers or outside advocates: "Why can't we get a deal? Guys, where's the deal? Why can't you get this done?" Trump also cajoled Republicans on Twitter and those tweets provided a road map of his cheerleading, pleading and disgust about and with the process and outcome. ·

One of the reasons Trump was so pleased during that May 4 Rose Garden ceremony, so brimming with what turned out to be misplaced ebullience, was that the House health care victory, fragile though it was, constituted a triumph as well for a White House still learning how to function together. But first came a moment of reckoning. Trump did not ask for it but one of his most important White House lieutenants, Budget Director Mick Mulvaney, offered it anyway.

"I told the president I effed up," Mulvaney said. "I told him I misread the House. It is dysfunctional."

In mid-March Mulvaney had talked Trump into demanding a House vote on the health care bill that narrowly emerged from three committees—Budget; Ways and Means; and Energy and Commerce. Passage in the Budget Committee was uncertain as three Republicans, all members of the Tea Party–inspired Freedom Caucus, had voted no. Ryan and other House GOP leaders cautioned Mulvaney against pushing for a vote. Mulvaney concluded they were stalling and the longer Trump waited the more likely he was to lose votes rather than gain them. He told Trump that the force of his personality, the historic nature of his election and the imperative to perform would knock Republican fence-sitters and soft "no" votes to "yes."

Trump not only thought this was a solid strategy, it amplified his sense of self and reinforced the potent image he wanted his presidency to project. Not incidentally, Trump wanted a win. A TV win. A celebration with comeuppance à la mode for cable news critics who had been hounding his infant presidency. Somewhat predictably, Trump, a rank amateur on legislative maneuvering, had little sense of timing, nuance, persuasion or legislative tactics. He was Lyndon Johnson with his telephone and bank of TVs, yes, but he was still a fallible mind reader of his own party.

Mulvaney was wrong. Trump's demand for a vote—delivered by Mulvaney in person—hardened opposition and led members to test their own political clout against Trump's, precisely the opposite of what Mulvaney predicted. Now Mulvaney had to own the failure. Mulvaney was recruited in part because it was assumed he could count conservative Republican votes because, after all, he was a member of all the various hard-liner caucuses and ad hoc groups and, as a result, knew their districts, their impulses and their fears. It was assumed, therefore, Mulvaney knew all the hard-to-find cul-de-sacs of conservative votes. He also knew all the players in the House GOP leadership and, even better, knew all the rivalries, bruised egos and feelings of alienation conservatives nursed in their ongoing battles with House Speaker Paul Ryan. Mulvaney thought he could harness that anger and put one over on Ryan and make Trump the ultimate Washington change maker, deal cutter and visionary. But when the moment came for Mulvaney's big reveal, he turned into the political equivalent of Geraldo Rivera staring inside an empty Al Capone vault . . . a young buck full of brash confidence, a big audience and nothing but darkness, dust and silence.

That left Trump to glumly swallow the collapse of the House health care bill. He did so the afternoon in March that Ryan pulled the bill. He sat behind the Oval Office's Resolute Desk and spoke dryly.

"[I]t certainly was an interesting period of time. We all learned a lot. We learned about loyalty, we learned a lot about the vote-getting process. We learned a lot about some very arcane rules obviously in both the Senate and in the House. And so it's been, certainly for me, it's been a very interesting experience."

Trump did not fire Mulvaney, which is instructive considering how many cabinet secretaries, senior advisors and other White House staff became casualties in Trump's first year. Mulvaney remained because he was devoted to the Trump agenda and even agreed to take on a second job, head of the Consumer Financial Protection Bureau, where he was just as zealous and pro-business as he had been reducing regulations (one of his key responsibilities as head of the Office of Management and Budget).

In the aftermath, Trump told Mulvaney not to worry and to go back to work—on the budget and health care. Trump hated to lose and demanded a victory on health care—preferably before his first 100 days in office were over. That meant refocusing his team and streamlining its efforts. Mulvaney, Vice President Mike Pence and Chief of Staff Reince Priebus became the chief White House facilitators and negotiators. The three, stung by their own failure (Pence was also assumed to be a House conservative whisperer), developed a new, two-stage process with conservatives and moderates to rewrite objectionable parts of the bill.

Trump prodded them on Twitter before 9 a.m. on April 2: "Anybody (especially Fake News media) who thinks that Repeal & Replace of ObamaCare is dead does not know the love and strength in R Party!" And this: "Talks on Repealing and Replacing ObamaCare are, and have been, going on, and will continue until such time as a deal is hopefully struck."

The trio—Pence, Priebus and Mulvaney—enlisted the help of Rep. Mark Meadows of North Carolina, chairman of the conservative House Freedom Caucus, and Rep. Tom MacArthur of New Jersey, head of the moderate Tuesday Group. Priebus initiated talks between the two and worked with Pence and Mulvaney to keep the process on track. Countless meetings were held and proposals exchanged. Each small area of agreement was run by House Majority Whip Steve Scalise of Louisiana to test its appeal among all House Republicans. On a parallel track the newly drafted bill was communicated to the Senate Budget Committee to ensure it would meet parliamentary requirements for consideration under reconciliation, one of the "arcane" rules and procedures Trump had referred to.

"Sometimes, you're going to have to eat some things you don't want to eat to get most of what you want," Priebus told me, by way of explanation of Trump's newly humble approach.

The key issue was giving states the option to opt out of some of the bill's health coverage requirements. A balance had to be struck to keep enough coverage to satisfy moderates but allow enough freedom for very conservative states—from which Freedom Caucus members tended to come—to opt out. When the rewrite was complete, conservatives and moderates achieved a political truce sufficient to bring the bill to the cusp of passage. A few moderate holdouts remained. Mulvaney tartly described the situation this way.

"This is how it always goes—you get the conservatives on the principle of the policy because that's what they care about and then you buy off moderates because they don't care about anything."

The moderate in the way in this case was Rep. Fred Upton of Michigan, the former chairman of the Energy and Commerce Committee, who had withdrawn his support for the conservative-preferred language allowing states to opt out of mandatory coverage for patients with preexisting conditions. Upton never supported Trump in Michigan and at the time was considering a run for the U.S. Senate. If he ran, Upton would very much want Trump's endorsement and was also looking to position himself as the bill's savior—the final negotiator who put it over the top. These motives congealed into a deal whereby the White House allowed Meadows and MacArthur to set aside $8 billion in a reserve fund for coverage of preexisting conditions. Upton withdrew his opposition.

As the House vote approached on May 4, the head of White House legislative affairs, Marc Short, nervously trafficked between Ryan's office, the House floor and the office of Majority Leader Kevin McCarthy. Short ran his own bed check on House votes—refusing to leave the vote counting to Ryan or McCarthy. His tally stood at 217—one more than the bare minimum of 216 required for passage. Short knew he needed that extra vote—not for passage but for political protection. If the bill passed with 216 votes, then every House Republican could be accurately described as "the deciding vote" abolishing Obamacare. While that would prove helpful in heavily conservative districts, it would likely be dangerous for Republicans in swing districts—many of whom had already been pummeled during town-hall meetings on the future of post-Obamacare coverage, premiums and access.

"Hope we get to celebrate," Short told me hours before the floor vote.

I thought Short was stringing me along. There's no way they don't have the votes, I thought. No way Trump would risk another defeat—losing a floor vote would kill Obamacare repeal and almost certainly bury tax reform. The losses would cripple the Trump presidency by mid-May. They were not that reckless, were they? They weren't. The bill passed 217–213 and White House stewards began preparing the Rose Garden. The White House dispatched a tour bus to bring House Republicans—like roadies from a successful concert tour—from the Capitol. Priebus green-lit the party. He wanted to be recognized for putting the bill back together and giving Trump that victory he craved.

"It almost felt like we won," Priebus said. "We wanted to savor it. It felt good."

Remembering Mulvaney's frustration with Speaker Ryan, Trump also used the moment to torment the Wisconsin Republican and close friend of Priebus. Trump's inclination toward one-upsmanship was never far away.

"I was joking, I said, you know, Paul, for the last week I've been hearing 'Paul Ryan doesn't have it. It's not working with Paul Ryan. He's going to get rid of Paul Ryan.' And then today I heard, 'Paul Ryan is a genius, he's come a long way.'"

Ryan stood less than two feet away. His fellow Republicans laughed nervously, confident in that moment of just one thing—only they (not Trump) had the power to take the speakership from Ryan.

Trump looked at the Republicans.

"Right?"

Ryan stepped to the microphone: "I'll take whatever."

A bit later, McCarthy, the Majority Leader, said he'd never seen a president so "hands on" in the vote-counting process. Standing over McCarthy's shoulder, Trump smiled rakishly and tilted his head knowingly. "Hands on" had—as everyone knew—a Billy Bush sex tape reverberation that did not shame Trump or elicit even the faintest prudish gasp from the many female GOP lawmakers standing nearby. No one reacted at all, except Trump—and his face told the world, "You can't touch me. And I am laughing."

The next week Trump fired FBI Director James Comey and the laughter over a hands-on presidency stopped. Abruptly.

The old saying in Washington is victory has a thousand parents, but defeat is an orphan. Not true here. Ask Republicans when repeal-and-replace died and they will give you several milestones. Some will point to Trump's early December 2016 conference call with top transition officials informing them that his strategy would be to push for a repeal-and-replace bill—not just straight repeal. Some have pointed to the first House bill's defeat because it signaled defiance of Trump and GOP division, and exposed the limited ability of two former House members in the Trump cabinet, Mulvaney and Price, to pigeonhole and persuade. Of course, most point to Arizona Republican Sen. John McCain's dramatic vote, killing the Senate repeal-and-replace bill at 1:29 a.m. on July 28.

Early in December, Trump called a senior staff meeting on health care. Most attendees were in Trump Tower (Bannon, Kushner, Conway, Katie Walsh and Miller) but two were in Washington—Priebus and economic advisor Gary Cohn. They dialed in from Priebus's office at the RNC. On that call, Trump made among the most important decisions of his transition, announcing he would not support a repeal-only approach to Obamacare. His administration, he said, would only support a simultaneous repeal-and-replace effort.

"That changed everything," Priebus told me.

The call verified that Trump meant what he had told Leslie Stahl of *60 Minutes* in his first post-election interview about his health care intentions.

"We're going to do it simultaneously," Trump said, referring to repealing and replacing Obamacare. "It'll be just fine. We're not going to have, like, a two-day period and not going to have a two-year period where there's nothing. It will be repealed and replaced."

Priebus offered the first hint of this new thinking during a mid-December interview on Hugh Hewitt's national radio show, an important showcase for Trump initiatives then and now. Trump reinforced his inflexibility on repeal-and-replace during a late December dinner with Ryan, saying he would not suffer the chaotic politics (doesn't that sound faintly amusing now?) wrought by ending Obamacare without a replacement that gave insurance markets, hospitals and doctors guidelines for the future.

It was a sensible position. It also, in a very real sense, tried to cure Republicans of their allergic political reaction to actually drafting detailed and politically durable *replacement* legislation that could pass the House and Senate. Since the passage of Obamacare, Republicans had taken more than 50 repeal votes in the House and Senate. But the GOP-led House had taken only one vote on a bill to replace Obamacare. The GOP-led Senate had taken none. Oddly, Trump was calling the GOP's Obamacare bluff.

Ryan and McConnell had planned to hold a straight repeal vote in early January—preferably before Inauguration Day to fulfill years of GOP hostility to Obamacare and usher in the Trump presidency with one promise already kept. With repeal on Trump's desk, Republicans contemplated a series of listening tours around the country and a lengthy process to replace Obamacare. How long would Republicans have spent cogitating on Obamacare replacement? That's a hard answer to come by as it never got that far and therefore was never tested. The soonest would have been August 2017 and they could easily have continued discussing it beyond the 2018 midterms.

Trump's "simultaneously" edict jostled matters considerably for Ryan. When his leadership team asked for an internal vote count on repeal-*and*-replace legislation, 50 to 60 votes that had been there for a simple repeal bill simply vanished. Republicans were not prepared, at that moment, to commit to replacement legislation that had not been drafted. In sum, House Republicans were united in repeal and splintered on replace. In the Senate, McConnell begged Trump for a straight repeal strategy. He had the votes for that. Repeal-and-replace, McConnell correctly sensed, would be next to impossible because the Senate had never seriously considered taking up the task. A bill to replace Obamacare would have to be written from scratch. And that drafting process, McConnell feared, would occur against a backdrop of conservative activists, reporters and (yikes!) voters asking what was happening, who would be affected and which states might lose the most coverage. That is precisely what happened. McConnell and Ryan both lost the repeal-only fight and from then on chased a repeal-and-replace unicorn.

While they chased, Trump urged them on via Twitter, providing almost weekly commentary on the Senate legislative gyrations, his sense of anxiety seemingly building with each tweet. It began on May 31: "Hopefully Republican Senators, good people all, can quickly get together and pass a new (repeal & replace) HEALTHCARE bill. Add Saved $'s." The tweet conveyed Trump's realization the Senate would draft something new. The method used would be key to the outcome.

You could almost hear the clattering of the Wild Ride rails. Down in defeat in March, up in victory in April, swerving to oblivion in May. Someone had to declare last rites on the process and it might as well have been McCain—a lawmaker known for his cranky independence, hot temper and iconoclastic interpretation of partisan loyalty. When McCain delivered the lethal blow, repeal-and-replace was ailing but still alive. In the immediate aftermath, McCain's gasp-inducing "No" vote was viewed as revenge against Trump for their many clashes over policy and Trump's July 2015 ("I like people who weren't captured") insult of McCain's five and a half years of Vietnam POW captivity. Based on my numerous conversations with those directly involved, whatever animosity that existed between McCain and Trump played a miniscule role. As it was described to me, the motives and animosities were apportioned in thirds: one-third Trump, one-third process and one-third McConnell. In truth, that would make the ratio one-third Trump and two-thirds McConnell because McConnell, the Majority Leader, ran the entire legislative process that produced the bill McCain blew up.

I spent many years covering the U.S. Senate and I can tell you, though it may not be patently obvious, that the legislative process means a great deal to each senator. In the House, the majority party runs the committees and the floor schedule and once bills reach the floor they are voted on and debated under rules determined entirely by the majority party. In the Senate, there is more flexibility and more room for innovation, especially as bills move through committee and to the Senate floor. Yes, the majority party decides the size of the various committees of jurisdiction. But the unique power each senator possesses, to hold up legislation through a filibuster, or to deny simple motions to move the process along, forces even those who run the committees to heed minority party objections if they want to produce a bill that can pass. This dynamic governs all legislation in the Senate. It was particularly important when it came to McCain and repeal-and-replace.

McConnell refused to send the House bill, the one Trump praised with such gusto, to either of the relevant committees. McConnell decided the House bill could not pass the Senate and could not even make it through a committee review process because the Finance and HELP (Health, Education, Labor and Pensions) committees would not be able to rewrite the bill in a way McConnell could be sure would win floor passage. McConnell simply had no faith that his Republican Senate colleagues could handle the delicate political and policy task under the rules of regular order. So, he subverted the process by creating an ad hoc committee of 13 Republicans to draft a bill in private. Under this approach, there would be public hearings and no committee amendment votes and no committee votes to move the bill to the floor. While not unprecedented, this approach was inconsistent with McConnell's pledge to revive regular order in the Senate—that being defined as an open legislative process in which committees would in fact hold hearings, draft a bill, allow amendments and hold a final vote expressing the will of all committee members.

When Senate Democrats passed Obamacare, they did much of this work in public on the first version of the legislation. In the end, Democrats produced their version of Obamacare in a secretive leadership-driven drafting process that doled out last-minute legislative goodies (see, Kickback, Cornhusker; and Purchase, Louisiana). By the time Senate Democrats voted on final passage, a special election loss in Massachusetts cut their effective majority from 60 seats to 59 and that, they said, forced them to use the budget reconciliation and its 51-vote simple majority glide path. These final two steps infuriated Republicans, chiefly McConnell, who denounced it as an abandonment of regular order and a shocking application of win-at-all-costs, brass-knuckle legislative maneuvering.

That was then. When McConnell approached his health care task under Trump, he created a process for repealing and replacing Obamacare that was, by any measure, more secretive, and abandoned any pretense of regular order or transparency.

Success or failure of legislation is usually analyzed at the end of the process. In fact, decisions made at the beginning frequently have more to do with victory or defeat than a roll call vote. In the case of health care, McConnell's process reflected the limited options he believed he was left with after Trump demanded a repeal-and-replace approach. He constructed a process that in retrospect may well have been designed to fail. The secrecy wasn't the biggest problem, but it was an irritant. Lawmakers wanted to know where the emerging bill was and what it would contain. Those answers were elusive throughout. The ad hoc committee of 13 initially kept its own counsel and offered few details. That led to demands from other Republicans who wanted to be allowed to participate. Shrewdly, McConnell opened the doors to any who had an interest.

"It was a committee of 52," Tennessee Sen. Bob Corker told me, referring to the number of Senate Republicans at the time.

In Congress, as in life, when everyone is involved no one is in charge. Weekly GOP Senate lunches devolved into spat sessions over replace legislation. Lots of cross talk and no resolution. At 5:37 a.m. on June 30, having been advised of the disarray, Trump tweeted a new recommendation, one that left McConnell positively cold: "If Republican Senators are unable to pass what they are working on now, they should immediately REPEAL, and then REPLACE at a later date!"

That was McConnell's preference all along. Trump had been leaning on Republicans for repeal-and-replace for six straight months. Now, smelling defeat, he reversed course. But it was too late. House Republicans had already taken a repeal-and-replace vote and if the Senate moved a repeal-only bill the House Republicans would own the vote on replacing Obamacare, leaving them vulnerable to charges of reducing access and allowing states to flee from coverage requirements, thereby reducing health care coverage. Republican senators were already invested in McConnell's legislative process, such as it was, and were disinclined to turn back. Trump's overreach was a desperate gamble and made no difference to McConnell's calculations or approach.

If this hyperactive Trump turn displeased McConnell he gave no sign of it. In private, Senate Republicans were seething at the situation and occasionally at one another. Irregular order. Through fits and starts a bill was stitched together. The minor miracle of McConnell's method, strained and secretive as it was, is that it attracted 49 Republican votes.

Trump offered more cheerleading on July 22: "The Republican Senators must step up to the plate and, after 7 years, vote to Repeal and Replace. Next, Tax Reform and Infrastructure. WIN!"

Trump was now, apparently, back on repeal-and-replace. By this time, his vacillations had become white noise. Trump was not driving the process or outcome. He was, in a very real sense, a bystander whose fate would rest in the hands of the key GOP holdout, McCain.

It was never clear how McCain would vote—at least never *absolutely* clear. He was regarded as a likely no, but no one could be positive. Every senator knows how to count. McCain was the 50th vote (Susan Collins of Maine and Lisa Murkowski of Alaska were already out). McCain's opacity gave other Republicans in the "yes" column special protection. If McCain voted no, the bill would die and they *would not be blamed*. McCain, according to more than a dozen Republicans directly involved in the process, might well have been a proxy "no" vote for half a dozen Senate Republicans, taking the heat so they wouldn't have to explain.

Four days before the climactic vote McCain gave a speech on the Senate floor that, many years from now, may be regarded as one of the most important of the Trump era. Unlike his Arizona colleague Jeff Flake, who took after Trump personally as part of an undisguised effort to position himself as the GOP alternative in 2020, McCain spoke of institutional decay.

But that was not the most dramatic part of the speech. The most dramatic part was that McCain was able to give it at all. On July 14, McCain completed what he thought was a routine physical in Phoenix and was driving to his home in Sedona when his cell phone rang. McCain's doctor told him to turn the car around and return to the Mayo Clinic in Scottsdale. Rick Davis, campaign manager for McCain's 2008 campaign and close family friend, related the conversation as explained to him moments later by McCain.

"He said to his doctors, 'I'm almost there. Can't it wait until Monday?'"

McCain asked why he had to come back. "They said, 'We're going to have an operation on you tonight. We found something on the CT scan and we've got to take it out of your head.'"

When McCain went in for his physical, the only complaint he had registered was that he hadn't been able to sleep well lately. He did not complain of pain in his head or over his left eye, where the CT scan detected a mass. McCain turned around and called Davis. Both thought it might be another melanoma, a type of skin cancer McCain had battled for years. As a follow-up, Davis called McCain's doctors and was told it was potentially more serious. Davis, in Los Angeles, called McCain's wife, Cindy, who was in San Diego. Both jumped on flights to Phoenix.

McCain returned to the Mayo Clinic about 5 p.m. and was in surgery about 5:30 p.m. and was out shortly after 11 p.m. Mayo put its top neurological surgery team together in the time it took McCain to drive back from Sedona.

In the procedure, a small hole was drilled over McCain's eye. A tumor was extracted. It was about the size of an adult man's thumb. It appeared the tumor had bled before, a worrisome sign. The surgeon folded back the layers of skin and stitched them in a kind of ragged, cross-hatch method that he had found healed better and looked less frightening. McCain awoke the next morning about 7:30 a.m. and was able to say his name, remember what day it was (highly unusual after this surgery) and ask for food because he was hungry. Impressed, hospital staff released McCain at 3 p.m. that Saturday afternoon.

On Wednesday, McCain's doctors asked to meet with him in person and delivered the news—glioblastoma, a deadly form of brain cancer, had been confirmed. It was the same cancerous brain tumor that killed Sen. Edward M. Kennedy, a close friend of McCain's despite their partisan differences, in 2009. Though the tumor had been removed, glioblastoma tumors left strands of cancer cells behind that could not be detected and that often grew into separate tumors. McCain wanted to return to Washington. He was warned that flying so soon after brain surgery could be dangerous. He briefly discussed driving to Washington in an RV. Eventually, it was determined rest was best and that when he returned to the Senate it would be to deliver a speech—an important speech.

In between came two more Trump tweets. Neither referred to McCain, as Trump had been advised, but both spoke to the building drama. July 23: "If Republicans don't Repeal and Replace the disastrous ObamaCare, the repercussions will be far greater than any of them understand." Then, on July 24, the day McCain flew back to Washington: "Republicans have a last chance to do the right thing on Repeal & Replace after years of talking & campaigning on it."

McCain landed in Washington that afternoon and was driven straight to the Capitol. He entered the Senate chamber to a standing ovation, something Davis and others told him to anticipate, but that he doubted would materialize. McCain, 80, stood at his desk and sought recognition immediately after Republicans had (with his help) approved a procedural measure setting the stage for an Obamacare repeal-and-replace vote in mere days. That vote passed 51 to 50, with Vice President Mike Pence presiding to cast the tie-breaking vote. Everyone knew the looming health care vote would be just as tight and that McCain would be the fulcrum.

The senator who had served for 30 years and had a reputation for a quick wit and quicker temper wore a charcoal suit, pale blue shirt and gray silk tie. It all looked very familiar. But McCain's face did not. Below his left eye a yellowish bruise had been touched up with makeup, the flesh there puffy. Over his left eyebrow a scar of reddish brown stitches arched up and then curled downward toward his temple. In the TV-lit Senate amphitheater both looked frightening—as if McCain had been in a bar fight and caught the nasty end of a broken beer bottle. At first, it was hard to concentrate on what McCain was saying. McCain's bearing was the same, his arms gripping the side of the wooden easel upon which all senators place their written speeches. Characteristically, McCain absentmindedly motioned toward the rostrum with his right arm and then appeared to give himself a handshake. This was a tic, informal and sweet. In purely physical terms it said—I'm still kind of nervous after all these years.

McCain cast his eyes as before on the presiding officer, ritually referred to as Mr. President because the vice president is the constitutionally designated president of the body and anyone who takes up that role is addressed as such.

"The senior senator from Arizona is recognized," Pence said to a hushed chamber, gripped in mournful regard for their scarred colleague.

"Mr. President," McCain said, "I've stood in this place many times and addressed as 'president' many presiding officers. I have been so addressed when I have sat in that chair. And that's as close as I will ever be to a presidency."

McCain looked up and smiled broadly as relieved and appreciative laughter rose from the floor. He was not well. But McCain was himself.

"I voted for the motion to proceed to allow debate to continue and amendments to be offered. I will not vote for the bill as it is today. It's a shell of a bill right now. We all know that."

McCain drew out the words "I—Will—Not—Vote—For—This— Bill" as if in verbal Morse code. McCain had not rehearsed the speech beforehand. Davis and others were surprised by McCain's improvisational intensity.

"I have changes urged by my state's governor that will have to be included to earn my support for final passage of any bill. I know many of you will have to see the bill changed substantially for you to support it. We've tried to do this by coming up with a proposal behind closed doors in consultation with the administration, then springing it on skeptical members, trying to convince them that it's better than nothing. That it's better than nothing? Asking us to swallow our doubts and force it past a unified opposition. I don't think that's going to work in the end. And probably shouldn't."

With "probably shouldn't" McCain leaned forward over his lectern for emphasis and scowled.

The White House thought McCain was still in play and worked to move him to yes. Four days later, when the vote was hours away, South Carolina Sen. Lindsey Graham, McCain's best friend in the Senate, acted as a shuttle diplomat with McConnell and Ryan. The question was always simple: What does McCain want? The answer drifted through the day but finally landed on a simple process question. If the Senate passes its bill, will the House accept it without changes? Ryan knew he would have to massage the bill at some level with conservatives. But McCain wanted the House-Senate conference committee to enlarge the Senate bill and nullify some of the most conservative elements of the House bill. McCain wanted a public commitment for a full-fledged conference committee where, essentially, the bill could be rewritten more to his liking. At a press conference that afternoon, McCain asked for a statement from Ryan, which was produced about two hours later.

Hours passed and as Senate debate approached midnight, McCain was still publicly uncommitted. But Priebus thought victory was in sight.

"I thought it was done," Priebus told me. "I thought McCain was a yes at midnight."

McConnell's office did not believe McCain was a yes. Neither did Trump's legislative team—though it tried everything to turn McCain around.

Months later, Priebus still said he thought McCain would be a yes vote. He sounded like he believed it. The wound he suffered was harmful. Conspicuous losses with Trump typically were.

At 11 p.m. reporters spotted McCain and asked him if he had made up his mind.

"Yes," he said. "Wait for the show."

McCain entered the Senate about midnight and spoke to Senate Minority Leader Chuck Schumer, whom he had called previously to share the news. When McCain walked away, Schumer smiled. McCain then conferred with Murkoswki and Collins, the two confirmed Republican no votes. At 12:44 a.m. Pence came to McCain's desk. They conferred there for 21 minutes, Pence lobbying the three senators simultaneously. At 1:10 a.m. McCain walked over to Schumer and a clutch of other Democrats—Amy Klobuchar of Minnesota, Elizabeth Warren of Massachusetts, Dianne Feinstein of California and Dick Durbin of Illinois. With reporters peering down from the press gallery above the rostrum, McCain jokingly looked up to the glass ceiling and said "No." The Democrats laughed. Feinstein offered a hug.

At about 1:20 a.m. Pence motioned for McCain to come off the Senate floor and into his ceremonial office. The president was calling on the hardline phone on Pence's desk and wanted to speak to McCain. The call was cordial but inconclusive. It lasted only a few moments. According to Davis, Trump said the vote was important and asked for McCain's help. No threats were issued, no harsh words exchanged.

"He wasn't getting his arm twisted," Davis said. "There was no 'I'll fuck you.' No [Lyndon] Johnson kind of stuff."

McCain thanked Trump but told him "No."

"He didn't even consider the administration position at all," Davis said. "It wasn't Trump's bill. It was Mitch's bill. If McCain had a problem, he had a problem with Mitch."

What McCain wanted was an open process and a different bill than McConnell's process produced. Four days earlier, McCain warned McConnell he would oppose it. And McConnell brought the same bill back to McCain.

"They just said this is the way we are doing it," Davis said. "That was loud and clear. The White House just got in the way. It was like a drive-by shooting for them."

McCain walked toward the rostrum and stopped feet away from McConnell. His glance was into the expectant eyes of Democratic senators staring right back at him. Before McCain gestured, Vermont Sen. Bernie Sanders, seated next to New Hampshire Sen. Jeanne Shaheen, tapped Shaheen's arm as if to say *something big is about to happen*. At 1:29 a.m. McCain raised his right arm out straight. It hung there with McCain's four outstretched fingers, seeking recognition from the clerk. "Mr. Peters," the clerk read, referring to Gary Peters, the junior senator from Michigan who had never been this close to history in his political life. The clerk looked at McCain and did not speak his name, as is customary. McCain clenched his hand into a fist and voted "no." Another bit of protocol was skipped when McCain's no vote was not read aloud. Normally, the clerk would say "Mr. McCain . . . Mr. McCain . . . No."

But there was a gasp. Few things in politics are truly unexpected. And even though Democrats *sensed* McCain would vote no, it wasn't real until it happened. When it did, even the cynics had their breath taken away.

Gasp!

Warren clapped her hands at her desk. Feinstein gave one cracking hand clap. Ohio Democrat Sherrod Brown slammed his desk exultantly. Schumer turned and waved his right arm twice to silence the gloating.

In a gasp-inducing presidency like Trump's, McCain may have won the battle of gasps.

Trump's Twitter feed never blamed McCain. From late July to late August, Trump's fury with McConnell grew as the realization sunk in that the effort might not have been as strenuous or genuine as Trump imagined or hoped.

July 29—"Unless the Republican Senators are total quitters, Repeal & Replace is not dead! Demand another vote before voting on any other bill!"

July 30—"Don't give up Republican Senators, the World is watching: Repeal & Replace . . . and go to 51 votes [nuke option], get Cross State Lines & more."

Trump by this time was driven to distraction by the Senate's 60-vote requirement to pass most substantive legislation. Throughout his first year, Trump hectored McConnell to abandon the legislative filibuster and pass all legislation with a simple 51-vote majority. Trump referred to it as the "nuke option" because it is the legislative equivalent of blowing up the Senate's role as the guardian of minority party rights. The House is structured to pass legislation on a simple majority basis. The Senate is designed to empower the minority party by giving it wide discretion to offer floor amendments and use procedural tactics to require a 60-vote majority. If the majority party has 60 votes, it can rule with an iron hand, as Senate Democrats did during Obama's first year in office. If the majority party has fewer than 60 votes, it must accommodate the minority party. In this era of entrenched partisanship, the minority party tends to stick together. That requires the majority party to bend considerably or fall short of 60 votes. Trump, as he said, found this process "arcane" and maddening. He wanted results. Balance-of-power issues, congressional customs and the maintenance of two distinct legislative bodies meant far less to him than being deprived of victories. McConnell adamantly opposed Trump on the question of abolishing the legislative filibuster.

On August 7, while in Kentucky for the August recess, McConnell gently lowered the boom on Trump. "I won't ask for a show of hands, but I know everyone is saying you've been there and haven't done anything," McConnell said to the Florence, Kentucky, Rotary Club. "Which, I find, extremely irritating. And I'm going to tell you why. Now, our president has, of course, not been in this line of work before and I think he had excessive expectations about how quickly things happen in the democratic process. Part of the reason, I think, people feel like we're underperforming is because too many artificial deadlines unrelated to the reality and the complexity of legislating may not have been fully understood."

That sent Trump through the roof and through August his animosity toward McConnell took Twitter flight.

August 9—"Senator Mitch McConnell said I had 'excessive expectations,' but I don't think so. After hearing 7 years of Repeal & Replace why not done?"

August 10—"Mitch, get back to work and put Repeal & Replace, Tax Reform & Cuts and a great Infrastructure Bill on my desk for signing. You can do it!"

And August 24—"The only problem I have with Mitch McConnell is that, after hearing Repeal & Replace for 7 years, he failed! That should NEVER have happened!"

While Trump and McConnell sparred publicly, efforts were being made to prepare for the next battle, the defining legislative accomplishment of Trump's first year—tax reform. When that celebration came it was as if the failure to repeal-and-replace Obamacare NEVER happened.

TEN

Race

The first week of the Trump presidency began with the travel ban. The last two weeks of his first year were defined, at least in part, by the supposed shitholery of Haiti, El Salvador and unspecified parts of Africa. Midway through 2018 the White House found itself engulfed in a crisis of its own creation, the separation of families stopped at the border under its "zero tolerance" policy of prosecuting all undocumented border crossers. Trump warned that illegals would "infest" America if not stopped.

Each episode carried unmistakable and, for some, haunting racial overtones that exemplified racism. Because the Trump effect on American life is to provoke out-sized and at times outrageous counter-reactions, liberals, amid the family separation debate, found themselves cheering when White House officials were denied service at a restaurant or hounded out of restaurants where they had been seated. Wait a minute. Could that be true? Did that happen? The spirit of liberalism that fought to protect the rights of African Americans at lunch counters in the Deep South during the civil rights movement found itself so unhinged by Trump that denying someone a meal was justified simply because the person worked for him? In the tense days when debate over family separations burned hottest, some activists publicized the phone numbers and addresses of Homeland Security employees. Some were shouted down in public. Homeland Security sent out a memo warning employees not to wear their badges in public, discuss their work or participate in social media forums—lest they risk their personal safety. A strange, morally righteous vengeance hung in the air, one seemingly indifferent to the spirit of acceptance, diversity of opinion and inclusion from which it supposedly sprang.

To put it bluntly, assessing the question of race, racism, hostility, indignation, offensiveness and intent in the Trump era, on many sides, is difficult. Where Trump is concerned the irrational can seem rational. That does not make it so. But it feels that way in a culture where feelings carry an equal or greater weight than thought—and who better illustrates that than Trump?—and where sentiments about race, racism and Trump's influence on this ongoing debate are pronounced, piercing and, alas, unresolved.

Is Trump a racist? No one can know but Trump. People close to him deny it vehemently. The allegation has been leveled frequently. It is a topic of active discussion and that, by itself, is a stark contrast to decades of American commentary, on TV or around the dinner table, about the presidency. Of course, for a sizable portion of the nation's history, the question never came up because the power structure did not consider it relevant. President Woodrow Wilson, for generations a hero of progressives, has had his actions on racial matters assailed only relatively recently. Safe to say there has never been as active a debate over the alleged racism of a sitting president in the post–civil rights era. That places Trump in a unique space. Is he a throwback or an active foe of modernity when it comes to race? Could he be both, neither of which is necessarily morally racist but is nevertheless hostile to the evolution in race relations symbolized by Bill Clinton, America's "first black president," and realized by President Obama? By the middle of 2018, prominent Republicans, albeit mostly in private, began to fret about Trump's influence on the Party of Lincoln and the racial hostility apparent in some sectors of support for Trump's immigration agenda. George Will, a prominent conservative columnist, urged voters to reject Republicans in the midterms. "In today's GOP, which is the president's plaything, he *is* the mainstream," Will wrote on June 22, 2018. "So, to vote against his party's cowering congressional caucuses is to affirm the nation's honor while quarantining him." Longtime GOP strategist Steve Schmidt, a veteran of the George W. Bush White House and senior strategist of McCain's 2008 presidential campaign, quit the party in disgust over Trump's "evil" immigration policies. On his Twitter feed, Schmidt called for the "absolute and utter repudiation" of Trump and his "vile enablers" during the midterms. On July 4, conservative author and columnist Max Boot wrote this warning to "any Republican with a glimmer of conscience": "You used to belong to a conservative party with a white-nationalist fringe. Now it's a white-nationalist party with a conservative fringe."

The events mentioned above—the travel ban, the "shithole" comment and family separation—had distinct and searing racial overtones, raising questions about Trump's attitudes toward immigrants and people of color as well as about the attitudes of those aggrieved by Trump. Trump was at the center of this storm, and he at times appeared to relish his role as a provocateur reshaping or making louder and more contested seemingly settled approaches to racial sensitivity, inclusion and civility. In between the travel ban and the "shithole" comment of 2017 came the late-summer storm spawned by Trump's unwillingness to find more fault with torch-carrying white nationalists than he found with hard-left counterprotesters. Early in the fall of 2017, Trump said NFL owners should fire any "son of a bitch" player who knelt during the national anthem to protest racial injustice. Throughout the year, Trump touted economic and stock market gains as his gift to African American and Hispanic workers, leaving the impression that what he cared about most was their economic destiny and not their racial sensitivities.

At the Justice Department, Trump scaled back civil rights enforcement. At the Department of Housing and Urban Development he allowed tighter restrictions on access to subsidized housing. He backed efforts in Congress and at the Department of Health and Human Services to scale back food stamps. These were not definitionally race-based decisions, but the consequences stood to disproportionately fall on people of color. Those close to Trump would bristle at allegations of racial hostility. Trump, they would say, was not against people of color as much as he was against handouts, subsidies and welfare. It was, however, nearly impossible to find the same hostility toward corporate welfare, tax subsidies for wealthy hedge fund managers, profitable drug companies or industries that benefited from Trump's regulatory relief.

When it came to race, Trump raised more questions with deeper meaning and ramifications than he did on almost any other topic—and did so precisely when the country thought it had achieved or at least begun to enter a new era of tolerance, inclusion and insight. It's not just that Trump's rhetoric was insensitive or abrasive or that it did violence to the 21st-century ethic of racial sensitivity; it's not even that Trump's "America First" slogan carried historical echoes of anti-Semitism and isolation. What marked Trump's approach to race was that it gave off the appearance that race played a role in judgments he made about immigration, housing, welfare and civil rights policy. Trump's approach to immigration is unquestionably more nationalist and inclined toward white European favoritism than any other president's in at least two generations. As it did during the campaign and the first year of Trump's presidency, "America First" and similar statements in relation to race subconsciously spoke to a cultural and nostalgic yearning for an earlier, whiter America.

At a White House dinner on September 25, Trump was joined by a small group of conservative leaders, including Ed Feulner of The Heritage Foundation, Leonard Leo of the Federalist Society, Marjorie Dannenfelser of the Susan B. Anthony List, Tim Phillips of Americans for Prosperity, as well as Conway and Short. At one point, Trump mentioned his speech the Friday before in Huntsville, Alabama, for Luther Strange, the appointed Republican successor to Attorney General Jeff Sessions. Strange was locked in a bruising primary fight with former State Supreme Court Justice Roy Moore and Trump held a rafter-raising rally for Strange to boost his campaign. The NFL season was less than a month old and some African American players had begun to kneel during the national anthem. It was a silent act of protest against many things: excessive police force, racial discrimination generally and what appeared to be the league's punishment of Colin Kaepernick, a former star quarterback who could not land on an NFL roster, players assumed, because he had started the anthem-kneel movement the season before. Kneeling had become a small on-field distraction but not a national or even league-wide issue. Until Trump jumped in with both boots.

"Wouldn't you love to see one of these NFL owners, when somebody disrespects our flag, to say 'Get that son of a bitch off the field, right now. Out. He's fired. He's fired'" Trump roared. At Trump's last mention of "fired," his voice turned hoarse for just a moment as the crowd chanted USA, USA, USA. "You know, some owner is going to do that. He's gonna say that guy that disrespects our flag, he's fired. And that owner . . . they'll be the most popular person in this country. Because that is a total disrespect of our heritage, that is a total disrespect of everything that we stand for. Okay? Everything that we stand for. And I know we have freedoms and we have freedom of choice and many, many different freedoms. But you know what? It's still totally disrespectful."

The outburst drove political and sports coverage through the weekend and made the anthem protests a searing issue for the NFL owners, the players unions, sportscasters and fans. As was so often the case in his first year, Trump saw an opening and exploited it. He made the anthem protests a national topic and largely succeeded in reducing the complex underlying issues into a referendum on patriotism, loyalty—and, none-too-subtly, race. In that same speech, Trump said the NFL game had become too soft (a point he frequently made about America as a country). "Because you know, today, if you hit too hard, right, they hit too hard, 15 yards, throw him out of the game. They're ruining the game." Trump also spoke to so-called Alabama values, which he did not define. In the context of his earlier remarks about kneeling NFL players, that values reference, for some, carried racial overtones. "I understand the people of Alabama. I feel like I am from Alabama, frankly. Isn't it a little weird when a guy who lives on Fifth Avenue in the most beautiful apartment you've ever seen comes down to Alabama and Alabama loves that guy, I mean, it's crazy, it's crazy. But I do understand your values, I love your values and those are the values that I believe in. Those are the values that made this country great."

At the dinner with his conservative friends, Trump asked if anyone had seen his anthem remarks in Alabama. "Did you guys like that?" Many said they did. Trump then explained his gambit. "It worked. I'm going to double down on it. I tried the cultural heritage stuff. Didn't work. But this worked." The "cultural heritage stuff" was Trump's reference to his defense of Confederate statues and Confederate history as part of the struggle that led to the clashes and a death weeks before in Charlottesville, Virginia. Trump did, as he promised, "double down" on the national anthem protests, drawing the ire of NFL players as well as NBA superstar Stephen Curry, who said the night of Trump's Alabama speech that he would not attend the White House ceremony to honor the Golden State Warriors' NBA championship. Trump took to Twitter the next day: "Going to the White House is considered a great honor for a championship team. Stephen Curry is hesitating, therefore invitation is withdrawn." That prompted LeBron James, the NBA's biggest star, to call Trump a "bum" and say that "going to White House was a great honor until you showed up!"

And so it went as Trump continued to denounce anthem protests; professional athletes, the vast majority of them African American, stood up to defend the kneeling as a form of free expression and a constitutional right. Trump ignored questions of the freedom to protest, racial injustice, police brutality or any other related issue and turned the question into one of national respect. If you respected the country, you stood. If you disrespected the country, you knelt. His critics said that protesting over economic, racial or sexual injustice had a long and important history in America, longer in fact than standing at sporting events for the anthem, a practice that began for baseball at the 1918 World Series and at NFL games after World War II. In so many words, Trump said, sure, but not at work and not while ticket-buying customers, many of them white, don't want to be bothered by controversy. In the NFL protests, Trump found a way to drive a starkly simplistic, nationalistic message into the mainstream in a way he could not after Charlottesville. And it pleased him greatly.

After white supremacists clashed with counterprotesters in the city Thomas Jefferson once called home, Trump delivered remarks that reflected his own sense of justice when it came to apportioning blame. "We condemn in the strongest possible terms this egregious display of hatred, bigotry and violence, on many sides. On many sides. It's been going on for a long time in our country. Not Donald Trump, not Barack Obama. This has been going on for a long, long time." The reference to "many sides" shielded white supremacists from specific presidential condemnation. Trump said all violence is bad, a self-evident truth. But Trump intentionally refused to blame white supremacists. By the time of his remarks, Trump knew the "Unite the Right" rally had featured torch-carrying marchers who gave the Nazi salute, yelled "Sieg Heil" and used slogans like "Jews will not replace us," "White Lives Matter" and "One people, one nation, end immigration" as well as the anti-Semitic and racist Nazi chant "Blood and soil." Eyewitnesses reported hearing supremacists shout "Fuck you, faggots" at counterprotesters and use the N-word. But to listen to Trump in the immediate aftermath of this appalling fascist spectacle, you might have been led to believe counterprotesters had clashed violently with someone other than the white supremacists they specifically rallied to oppose.

In late August 2017, Politico was the first to report that Trump's own Department of Homeland Security sent a written warning to Charlottesville and Virginia State Police three days before the August 12 "Unite the Right" rally that white supremacists and anti-fascist Antifa forces were poised to do battle in what could make the clash "among the most violent to date." The August 9 memo was written by the Office of Intelligence and Analysis within the Department of Homeland Security. It read in part: "Anarchist extremists and white supremacist extremists alike online are calling on supporters to be prepared for or to instigate violence at the 12 August rally." This memo provided the basis for Trump's "many sides" response.

Charlottesville created genuine tension within the administration. Mnuchin, Cohn, Tillerson and others wondered if they could continue to work for someone who appeared to give such wide latitude to anti-Semitism and bigotry, someone who appeared to believe Antifa was as dangerous as the white nationalist movement attaching itself to the Trumpian cause. Mnuchin issued a public explanation. Tillerson refused to defend Trump. Cohn blasted Trump in public. Trump's tone deafness to Charlottesville's symbolism was consistent with and welled up from the underlying assumptions of his first travel ban executive order: for example, aliens are bad, whites are good and nationalists who dislike or demonize Muslims as terrorists—or both—are simply misunderstood.

During the campaign, Trump tolerated white nationalists' support and gave them a visibility and credibility no national candidate had since George Wallace in 1968. When pressed, Trump would attempt to distance himself, but did so with an unmistakable tepidness that gave haters reason to believe that, in his heart, Trump was with them—or at least wasn't going to call them out or banish them. It was the closest this fringe element had been to political legitimacy and power, again, since Wallace. Part and parcel of this was Trump's denunciation of "political correctness," by which he meant a growing cultural hostility and "safe space" aversion to the kind of sendup satire bigotry voiced by blue-collar patriarch Archie Bunker in the 1970s hit sitcom *All in the Family.* Trump identified with and spoke plainly to the pathos of blue-collar life, its barstool common sense, its "America, love it or leave it" lingo and its embedded, 1950s-era hostility to racial mixing, homosexuality and secularism. Trump placed most white nationalists into this category, considering them far less dangerous than liberal critics alleged and picked on by the forces of modernity that Trump distrusted and disliked. Bannon and others fed Trump's hostility to the cultural left, leading him to conflate academics and activists with Antifa, the violent, anti-free-speech fringe group on the left.

When violence erupted in Charlottesville, Trump saw counterprotesters as tools of Antifa, a more malevolent force, in his mind, than apprentice Archie Bunkers in Dockers with hardware-store tiki torches. Trump also fundamentally agreed with the purpose of the white nationalists' protest—blocking removal of a statue honoring Confederate Gen. Robert E. Lee. Trump wanted to preserve this and other Confederate statues, he said, to protect the nation's "history and culture." Trump doesn't know much about the Civil War, but saw aggrieved southerners and white nationalists who wanted to protect the statues as victims of leftist overreach and antiwhite purification. Trump did not see removal of Confederate statues as a remedy to racial grievance or a removal of hateful symbolism, but as an ad hominem attack on cherished southern "heritage"—a segregation-era code word Trump unfurled in common cause with white nationalist sensibilities.

On August 15, in the lobby of Trump Tower, the president held a memorably contentious press conference as top administration officials, there to discuss infrastructure issues, stood in paralyzed shock. Stung by criticism from Republicans and business leaders, Trump was defensive and feisty. He tried to rebuild his reputation by recasting the conversation about race as one defined by economics (not rhetoric) and the conversation about white supremacy as one defined by quiet southerners (not bigots, anti-Semites or thugs) who just wanted to keep a statue of a revered Confederate general.

A reporter asked Trump about Doug McMillon, CEO of Walmart, who had criticized Trump for not "unequivocally rejecting the appalling actions of white supremacists." McMillon had also said that Trump "missed a critical opportunity to help bring our country together."

Trump was asked if he had, in fact, missed such an opportunity.

"Not at all. I think the country—look, you take a look. I've created over 1 million jobs since I have been president. The country is booming. The stock market is setting records. We have the highest employment numbers we have ever had in the history of our country. So the head of Walmart, who I know, a very nice guy, was making a political statement."

Trump was asked if he had worsened race relations. Again, he answered in economic terms.

"I believe that the fact that I brought in, it will be soon, millions of jobs, you see where companies are moving back into our country. I think that's going to have a tremendous positive impact on race relations. You know why? It is jobs. What people want now, they want jobs. They want great jobs with good pay. When they have that, you watch how race relations will be."

Taken at face value, Trump argued that a country is happier when it is prosperous. His answer to questions about racial sensitivity then and ever since can be summarized as follows: Forget being sensitive or making "political statements," I am focused on job creation and nothing else. In conversations with those close to Trump, the impression you are left with is that Trump considers most of the "race" conversation beside the point and that he is fatalistic about his ability to shape it or solve it.

"They have been frayed for a long time," Trump said of race relations. "You can ask President Obama about that. He would make speeches about it."

Trump also harbored a sensitivity to aggrieved whites that permeated his "many sides" defense. Trump believed he had sufficiently denounced the white supremacists and the driver of the car that killed counterprotester Heather Heyer (when he called him "a murderer").

But Trump did not want those who rallied to keep the Lee statue in Charlottesville to be tarred, if you will, with the same brush as the chanting fascists. To Trump, it did not matter if those loyal to Lee's statue could have chosen to march without repugnant company. Trump made sure he reached down into the recesses of that crowd and said "I see you. It's okay. I will protect you." It was part of Trump's "forgotten men and women" motif.

"If you reported it accurately, you would say that the neo-Nazis started this thing," Trump said as he continued to do battle with White House reporters in the Trump Tower lobby. "They showed up in Charlottesville. Excuse me. They didn't put themselves down as neo-Nazis. You had some very bad people in that group. You also had some very fine people on both sides. You had people in that group that were there to protest the taking down of, to them, a very, very important statue and the renaming of a park from Robert E. Lee to another name."

Trump wanted to identify with sympathies toward Lee as a general and not necessarily a warrior for slavery. Trump lacked the capacity to make a nuanced argument but did arrive armed with the names of founding fathers who, viewed through the same lens, would fail the slavery test being applied to Lee's statue. It was an "Alabama values" argument through and through.

"Was George Washington a slave owner?" Trump asked tauntingly. "So will George Washington now lose his status? Are we going to take down—excuse me! Are we going to take down statues to George Washington? How about Thomas Jefferson? What do you think of Thomas Jefferson? You like him. Good. Are we going to take down his statue? He was a major slave owner. Are we going to take down his statue? It is fine. You are changing history and culture." It sounded like something Archie could have said while perched on a barstool inside Kelsey's Bar.

To Trump that history and culture was and is worth preserving, even if in the retelling that history has been, in the main, a celebration of white, protestant Christian dominance of America and, until recently, has sanitized (others have said whitewashed) the institutionalized racial brutality visited upon African Americans and Native Americans.

That question of cultural preservation arose amid a racial flashpoint for Trump's first year—the "shithole countries" saga. As a quick refresher, Trump was accused of describing Haiti, El Salvador and un-specified parts of Africa as "shithole countries" during an Oval Office negotiation session on immigration with a bipartisan group of sena-tors. Trump was quoted saying "shithole" on January 11, the birthday of immigrant and founding father Alexander Hamilton. This happened to be the day before the eighth anniversary of the Haiti earthquake. It was also the day before Trump would sign a proclamation honoring Martin Luther King Jr. and then-Secretary of State Rex Tillerson was to deliver a speech to Department of State employees on . . . wait for it . . . the importance of "respect and diversity."

At the very same "shithole" meeting, Trump asked lawmakers why America took so many immigrants from less-developed countries in-stead of places such as, well, Norway. It is often said even by people who admire Trump that the last voice he hears is often the most per-suasive. The day before he had welcomed Norwegian Prime Minister Erna Solberg to the White House. The proximity to Trump's question about immigration patterns mattered because Solberg was one of the most Trump-like politicians in Europe, leading her conservative party to reelection two months before Trump's stunning 2016 victory. In her campaign, Solberg criticized immigration flows in Europe and cut taxes. Trump likes allies. Wherever he can find them. When he asked lawmakers about why America didn't allow more immigration from places like, say, Norway (population 5.3 million and predominantly white) it is quite probable he meant more people like Solberg. That white preference—or should we say the privilege of white-preferential language—was one of the discordant, repetitive notes of Trump's first year in office. It continued unhesitatingly into 2018.

It must be noted that as the "shithole" controversy raged, some White House aides began to whisper that Trump actually said "shit-house" instead of "shithole"—as if there were a qualitative difference between "hole" or "house" as modified by "shit." "House" or "hole," the question that began to be asked on editorial pages and street corners in the developed world was, in effect: Is the shithole Haiti, El Salva-dor, countries in Africa or *the occupant of the Oval Office*? The "shit-hole" question was, then, as functional as it was metaphorical. It also spoke to one of the most consequential aspects of the Trump presi-dency—its coarsening influence on political dialogue and its effect on our national ability to discuss and communicate about the vital issue of race. Before we go any further, we must acknowledge the accusation that an American president described Haiti, El Salvador and all of Africa as a "shithole" would have for weeks paralyzed any previous modern presidency—subjecting it to widespread criticism, party defections, voter outrage and international condemnation. Some of that was visited upon Trump, but in muted forms, because the revelation seemed, oddly, neither unexpected nor out of place . . . for Trump. That is original and important. And quite possibly worrisome.

On the eve of the one-year anniversary of his inauguration, Trump was facing the prospect of a government shutdown. His relationship with congressional Democrats was so frayed he could parlay no compromise—in part because of his immigration-fueled expletive the week before. Amidst this, Trump planned to fly to Mar-a-Lago on his one-year anniversary eve to toast himself at an anniversary fundraiser. Instead, he hunkered in the Oval Office and invited Senate Majority Leader Chuck Schumer to the White House on January 19 to see if he could strike an 11th-hour deal.

The shutdown was a three-day skirmish that illustrated how much Trump has changed politics by using tactics unimaginable just two years earlier. On the shutdown's first day, Trump released an ad for his reelection and its contents must be recorded as confirmation that Trump knows one kind of politics—reductionist politics. The ad used news footage of an illegal immigrant accused of murdering two Sacramento police officers in 2014. In court the suspect, Luis Bracamontes, can be heard saying he wished he "killed more of those motherfuckers." The outburst tended to validate concerns raised by Bracamontes's attorneys that he was mentally unfit for trial. The Trump reelection ad described Bracamontes as "pure evil" and said Democrats who refused to fund a border wall would be "complicit" in every future murder committed by "illegal immigrants."

The accusation that Democratic opponents would be "complicit" in murder was a clever redirection of *Saturday Night Live*'s mockery of Trump daughter Ivanka, who, in a satirical commercial, dazzles the elite while wearing a perfume named "Complicit." The Bracamontes ad also conveyed neo-McCarthyite notes of guilt by association. It passed by with barely a whimper of protest. Moreover, it worked. By midday on the shutdown's first workday, January 22, Senate Democrats caved.

The tipping-point issue for the shutdown was a clash over legal status for children brought into the country illegally by their parents, children who have grown to adulthood knowing no other country but America but nevertheless subject, under Trump, to the threat of deportation. Democrats wanted to provide permanent legal status to these so-called Dreamers after Trump ended Obama-era executive (as opposed to legislative) deportation protections. Trump wanted guaranteed border wall funding and changes to legal immigration policy through the Visa lottery system and family reunification rules. These are big issues with a long history and multigenerational political constituencies.

Trump's ad reduced the debate to one accused murderer and conflated every "Dreamer" with criminality and every Democrat who disagreed with Trump with an aider and abettor of murder. Textbook reductionism, its crudity self-evident. It was also radical on the underlying issue of "Dreamers." Trump in the past said he had "great compassion" and wanted to treat them with "love." But Trump got caught between this rhetoric and his base. He offered "Dreamers" permanent legal status by codifying Obama's executive action. Trump's base alleged he was toying with "amnesty." Trump recoiled and boosted his original $1.8 billion ask for the border wall to $25 billion. Democrats and even some Republicans balked. But Trump hewed closely to his base, fearful of decoupling himself from the only part of America relentlessly with him.

"Trump has an adopted base that he is uneasy about," Tennessee Sen. Bob Corker told me. "He's kind of intimidated by them. Every single decision he makes is about the base. He's constantly worried about showing weakness."

Corker and Trump clashed famously during Trump's first year but this sentiment is shared by dozens of Republicans inside and outside the administration and Congress. The presidency is a majoritarian office. Oddly, Trump may be the most operationally quota-oriented president in modern history—with nearly every decision calculated to cater to the roughly one third of the nation that adores him. It doesn't seem possible that an American president could allege that the opposition political party that captured three million more votes than he did in the last election was aiding and abetting murder. But Trump did. And the shutdown was settled largely on his terms.

Ironically, Trump's speeches and tweets in 2017 echoed late 1950s and early 1960s conservative movie demagogues—Andy Griffith's Lonesome Rhodes from *A Face in the Crowd* (1957); Cliff Robertson's Joe Cantwell from *The Best Man* (1964); and Burt Lancaster's Air Force General James Mattoon Scott (who had his own Sean Hannity–like TV ally) in *Seven Days in May* (1964). To watch these movies now is to see parts of Trump shine through the celluloid and crackle across the speakers. The movie demagogues were conservative caricatures created by liberal writers and directors like Gore Vidal, Elia Kazan and Fletcher Knebel. Griffith's character, Lonesome Rhodes, rises from the life of a drifter to TV sensation because of his homespun wit and supposed front-porch common sense. In one scene, Rhodes describes his appeal. "This whole country is like my flock of sheep. Rednecks, crackers, hillbillies, hausfraus, shut-ins, pea-pickers—everybody that's got to jump when somebody else blows the whistle." Rhodes speaks of his ownership of the adoring audience. "They're mine! I own 'em! They think like I do. Only they're even more stupid than I am, so I gotta think for 'em." Another character in the movie, Mel Miller, says of Rhodes, "I'll say one thing for him, he's got the courage of his ignorance." In *The Best Man*, the character William Russell, played by Henry Fonda, responds to a reporter's question about his political rival, Cantwell, and attempts to deal with the charge that he is an intellectual and that Cantwell is closer to the people. "Intellectual? You mean I wrote a book," Russell says. "Well, as Bertrand Russell said, 'people in a democracy tend to think they have less to fear from a stupid man than an intelligent one.' Actually, it's the other way around. It's the stupid man." In *Seven Days in May*, the plot revolves around Gen. Scott's plot to overthrow the government because he opposes a nuclear treaty with the Soviet Union. President Jordan Lyman is played by Fredric March, who disputes an allegation that Gen. Scott and those who agree with him are the "enemy." "The enemy's an age—a nuclear age," President Lyman says. "It happens to have killed man's faith in his ability to influence what happens to him. And out of this comes a sickness, and out of sickness a frustration, a feeling of impotence, helplessness, weakness. And from this, this desperation, we look for a champion in red, white, and blue. Every now and then a man on a white horse rides by, and we appoint him to be our personal god for the duration." President Lyman's "nuclear age" might as well be today's "terrorism age" or "age of digital economic disruption."

Decades later, it is as if, for these liberal doomsayers, the caricature has come to life and the horrors are no longer celluloid but stalking the countryside. The critique of the conservative demagogues asserted they were simplistic, ruthless, dangerous and hypocritical. The left sees all of this and much more in Trump. As to the black-and-white movie demagogues of the 1950s and early 1960s, Trump bears somewhat of a resemblance. When it came to debates over immigration and border security, for example, Trump simplified all choices to us versus them. Racial appeals were less visible in other policy areas. It does not therefore seem a stretch to observe that on one of his most important issues, immigration, Trump popularized, or came to personify, atonal politics—the symphony of a great immigrant nation reduced to one "America First" note repeated with clanging simplicity.

I had heard some of this before. My first presidential campaign was in 1992. I covered Democrats throughout New Hampshire and beyond and then picked up Ross Perot's surprisingly strong third-party bid for the presidency that spring. In New Hampshire, my stops with Democrats brought me within shouting distance of Pat Buchanan's primary challenge to President Bush. Buchanan had a nativist streak to his politics and was a hard-liner on illegal immigration. He was also a cultural warrior who spoke of the American experience as improving upon European political and intellectual traditions—emphasis on European roots.

On February 8, 1992, Buchanan appeared on *Face the Nation*. Asked about Bush's economic program Buchanan said the following: "It's certainly not the long-term strategy to make America first again in manufacturing, industry and business the way we once were." Buchanan called for a freeze in federal hiring and deep cuts in nondefense spending and federal taxes. "We are losing industries like autos and steel. Where is the administration plan to make America first again in manufacturing? All of us see our manufacturing base declining." Buchanan was asked how he could work with Congress. "There is no substitute for a president who will fight. The people are fed up with a professional political class whose main expertise is getting itself returned to office." Buchanan had a word of advice, utterly unsolicited, for the news media. "The American press corps, national press corps, get with it. Our country is in deep trouble."

Sound familiar? Pat Buchanan lost the New Hampshire primary but attracted 37 percent of the protest vote, a stiff rebuke for Bush's presidency and a warning shot from conservatives. That was the high-water mark until Buchanan gave a stem-winder at Bush's renomination convention that petrified suburban Republicans. One of the great questions facing Republicans in the 2018 midterms will be whether suburban Republicans, almost all of whom fell in with Trump in 2016, will recoil and stay home. A complementary question will be if Democratic or independent voters who crossed over for Trump will reconsider. Trump, it could be argued, is Buchanan on racial, economic and nationalist steroids. That he is president alone makes Trump historic, and the aftereffects of his presidency will either become a new norm or the dying gasp of a fading America, its white demography and 1950s-era iconography laid to rest one obituary at a time. For those who would like to believe or already believe that there is or was a demographic destiny that dooms or will doom racial animosity and violence, Trump's travel ban and his comments on the violence in Charlottesville, NFL kneelers and "shithole countries" stirred some of the deepest, most scarring anxieties of his first year in office.

ELEVEN

North Korea

One year after Election Night and it felt like Trump's velocity, recklessness and arrogance were about to topple the enterprise. We were in Seoul, South Korea, and events there and back home signaled what looked like the beginning of a coming apart, a seam-splitting series of seemingly random events, each and in combination an omen that the enterprise could crumble upon itself.

This was not a new experience covering the Trump White House. It felt a bit like that when the White House tried to prove its inauguration crowd was larger than Obama's and the travel ban debuted as a disorganized mess. It felt that way in May when Trump fired Comey and the White House became tangled in its conflicting explanations. It felt that way in August when Trump was still seething over the health care failure, feuding with Senate Majority Leader Mitch McConnell and threatening to unleash nuclear "fire and fury" on North Korea. Even with this history, things felt especially unstable in Seoul. The omens seemed to multiply.

That morning, under a morning sky draped with clouds and fog, Trump had boarded Marine One for what was to have been a surprise visit to the demilitarized zone (DMZ) separating North and South Korea. Cloaked in secrecy as thick as the skies, the mission was to feature a historic hook. Trump would meet South Korean President Moon Jae-in at the DMZ, a first for the two nations. But this ambitious photo op, heavy with symbolism, would soon disappear into the indifferent peninsular vapor. Omen one.

In Washington, Special Counsel Robert Mueller had just interviewed Stephen Miller, top White House domestic policy advisor and, during the campaign, speechwriter and immigration jackhammer. Mueller's Miller interview brought the probe closer to the Oval Office. Hope Hicks, at the time Trump's most trusted communications advisor, was due for questioning after the Asia trip and that would bring Mueller's team even closer. In Asia, Hicks wept at the prospect, fretting over the legal vise each question might represent and the weighty implications of wrong answers—as well as truthful ones. Miller and Hicks represented omens two and three.

The day before, in Virginia, in the nation's only competitive governor's race, a bland Democrat, Ralph Northam, defeated Trump-backed Republican Ed Gillespie by nine points. Gillespie won more votes than any other candidate in Virginia gubernatorial history and was still clobbered. Gillespie would later tell friends: "I have met The Resistance and it is real." Over 500,000 more voters cast ballots for the two major candidates than in 2013, and some post-election surveys revealed that the No. 1 issue driving turnout was opposition to Trump. Omen four.

Meanwhile, in Alabama, the state that hosted Trump's first nationally televised outdoor stadium campaign rally and boasted his only U.S. Senate endorsement (Sessions), nasty news had sprung up about the surprise GOP nominee vying to replace Sessions. Serious and credible allegations of sexual misconduct and misjudgments involving teenage girls in the 1970s surfaced against Roy Moore. ("Serious and credible" is what Senate Republicans called the charges.) In Asia, Trump murmured that he hadn't heard much about the Moore story. Trump's hesitancy spoke volumes about the new moral compass of a party with a history of advertising its values, accountability and maturity. Omen five.

Amid these portents of doom Trump tried to find Moon in the fog.

The mission had all the hallmarks of Trump bravado, for it was designed to surprise traveling reporters, thereby garnering maximum publicity. It was also built to paper over serious differences in style and policy about confronting the North. Moon, the newly elected center-left president, was eager to dialogue with Kim, skeptical of Trump's bluster and fearful of increased U.S. muscle flexing. A photo op with Trump at the DMZ would produce an image bigger than the truth, a Trump hallmark if ever there was one. It would also signal unity and shared purpose, as no South Korean president had appeared before with an American president at the DMZ—the feeling being Koreans lived daily with the threat of war and the grief of separation and did not need to pose with an American commander-in-chief to be reminded. Moon wanted to give Trump the photo op and gain his ear on efforts to resolve the conflict with the North rather than destabilize it with Twitter jargon.

Trump had been coy about the possibility of a visit. Pentagon and State Department advisors, including Secretary of State Tillerson, cautioned against it as too provocative, a potential powder keg of our own making.

For anyone who has ever been to the DMZ, as I had been as part of President Obama's 2009 trip to Seoul, the tension is almost unbearable. Forces on both sides—even in that time of comparative calm—were taut, aggressive and tense. It felt as if both sets of national bayonets were pitched at a sharp angle, right beneath each other's throat. Resting uneasily between a craggy, undulating border lay the flimsiest word modern warfare ever invented—"armistice." It means nobody won and everyone is snarling and twitchy-fingered—forever. That's the DMZ. To senior Trump advisors it felt like no place for idle threats or mocking tweets.

Even so, Trump was determined to place his personal machismo on the line and climbed aboard Marine One, eager to achieve a defining image of his first year in office. There was another motive. Trump wanted that picture to ricochet while he flew from Seoul to Beijing, where he would lobby Kim Jong-un's biggest benefactor, Chinese President Xi Jinping, on the biggest ask of his presidency: help me throttle North Korea into denuclearized submission.

While we were in Seoul, this DMZ mission was treated like a state secret. Most reporters, White House staff and South Korean dignitaries were kept in the dark. Only a handful of U.S. reporters were made aware and they were sworn to absolute secrecy. My CBS colleague, Steven Portnoy, was part of the traveling White House press pool (he occupied the seat reserved for radio reporters) and has provided this recollection from his notes.

> The out-of-town travel pool received the following off-the-record email, sent by Sarah Sanders at 11:23 pm local time Tuesday: OFF THE RECORD and not to be shared with anyone not on this chain. Call time tomorrow morning will be at 6:45 and you all will need to gather at 5:45 am. Janet will follow up with additional logistics. Thanks and see y'all in the morning.

That was Portnoy's first inkling something unusual was being added to Trump's schedule. In White House parlance, the "call time" is when reporters move with the president. The gather time is when they assemble at an assigned location to have their gear inspected or "swept" by the Secret Service. Under the rules communicated, Portnoy could not alert anyone at CBS about this budding news event. Portnoy and other reporters gathered in the lower level of the Grand Hyatt Hotel in Seoul. The Secret Service, as is custom, checked their phones, cameras, satchels and workday belongings. Press Secretary Sarah Sanders then marched reporters into a cavernous hotel conference room with rows of tables. Portnoy noticed notepads and pens at each seat. He began taking notes.

"What I'm about to tell you is off the record until we return to Seoul, and can't be shared with anyone outside this room," Sanders said. "As you may have guessed, we're going someplace."

Sanders then took out a scrap of paper, unfolded it and raised it so each reporter and photographer could see it. Three scrawled letters spelled out "DMZ."

"This," Sanders said, "is where we're going."

It was clear to Portnoy that Sanders did not want to say the location out loud, prompting him to wonder if the United States feared the conference room in Seoul might be surveilled. About 7 a.m. local time, Portnoy and the other reporters were hustled into prestaged vans deployed at every presidential event to move reporters within the motorcade. The reporters waited inside, unsure what was next. Portnoy noticed the van's windows were left open. Muggy air fogged the windows and soon mosquitos appeared. No one from the White House was in the vans. Just reporters, fog and insects.

At 7:08 a.m., Portnoy looked out the window and saw Trump enter his limousine with Tillerson, McMaster, Kelly, Miller and Sanders in tow. At 7:09 a.m., the motorcade left the hotel and sped through sleepy Seoul streets without sirens. Trump arrived at Yongsang Garrison, the U.S. Army headquarters, at 7:19 a.m. Reporters dashed to two waiting CH-47 Chinook helicopters. Trump walked to Marine One and reporters swiftly lost sight of him.

The helicopter armada carrying Trump in Marine One and reporters, support staff and others in two chase Chinooks lifted off at 7:43 a.m. for what was to be a 15-minute flight to the DMZ. The overcast sky obscured the tops of Seoul's skyscrapers. Portnoy waited for the DMZ descent that never came.

About 20 minutes in, the chopper banked a hard right into more gray nothingness. As a precaution, Portnoy tried to record one story on the flight and its unknown and unknowable outcome—if only for posterity, as this was all beginning to feel unhinged and weird (he later discovered the radio dispatch he tried to record was drowned out by the roar of the helicopter rotors).

Portnoy then noticed an intense conversation between Army personnel, the Secret Service and a White House aide. A cell phone was soon passed around with a text message for each reporter to read, the phone moving one by one down the line of reporters buckled tightly in fold-down seats bolted to the inner hull of the helicopter. The text message said the helos were heading back to Seoul and that the flight would be tried a second time. Portnoy could not believe it. The leader of the free world took off for the DMZ without assurances he could land safely? Who does that? Who takes that kind of risk for a photo? Trump.

Marine One and the other choppers landed back at Yongsan Garrison at 8:08 a.m. The rear door opened. Reporters and photographers spilled out into the grassy field from which they had just taken off. Bleachers were nearby. Marine One and the limousine were positioned about 100 yards beyond the bleachers. Sanders, wearing an Army Ranger's jacket to ward off the cold, admonished reporters they were still under a strict no-news embargo. No calls. No texts. No emails. No communication to anyone.

The chopper pilots, Sanders said, were holding out hope the skies would soon clear. Trump was disappointed but eager to continue, she said. Photographers climbed to the top of the bleachers to shoot Trump's limousine as it idled next to Marine One. They reported some movements every few minutes, but nothing indicating another takeoff. The clouds never parted, the morning sun still a rumor.

As Portnoy recalled, reporters began to discuss the news value of the aborted landing at the DMZ and made a pact not to allow the White House, à la the movie *Men in Black,* to pretend the flight never happened. It didn't come to that. Sanders lifted the embargo when Trump decided to ditch a second attempt. Everyone was stuffed back into waiting vans at 8:55 a.m.

Traveling reporters were at somewhat of a loss as to what to report. Is it a surprise if there is no surprise? Is there a photo op if there is no photo? Is there history with no story? Is there a myth without even so much as a half-truth? It felt as if these questions suffused the entire first year of the Trump presidency, an odd place where they commingled with metaphor and where answers proved elusive.

As Marine One banked away from the grassy landing zone, this sense of something larger at work became inescapable. It wasn't just that fog triumphed over a photo op; it was the nagging notion that perhaps, just perhaps, Trump's tenacity and bluster, his ego and self-glorification were losing their vitality. Legal jeopardy. Political rot. Legislative impotence. All that was left was Trump's mania—the last, inexhaustible commodity. That's how it felt.

That's not how it turned out. In five weeks Trump would sign a bill cutting corporate and individual tax rates, his biggest legislative victory of the year. That bill also opened for oil exploration the Arctic National Wildlife refuge, a goal of congressional Republicans for more than 30 years. The bill also repealed the Obamacare mandate, one of the unmet goals of the repeal-and-replace spectacle. These achievements had appeared unreachable amid missed opportunities in Asia and mounting storm clouds back home. The bill was yet another reminder of Trump's ability to change the rules of the game—and how his indifference to norms yields unexpected results.

This book is due for release in mid-September 2018. By that time, it is very likely that either military conflict will have broken out or direct talks between the United States and North Korea will have commenced with the goal of diffusing the nuclear threat. In mid-June of 2018, after announcing and then canceling a summit with Kim Jong-un, Trump met Kim in Singapore for a five-hour summit that included no fewer than eight on-camera handshakes. Kim gained worldwide stature from the summit. Trump reinforced a reputation for risk-taking and improvisation. Historically, interactions with the North Koreans were confined to lower levels of both governments, with rare exceptions made when agreements neared completion (there have been many, all unfulfilled by the North). Trump trashed that approach and decided to start at the top with Kim. The summit produced global headlines and saw the Trump National Security Council produce what can only be described as a pro-summit propaganda film designed to flatter and seduce Kim into a peace deal with Trump.

In a moment without precedent in my time as a White House correspondent, Trump had the video played—first in Korean and then in English—for reporters awaiting his post-summit press conference. No explanation was provided. The video just rolled as a sappy voice-over spoke of the new destiny Kim and Trump could forge for the world. Trump responds to videos, not words. He assumed Kim would too. Trump told reporters he showed Kim the video on an iPad. The video was pro–North Korea or at least pro-Kim. It was the first such propaganda device ever devoted to the North Korean regime by an American president. At the summit, Kim made no new public promises and disclosed no new information about nuclear weapons, their production or their location. He did not agree to reduce the production of highly enriched uranium or agree to allow inspections of existing stockpiles for the purposes of having them removed. Publicly, Kim conceded nothing new. Trump implied he made deals in private. In the weeks after the summit, no details emerged and no new negotiations were scheduled, even though Trump said they had been agreed to and that U.S. inspectors were ready to arrive in North Korea within weeks. The crisis atmosphere around North Korea felt suddenly calm, not because North Korea disarmed or took initial steps in that direction, but because Trump decided the North was going to disarm. He spoke of the standoff as being "solved" and said he should be hailed for saving "millions of lives." As if watching TV, Trump appeared to have changed the channel from North Korea War to North Korea Peace.

The long-term effect of Trump's made-for-TV summitry is unknowable. Trump seemed inordinately pleased that it happened and less focused on or concerned about what came next. If it sets in motion denuclearization of the North and reunification with South Korea, Trump will have achieved one of the great feats in American diplomacy and could qualify for the Nobel Peace Prize. If the summit fails and suspicions deepen, war may come. If conflict arises, the U.S. military will probably strike first, launching an aerial preemptive attack on nuclear facilities, ballistic missiles, missile launchers and antiaircraft weapons.

Trump warned the world about this possibility in blunt and, to some, hyperbolic terms during his September 19, 2017, address to the United Nations General Assembly, his first as commander-in-chief: "North Korea's reckless pursuit of nuclear weapons and ballistic missiles threatens the entire world with unthinkable loss of human life. The United States has great strength and patience, but if it is forced to defend itself or its allies, we will have no choice but to totally destroy North Korea. Rocket Man is on a suicide mission for himself and for his regime."

Trump's approach to North Korea pivoted off his relationship with China. Well before Election Day, Chinese emissaries tried to develop some insight about a potential Trump presidency. The most direct route, they quickly discovered, was through Kushner. Through former Nixon national security advisor and long-time U.S.–China whisperer Henry Kissinger, the Chinese Ambassador Cui Tiankai met with Kushner in Trump Tower in September and October of 2016.

"The advice that Kissinger gave me was, look, they are all nervous because they don't know what it will be if Trump's there and that's an advantage so don't try to assuage people," Kushner told me. "So just listen and say, look we'll see what happens. Obviously, during the campaign the president had a lot of rhetoric around China which was very tough."

After Trump won, the Chinese requested more meetings and more than before viewed him as a wild card.

"I got together with them and basically I said everywhere I go around the world . . . people are basically playing us against each other and we should be working together," Kushner recalled. "We share very similar macro goals. We want to have as much peace as possible and want to have as much prosperity as possible and so if we can figure out how to work together on these things people can't play us against each other and we can solve a lot of the world's problems."

And yet something was brewing that alarmed the Chinese. World leaders were calling Trump, and the Chinese detected that pro-Taiwan Republicans were laying the groundwork for a call between pro-American Taiwanese President Tsai Ing-wen and the president-elect. Assisted by Bob Dole, the former Senate Majority Leader and 1996 GOP presidential nominee, intermediaries spent days setting up the call, hoping China would view it as a new wrinkle in its relationship with America. No U.S. president had spoken to a Taiwanese leader and no high-level meetings had occurred between the two since President Carter severed diplomatic ties in 1978 (an outgrowth of Nixon's 1972 visit to mainland China that cemented the "One China" policy whereby the United States recognized only the People's Republic of China and not Taiwan, also known as the Republic of China). Tsai won her election in January of 2016. Her Democratic Progressive Party defeated the Kuomintang, which had historically called for closer ties with China.

The absence of formal diplomatic relations obscured the reality that the United States, through the 1979 Taiwan Relations Act, carried out de facto diplomatic relations with the Taiwanese government. What's more, the law required "the United States to make available to Taiwan such defense articles and defense services in such quantity as may be necessary to enable Taiwan to maintain sufficient self-defense capabilities." Under the umbrella of so-called strategic ambiguity, U.S. policy has since then been to make sure Taiwan did not declare independence and China did not invade. Trump wanted to take Tsai's call, describing it as polite but knowing its larger significance—in the Kissinger sense of being unpredictable early and watching what new possibilities might emerge.

"The president thought, you know, he was taking all the calls from the leaders who were calling him and again, with him, he wasn't very bent on protocol and said if they want to call me I'll take the phone call," Kushner recalled. "It's not respectful not to take the phone call. The Chinese called me about eight or nine times that morning before the call saying we heard a rumor this is happening and [that] this would be terrible [and] warning me. So I called the president and I said this is what they are saying. He said, 'Look, I have a scheduled phone call, I'm not going to cancel the call.' Strategically, he had no relationship with China and there's no reason for him not to take a phone call if someone requests a phone call. It is what it is."

The December 2 call, which lasted about 10 minutes, became an instant global sensation and an early litmus test of political/foreign policy interpretations of Trump. Traditionalists in both parties were aghast, seeing it as confirmation Trump was naïve or clumsy—possibly both. Trump conservatives, an emerging breed, were delighted. Dole was neither but was supportive of Trump rattling Beijing's cage and seeing what the reaction would be. China reacted with due speed, asking Kushner to meet with Foreign Minister Wang Yi.

"We had another long meeting where they kind of read their scripts—the sovereignty of China is nonnegotiable, basically very, very hot in that regard," Kushner recalled, saying that meeting and two others with Chinese officials yielded few results. "We weren't getting anywhere. A lot of layers. They do that intentionally so they don't have to make decisions in the moment. I went to the president and said 'This isn't really going anywhere. If we want to have real discussions it seems like their system is going to have to be top down, right, not bottom up.'"

Kushner got Trump's approval to pitch the Chinese on a summit with President Xi.

"The deal I made with them was that we would recognize the One China policy, which really wasn't giving much because you could always backtrack from that, in exchange for President Xi coming down to Mar-a-Lago for a visit. I liked Mar-a-Lago because it was more personal, more casual. Japan had come down to Mar-a-Lago and they [the Chinese] wanted to make sure it was equal to or greater than what happened to Japan. The whole crux of it was to try to create one-on-one time between the two leaders and let them talk through ideas. One thing with the president, obviously, he's very personable. We have a weird dynamic with world leaders. They all love him, they all want to be his friend, all like him in person but they are all nervous where things will go."

Trump and Xi spent about four hours together alone with translators, highly unusual for Chinese leaders who prefer to be surrounded by interlocutors and, as Kushner refers to them, "layers" of bureaucrats. The two leaders talk frequently by phone and Trump's admiration for Xi has sometimes suggested China has regained the upper hand. In April of 2017 Trump told Reuters he would not speak to Tsai again without checking with Xi first. Trump was responding to Tsai's saying she was open to a second call with Trump. "I wouldn't want to be causing any difficulty right now for him [Xi]," Trump told Reuters. "I think he's doing an amazing job as a leader and I wouldn't want to do anything that comes in the way of that. So I would certainly want to speak to him first."

Kushner knows the future of this relationship and possibly all of Trump's first term will turn on Xi's cooperation with Trump on North Korea.

"They built a very, very strong relationship," Kushner said. "We still have North Korea, which is almost like a test case. At least there is a foundation. Xi couldn't call [Trump] because of the One China policy. They weren't starting discussions because they were in their corner on that. That was kind of the evolution. There is one person who is the final sign-off on decision matters in this government [Trump] and I think it's the same with the Chinese government."

Kushner also offered a general assessment of why China may be more inclined than some experts believe to exert pressure on North Korea—not to please Trump or the West but to advance its own economic and regional goals.

"China, in my view, just wants 10 years of quiet," Kushner said. "They've taken 300 million people out of poverty. They've made great progress. They've gotten more centralized control. And I think they just don't want disruption. And they recognize that America still has a lot of power over them. And we also have a lot of grievances. We want to rebalance the relationship and I think that they know there's lots of different ways that that could happen. Trump's a wild card, which, again, is a great advantage as a negotiator."

Before Trump's summit with Xi, he had a fateful White House dinner that set much of his North Korea policy in stone. It was late February and Trump was joined by Defense Secretary Mattis, new National Security Advisor H. R. McMaster and South Carolina Sen. Lindsey Graham. At that dinner, Trump asked if his policy should be to contain North Korea's nuclear program or eliminate it. Containment would mean accepting the North as a nuclear power, which it already was, and tolerating its possession of long-range ballistic missiles capable of reaching Guam, Hawaii and the U.S. mainland (the Hwasong-15 fired on November 28, 2017, had an estimated range of 8,000 miles, exposing the continental United States). Containment would prioritize deterrence and blocking the export of nuclear technology to other nations or terrorist groups.

Over dinner, Graham told Trump he could not be the president who tolerated a persistent nuclear threat from a nation that repeatedly threatened to attack the United States and its allies. Throughout 2017, Trump complained that the North Korean problem "should have been solved a long time ago." Trump knew he inherited a bad situation. In their Oval Office meeting right after the election, Obama warned him North Korea would be his toughest issue. Kim Jong-un came to power in 2012 and he accelerated ballistic missile testing, overseeing 86 of the 117 ballistic missile tests carried out by North Korea through November 2017. Graham emphasized the situation was now more dangerous than ever and cautioned that containment/deterrence might not work against a dictator as young, volatile and aggressive as Kim. Mattis and McMaster agreed.

From then on, Trump's policy was to force North Korea to give up nuclear weapons, while repeating the long-standing U.S. policy that Washington had no interest in regime change. The Trump policy would be: Kim Jong-un can keep his government or its nuclear weapons; he cannot keep both.

That decision placed the United States and North Korea on a collision course. U.S. war planning increased in tempo and specificity. McMaster became a strong proponent of the so-called bloody nose strike on the North. The concept envisioned bombing runs so effective and startling that the North would lose much of its nuclear and ballistic missile capability, suffer a consequent loss of all the billions invested therein and be humiliated in the eyes of the region and most importantly China. Trump has given "bloody nose" serious consideration and it had been war-gamed repeatedly in the Pentagon and within Pacific Command.

It is tempting in that it envisions no sustained military response from the North, no conventional strike against South Korean or U.S. forces and no prolonged land war. The theory is that North Korea will develop a new appreciation for American might—and, like someone who's suffered a bloody nose in a bar fight, Kim Jong-un, having been so bloodied, will better remember the risks of provocation.

The Pentagon and Department of State have deep reservations, though, and disagreement over "bloody nose" led to a significant diplomatic setback for Trump late in 2017. His nominee as ambassador to South Korea, Victor Cha, became a casualty in a dispute over the policy. Trump never formally nominated Cha but he was the choice and being prepped for nomination and confirmation hearings. The White House dumped Cha over the disagreement. He formally withdrew on January 30, 2018, and *The Washington Post* published an extraordinary Cha op-ed critical of "bloody nose":

> . . . the answer is not, as some Trump administration officials have suggested, a preventative military strike. Instead there is a forceful military option available that can address the threat without escalating into a war that would likely kill tens, if not hundreds, of thousands of Americans. When I was under consideration for a position in this administration, I shared some of these views.

This was a remarkable event in the first year of the Trump presidency, almost without compare in national security deliberations. The administration had for nearly a year failed to nominate an ambassador for a long-standing ally on the front lines of war. The nominee it considered had been a trusted advisor to the previous Republican president (Cha was George W. Bush's top national security advisor on Korea policy). The White House then dumped the presumed nominee over a disagreement on policy. That policy and the deep disagreements it spawned were then unveiled for the world—most notably Kim—to scrutinize.

Trump, of course, was fully within his rights to dump Cha. It would be derelict, with questions of war and peace so near, to do otherwise. It remains, though, an extraordinary moment that passed, as so many did in 2017, with barely a ripple. Cha wrote the following about the flaws of "bloody nose" assumptions. "Some may argue that U.S. casualties and even a wider war on the Korean peninsula are risks worth taking, given what is at stake. But a strike, even a large one, would only delay North Korea's missile-building and nuclear programs, which are buried in deep, unknown places impenetrable to bunker-busting bombs."

Every military risk is calculated but in North Korea the equation is more difficult because we know so little about North Korean society, Kim's motives and his hold on power. The North also has much less to lose than the South. The proximity and prosperity of Seoul make it an inviting target. All of South Korea's prosperity makes it a source of North Korean envy and resentment. The North's constitution still calls for the revolutionary overthrow of the South (something the excitement over peace talks and summitry in May of 2018 inexplicably overlooked).

Under the anxious cloak of peace provided by the armistice, South Korea has prospered and democratized—its economic innovation, culture, transportation technology, music and dance are a marvel throughout Asia. North Korea, by contrast, has imprisoned and starved millions, siphoned wealth to build a nuclear arsenal and sought nuclear technology from proliferators in Pakistan and Iran. Without its military and without its nuclear capability, North Korea would recede from view to fester in its reclusive and repressive juices. In November 2017, a North Korean military defector was riddled with bullets by his "comrades" as he raced to freedom across the DMZ; the regime he fled is ideologically and morally riddled with parasites.

Every statement Trump made in 2017 was designed to rattle Kim and leave him uncertain how far Trump might go to achieve denuclearization. In Trump's world it is never easy to reconcile conflicting statements. There were many about North Korea—Tillerson and Trump appeared at odds and off script. Intentional or mismanaged? Those closest to Trump believe the former. "We're keeping them off their guard," Chief of Staff John Kelly said of the North in December of 2017. "There are all sorts of messages. There is a lot of messaging going on. There are a lot of people, to include the Chinese, that are convincing him [Kim Jong-un] that he is so far up that [nuclear escalation] ladder he doesn't really understand he's even on the ladder. He needs to be very careful. There's a lot of messaging. And not just the normal means."

Gingrich described Trump's thinking on North Korea. "Kim Jong-un has never faced a serious American. From '68 on they have never had a serious American president who followed through. So, their attitudes have been 'screw them.' He [Trump] believes it's just going to get worse and you can't risk an American city. He's not going to be the president who loses an American city. That forces you to think hard things that otherwise you could hide from."

Gingrich's argument that North Korea has never faced a U.S. president willing to "follow through" is based on two events at the height of the Cold War, one during Lyndon Johnson's presidency and the other during Richard Nixon's. On January 23, 1968, North Korea seized the USS *Pueblo,* an environmental research ship the Navy deployed as an intelligence-gathering vessel. North Koreans took 83 crew members prisoner and one died in the armed taking of the vessel. The seizure happened within a whirlwind of events battering Johnson and the U.S. military in Asia. A week before, Johnson had delivered his State of the Union address proclaiming military and political progress in South Vietnam while acknowledging that North Vietnam "continues to pour men and materiel across frontiers and into battle." One week later the North Vietnamese launched the Tet Offensive, a multilayered assault on South Vietnamese cities and fortifications that undercut optimistic appraisals of the war's progress. The *Pueblo* was taken in between these events and just three days after North Korean troops crossed the DMZ and stormed South Korea's presidential mansion, the Blue House, leaving 26 South Koreans dead. The North starved and tortured the *Pueblo* crew during their captivity. It never released the vessel (it is a museum now in Pyongyang). When the crew was freed Johnson issued a written apology admitting the *Pueblo* was spying and promising no further surveillance missions. The crew crossed the Bridge of No Return on December 23, 1968, exactly 11 months after being taken prisoner.

The next event occurred on April 15, 1969. A North Korean MiG-21 shot down a U.S. Navy Lockheed EC-121M Warning Star spy plane over the Sea of Japan, killing 30 sailors and one Marine. It was the largest loss of life to a U.S. air crew during the Cold War. The newly inaugurated Nixon administration was stunned. Nixon reviewed military options including nighttime bombing raids, a ground assault across the DMZ, mining North Korean territorial waters and imposing a blockade. Military advisors warned any reaction could lead the North to fire artillery on Seoul. Nixon chose to focus on Vietnam and did nothing. His national security advisor, Henry Kissinger, later called the administration's reaction "weak, indecisive and disorganized."

When Gingrich tells Trump that North Korea has never encountered a formidable U.S. president, this is the historical backdrop he references. In his speech to the South Korean National Assembly, Trump summarized this history and North Korea's shabby record at complying with agreements to stall its nuclear weapons program. He made an oblique reference to the Obama-era policy of "strategic patience" and warned Pyongyang that the days of diffidence were over. "The regime has pursued nuclear weapons with the deluded hope that it could blackmail its way to the ultimate objective. And that objective we are not going to let it have. We are not going to let it have."

Trump believes this rhetoric and active war-planning have shocked the North *and* led China to apply more diplomatic pressure (voting for two new UN Security Council Resolutions sanctioning the North) and economic pressure (ending coal shipments to the North and cutting off access to Bank of China loans). China's motives are unclear. The White House knows it could do more to chasten Kim. But Trump believes he has changed Beijing's calculus, motivating it to move more harshly against the North by keeping the threat of military action at the ready. Trump also believes his relationship with Xi has moved China to act.

"China is doing more to curtail economic support to North Korea," Ambassador Joseph DeTrani told me. From 2003 to 2006 DeTrani was the U.S. Special Envoy for Six Party Talks with North Korea. "Part of this is because the Trump administration, working primarily through the UN Security Council, has made North Korea a priority security issue for the global community. And with the rhetoric from the White House of 'all options on the table,' China realizes that the period of 'strategic patience' from the U.S. is over and things can get nasty quickly."

I also ran this theory by Robert Carlin, an 18-year CIA veteran and later intelligence officer for the Department of State with almost all of his CIA and State work in or about North Korea, a place he has visited more than 35 times. Carlin is now a CBS contributor. "Pyongyang would flip this around, and probably with more justification: 'Kim Jong-un is the first North Korean leader to seriously threaten the U.S.' That's why, they'd argue, they finally have Washington's attention."

Carlin argued that the ballistic missile technology and existing nuclear weapons give the North, for the first time, the ability to menace Tokyo as well as U.S. bases on Okinawa and Guam—not to mention the possibility of Hawaii and the mainland. A false missile alarm tripped in Hawaii in early May of 2018 sent panic across the island and told the North their capabilities were, for the first time, being taken seriously outside of the peninsula. In all likelihood, it provoked smiles in Pyongyang.

"They've won the psychological war," Carlin told me. "Sirens going off in Hawaii, people stocking supplies in Detroit. For weak, poor, little North Korea this is a significant win."

Carlin and DeTrani both fear war could come, and sooner than later. "We are one or two steps away from a war, and it could come upon us all of a sudden," Carlin told me. "That isn't inevitable, but I've seen nothing over the past several years that gives me any confidence that Washington understands the history and knows how to use those lessons to get us off this truly tragic path." DeTrani takes seriously warnings about a preemptive strike to avert a feared nuclear missile launch. "I think the possibility of a preventive strike is real, especially if there's intelligence that says North Korea is planning an attack that's viewed as an imminent threat to the U.S. or its allies in South Korea and Japan."

If Trump orders a preemptive attack of the "bloody nose" variety and the bombing runs are successful, North Korea will have suffered hundreds of military dead and a substantial setback to its nuclear arsenal (the United States estimated in 2018 North Korea had 60 nuclear weapons and sufficient highly enriched uranium to produce six more each year; the North tested what it said was a hydrogen bomb in September of 2017, a 100-kiloton yield that estimates suggest was 1,000 times more powerful than the U.S. atomic bombs dropped on Hiroshima and Nagasaki in Japan in 1945).

If Trump cut some new deal with Kim in Singapore that creates a new method of denuclearization and verification, then that international system will have been reset as well. If the North slow-walks Trump and fools him like it fooled American presidents before him, history will have repeated itself but with much higher TV ratings. No one knows how Trump, if he decides that he has been manipulated, will react. If it is war, Kim Jong-un will have been the provocateur and Trump the actor. And Trump alone will have rewritten the nuclear rule book. Preemptive attacks to extinguish the threat of nuclear attack will have been established as a defensible military strategy by the world's preeminent nuclear power. The nation with vast nuclear superiority in terms of numbers (4,480 warheads in 2017) and delivery systems (bombers, ballistic missiles and submarines) will have felt sufficiently threatened by a smaller stockpile and unverified delivery to launch a preemptive assault. If this comes to pass, the mere threat of nuclear attack from a rogue nation with a manic leader will become the new threshold for preemption and whatever it militarily spawns.

The alternative is to continue economic and diplomatic pressure while pursuing missile defense capability. "You need a crash program on three-layer missile defense so you can kill on launch, kill in space and kill on reentry," Gingrich told me. The wisest course of action may be for Trump to buy time with negotiations while the United States fortifies its intercept capability.

If war comes to pass—"bloody nose" or some bloodier and costlier variation—Trump will become the most consequential president of the 21st century and the most important warrior president since Harry S Truman unleashed atomic carnage upon Japan. This will be because Trump will have changed the preemptive war equation by acting unilaterally to blunt or eradicate a nuclear threat—after warning of the use of nuclear weapons beforehand. If he unleashes against the North, Trump will have fundamentally changed the nuclear calculus for the weak and the strong. During World War II, the United States won the race for the atomic bomb, ended the global conflagration on its own terms and laid the groundwork for the nuclear arms race and subsequent controls and communications channels. Truman's subsequent reluctance to use atomic weapons again during the Korean War frustrated his commanding general, Douglas MacArthur, and established the policy, tested thereafter but always upheld, of nuclear deterrence.

Truman. MacArthur. Taiwan. Trump. North Korea. Events are jumbled and never flow in a straight line; personalities draw from history they know and pivot in relation to events as they happen. Trump's knowledge of Korea is limited; his frustration with having to confront a North Korea capable, for the first time ever, of inflicting damage on the United States is palpable. Throughout 2017 Trump's inner circle became more convinced that Kim Jong-un did not comprehend U.S. military strength. They also concluded he harbored a gangland contempt for perceived U.S. weakness in dealing with the regime. "I have to tell you this is dangerous, dangerous business," Kelly said in December of 2017. "I don't think North Korea understands it at all. He [Kim Jong-un] actually thinks that he's very close to being able to deter the United States in all cases because he has a deliverable nuclear weapon. He couldn't be more wrong."

The question for Trump is not whether the United States can strike North Korea and degrade its nuclear test capabilities and its ballistic missile research. It can. The question is at what cost? What would North Korea do? Even after Trump's Singapore summit with Kim the answers remained elusive. What may or may not be clear is South Korea's will to fight back and the long-term ability of the U.S. military to defend and reinforce a South Korea at war with North Korea. If war breaks out, the deeper question about U.S. military readiness will shadow every decision Trump makes about conflict on the Korean peninsula. The simple fact is the United States is not ready to launch and sustain a new war anywhere. For all of Trump's talk about a rebuilt military, it's a work in progress. The military is overextended and underfunded for the type of conflict that war in Korea could require. Trump in 2017 did nothing to rebuild the military. He did not win one cent more for defense spending from the GOP-led Congress than Obama did. Right before the year ended, Trump secured $4 billion to replenish ballistic missile interceptor stockpiles and accelerate the production of new interceptor technology. Considering the rapid pace of North Korea's ballistic missile program in 2016 it is hard to imagine any U.S. president would not have sought or received such funding.

As for rebuilding the U.S. military, Trump in 2017 was mostly talk. For all the justifiable criticism of Trump's zest for exaggeration, criticism of his fact-free riffs about transforming the U.S. military have gone largely unremarked upon. At the end of the first year of Trump's presidency, the defense budget was the same as it would have been under Obama. Every new president inherits last year's budget from their predecessor, meaning they don't have any influence over federal spending until the new fiscal year begins on October 1 of their first year in office. But Trump and the GOP-led Congress couldn't fashion a budget to boost defense spending for the new fiscal year.

While it's true Trump called for more defense spending, he never got it from Congress in 2017. He did receive a defense authorization bill that reflected new Trump spending priorities, but without actual dollars appropriated, meaning what Trump had was a shiny wish list. Trump did secure an increase in defense spending in February of 2018, but it wasn't until late March that those bills were written and signed. In practical terms, the Pentagon did not receive the boost until the fiscal year was nearly half over . . . meaning Trump will have spent more than a third of his first term with Obama's defense budget. And that's not even the real problem.

The central issue is the paralysis that comes with fiscal drift. The Pentagon, as any budget analyst there will tell you, cannot plan with constant fits and starts in congressional funding. Every time Congress passes a temporary spending measure to avert a government shutdown, which happened four times in 2017, it must slow down decision-making on future programs and limp along with the current allocations. That means Trump's promises to expand the Army from 476,000 active duty troops to 540,000 and to increase the number of Navy warships from 275 to 355 and to add 100 Air Force combat aircraft are not only fictional, they aren't even previews of near-term coming attractions. The term in Washington is "continuing resolution." That means the same budget as before. Trump's promise to increase defense spending— and his relentless false hectoring throughout 2017 that this had happened—could not materialize until early 2018, when Congress agreed to boost defense spending by 16 percent and nondefense spending by 13 percent over two years. But with the details pending through March, the Pentagon remained uncertain how much money would go where—continuing the uncertain budget process.

For the military, the readiness crisis is upon us. The U.S. military is simply incapable of maintaining its force posture, readiness and preparation for war. That's not my opinion. That's the verdict of every service secretary in the Trump administration. CBS National Security Correspondent David Martin once quoted Air Force Secretary Heather Wilson following her first assessment of service readiness. The assessment was so appalling Wilson told subordinates it had to be wrong. It was not. As the saying goes in the Pentagon, the readiness crisis doesn't mean the U.S. military isn't No. 1. It still is. And it doesn't mean the military won't go where the president orders it to go. What it does mean is that when that order is given, fewer Americans will come home alive or uninjured.

For the layman, readiness sounds a little nebulous. What does readiness mean? Isn't every member of the military ready to carry out an order? Absolutely. The readiness of the personnel is never the issue. The issue is the readiness of the tools of war. Part of that equation is training and force fatigue. Never was that more vividly and tragically on display than in the summer of 2016, when in June the destroyer USS *Fitzgerald* collided with a container ship near Japan and seven soldiers died and in August the USS *John S. McCain,* another destroyer, collided with an oil tanker near Singapore, killing 10 sailors. Those sailors lost their lives in part because shipmates on their vessels and the commanding officers overseeing their training could not maintain operational tempo and staffing levels consistent with the demands of their assignments. Throughout the fall of 2017, top officials from each branch of the military testified to Congress about deep stresses on personnel and equipment. Many military planners consider this rather dry topic—force readiness and maintenance—the most important issue facing a fighting force at war nonstop since 9/11.

It is apt at this moment to bring Army Gen. George S. Patton back into the conversation. In his memoir, *War as I Knew It,* Patton declared, "fatigue makes cowards of us all." Fatigue can also make you lose track of things, lose focus or forget urgent tasks. One or a combination of these factors, according to subsequent Navy investigations, led to the tragedies of the USS *McCain* and *Fitzgerald*. During the very summer when Trump was trying to project to China and North Korea maximum readiness, maximum flexibility and maximum alertness, the U.S. Navy was incapable of sailing two vessels safely through international waters. Not only did America lose 17 of its best, the nation's prestige suffered and its ability to match Trump's bellicose and threatening rhetoric was visibly undermined. The Navy tragedies do not mean U.S. forces are incapable of carrying out coordinated and possibly effective strikes against North Korea. But they do suggest that Kim Jung-un, in his isolated and paranoid world, might be more prone to miscalculate about U.S. capability and nerve.

Nothing Trump could have accomplished in terms of military spending before October 1, 2017, would have changed the situation in the South China Sea. But those disasters will not be forgotten in Pyongyang or Beijing. What becomes of the collision course between Trump and North Korea—and what China decides to do or not do—will be influenced not only by Trump's decisions, but by the ability of the U.S. military to carry the fight in any direction for a week, a month or longer. The longer the duration of battle, the more brittle U.S. capabilities will become and the higher the toll will be in terms of equipment, personnel and strategic flexibility. If Trump launches a preemptive attack and North Korea responds with a conventional war in South Korea, Trump may not only have a bigger war on his hands than he bargained for; he may have to explain why he started it before the military was ready.

In either case, Trump has set history in motion and will be recorded as the president who confronted North Korea and all its risks, opacity and cruelty. To quote the president: "We'll see what happens."

TWELVE

Deregulation

I f you think watching President Trump drink a glass of water with
two hands looks awkward, you haven't studied him closely at his
most awkward—when he tries to look like a conventional politician
playacting through a made-for-TV stunt.

To his never-ending credit, Trump hates typical political show-
manship. Trump doesn't need a show. Other politicians do. Trump
needs only a microphone, his ochre skin, his suspension bridge hair
and his whirligig rhetoric.

But the White House still tried to shoehorn the showman into
Hush Puppies of political convention—a contrived stage, some grandiose object d' news and a device with which to interact with the
object.

Trump tried his best on December 14 when he ambled into the
Roosevelt Room and stood beneath the Tade Styka portrait *Rough
Rider* of a dusty but dashing Teddy Roosevelt, smiling atop a rearing
horse. Nixon named it the Roosevelt Room because Teddy built the
West Wing and Franklin, his fifth cousin, expanded it. FDR kept an

aquarium in the room and many mounted fish on the wall, prompting Kennedy to name it the "fish room."

Amid all the props, Trump looked most definitely like a fish out of water. But he pressed gamely on, his opening line betraying his state of mind.

"Regulations, oh boy," Trump said with a sigh. "That's a lot of regulations."

Aides had pre-positioned two dull piles of white paper (Washington's number one export) along the west wall of the Roosevelt Room. The point—supposedly—was that the piles of paper were conspicuously different in size. One pile was slightly more than a foot high with three stacks of white paper placed end to end—covering just under three feet of floor space. It represented the sum of federal regulations during Kennedy's presidency. The far larger pile stood six-and-a-half-feet high and was nearly six feet wide. It represented federal regulations today. One pile was suitable for a large college three-ring binder. The other was suitable for *Hoarder Garage*, Episode 11. A slightly sagging red ribbon ran across both piles.

"We've begun the most far-reaching regulatory reform in American history." Trump said. "The never-ending growth of red tape in America has come to a sudden, screeching and beautiful halt. Within our first 11 months, we canceled or delayed over 1,500 planned regulatory actions, more than any previous president by far. For every one new regulation, we have eliminated 22. Twenty-two. That's a big difference. I want every cabinet secretary, agency head and federal worker to push even harder to cut even more regulations in 2018, and that should just about do it."

The visual point was simple enough. Too many federal regulations. Trump was going to do something about it. What was the garish red ribbon about? Well, to make wretched political stage-managing even more wretched, politicians must interact with the props. White House aide Chris Liddell (he of the now-famous Romney transition book) handed Trump a pair of scissors that might have been surplus from the clown vault of the defunct Ringling Brothers Circus. So armed, Trump would cut through the ribbon. Get it?? He's cutting red tape! For all of those who complain that Trump's approach to politics is insulting in its simplicity or sledgehammer symbolism . . . let me say this . . . there were moments and places during Trump's first year when a fair and layered discussion on this could be had. However, you can take my word as someone who has covered politics up close for nearly 30 years, silly stuntery, phony props and playacting unworthy of summer stock in Keokuk mongrelized politics and political communication long before Trump came along.

"So, this is what we have now," Trump said as he stood between the two stacks of paper, the red ribbon that stretched across both stacks crossing over his knees like a misaligned beauty pageant sash. "This is where we were in 1960. And when we're finished, which won't be in too long a period of time, we will be less than where we were in 1960."

Trump wielded the scissors like a small-town mayor opening the town's first Dairy Queen and snapped them shut. The ribbon fell harmlessly and anticlimactically to the carpet as the cameras obediently captured the "drama." Trump waved to reporters as Interior Secretary Ryan Zinke and Transportation Secretary Elaine Chao clapped obediently.

When it comes to regulations and rewriting the federal government's relationship to federal lands, exploitation of natural resources, the internet, labor rights, worker safety and pollution control, Trump needs no toys. His approach is deadly serious and methodical—so much so that Politico said one of Trump's biggest accomplishments in his first year was undoing much of Obama's last year—effectively turning it into a seven-year presidency. It is a legacy that could last years and may remake the concept of the regulatory state—with unknown economic, environmental and safety consequences.

Some examples:

- Trump lifted regulations on net neutrality, giving service providers freedom to charge more for faster internet connections— something advocates say will accelerate innovation and increase consumer choice but opponents contend will ghettoize the poor with slower transmission speeds, fewer options and less access to entertainment and information (FCC Commissioner Ajit Pai and his wife received credible and repeated death threats while net neutrality was being repealed).
- He opened federal lands on coastlines in Florida, California and the mid-Atlantic to drilling for natural gas and oil.

- He reduced the size of two national monuments—Bear Ears and Grand Staircase-Escalanate—for private ranching and mineral extraction.
- He loosened restrictions on development on federal lands throughout the West and opened the Arctic National Wildlife Refuge for oil and gas drilling.
- He reduced the scope of rules protecting streams from coal mining waste and dramatically shortened environmental reviews of constructions projects and new chemicals.

Through it all one constant emerged—business and private interests won. Trump argued that preference had long been missing from Washington and the time had come to put the government behind instead of in the way of industry, entrepreneurs and capital. Trump and his cabinet secretaries—with varying degrees of passion and persuasiveness— told reporters and public interest groups that the deregulatory agenda served the public by creating jobs and economic growth. It is the most fundamental shift in nearly 40 years. Most of it you probably missed.

As you might have imagined, Trump hyped the numbers during his ribbon act—he didn't cut that many regulations—the White House double-counted and exaggerated. Even so, environmental, labor and civil rights groups could barely keep up with the pace and scope of regulatory retrenchment. Some came through executive order. Cabinet secretaries did some on their own—frequently with the help of lobbyists from affected industries. The Republican-led Congress did most of the work, using a previously obscure law written as part of the Contract with America. It is called the Congressional Review Act. House Speaker Newt Gingrich included the legislation in the Contract so as to allow the expunging of regulations written in the waning days of future Democratic presidencies. Bill Clinton signed the law in 1996 but Gingrich, remarkably, had to wait for Trump to dust off this regulatory eraser.

The law gives Congress the power to eradicate any regulation written in the previous 60 legislative days. This power is potent. No hearings are required. The move to nullify a new regulation can come straight to the House and Senate floor. No amendments are allowed. Simple majorities suffice—meaning no 60-vote requirement in the Senate. Once the rule is vanquished, no new rule can be substituted or reissued if it resembles the original in intent or effect. The only way around this hurdle is the passing of a new law authorizing a similar rule (impossible in a Congress that just killed the original).

From 1996 to 2017, the law had been used only once, when Bush reversed a Clinton-era regulation on ergonomics. Republicans sent Obama five disapproval resolutions—the formal name of the procedure—but he vetoed all of them (those vetoes represented nearly half of the 12 issued during Obama's two terms in office). Trump and the GOP Congress used the Congressional Review Act 15 times from February 14 to November 1 (13 of those were approved in Trump's first 100 days). Because Congress counts days abnormally (measuring by days in session instead of days on a calendar), the law's 60-legislative-day window allowed Trump and Republicans to strike Obama-era regulations dating as far back as May 2016—that's right, the last nine months of his presidency. Ryan and McConnell launched the effort with Trump transition advisors Short, Dearborn and Liddell.

"We thought of it immediately," McConnell told me. "President Obama was so sure Clinton was going to win he just kept spewing out regulations right up until the end. Thereby making a lot of this stuff eligible. We started writing them as soon as we knew Donald Trump was going to be president. We were going back 100 days and figuring out which ones were eligible and prioritizing the ones that we thought would provide the most relief."

According to the George Washington University Regulatory Studies Center, Obama issued 41 economically significant rules (defined as having a $100 million or more in annual economic impact) between November 1, 2016, and January 19, 2017, or 13.6 significant rules per month—three times the Obama administration's normal clip. Obama imposed 481 economically significant rules compared to 361 by Clinton and 358 by Bush. During Obama's presidency, when this topic arose, officials would defend against charges of a costly regulatory binge by complaining that the $100 million "economically significant" threshold had not been adjusted for inflation since the executive order that established it in 1993. According to GWU Regulatory Studies Center calculations, this does not absolve Obama, because half of Obama's 481 rules imposed yearly costs over $1 billion. Moreover, 96 percent of all

Obama rules would still be deemed economically significant even *after* adjusting for inflation.

Congressional Review Act nullifications removed the following rules: limiting and monitoring pollution to surface- and groundwater from coal mining; requiring the Social Security Administration to notify the National Instant Criminal History Background Check of anyone deemed mentally incapable of handling their finances (thus prohibiting sales of firearms to these individuals); imposing teacher accountability standards under the Elementary and Secondary Education Act; establishing data on state unemployment compensation for jobs that require drug testing; requiring telecommunications carriers to inform customers about their rights to protect confidential information; and requiring financial companies to limit the use of pre-arbitration agreements to avoid or settle class action suits.

Not counting Gorsuch on the Supreme Court, nothing Trump accomplished in his first year has resonated more with conservatives than his move against federal regulations. It far surpasses the sense of excitement or anticipation generated by the reduction of corporate and personal income tax rates and other simplifications of the tax code achieved in late December 2017. For pro-business conservatives— especially small businesses looking for a leg up amid economic dislocation—nothing matters more than fewer existing regulations and no fear of new ones.

"When I am on the road talking to both activists and donors," Tim Phillips, of Americans for Prosperity told me, "what I hear about more than anything, more than tax cuts, more than immigration, is the regulatory environment and how it has changed. The EPA. The National Labor Relations Board. That's what I hear about. Occupational Safety and Health Administration. It happens right away. It takes effect whenever they say it. Across the administration the departments are trimming back the dramatic overreach of the Obama years and to an extent the Bush appointments. When you look across the Trump administration, they are much better and much stronger when it comes to economic freedom."

The story of when federal regulations grew and under which presidencies is really about three presidencies: Nixon, Carter and Obama. According to federal records assembled by the George Washington

University Regulatory Studies Center, the Federal Register was 1,500 pages long in 1960. The companion Code of Federal Regulations, which publishes the detailed rules that implement each regulation in the Federal Register, was 22,000 pages long. Every regulation adds substantially to the list of pages in the Code of Federal Regulations. When, in 1968, the Federal Register grew to 3,000 pages the number of pages in the code was 58,000. By 1974, the last year of Nixon's presidency, pages in the Register had tripled to 4,500, while the code had expanded to 70,000 pages. By the end of Carter's presidency in 1980, the Register had risen to 7,200 pages and the code to 102,000. Reagan genuinely cut regulations back, reducing the Federal Register to 5,000 pages by 1988 (a reduction of 30 percent) even as the code increased to 118,000 pages. The Register was 5,800 pages and the code 130,000 pages by the end of Bush the elder's one term. Clinton boosted the Register to 7,400 pages and the code to 138,000 pages by 2000. Bush the younger brought it to 7,900 pages by 2008 (like his father, letting inertia take its course and adding a few items of his own) and the code to 158,000 pages. Obama added nearly 2,000 pages to the Register, the most since Carter, bringing the total to an eye-popping 9,600 pages. Under Obama the code grew to 184,000 pages. By the end of Trump's first year, pages in the Register shrank to 6,100 (a 36 percent cut, compared to Reagan's first-year reduction of 19 percent).

And yet, federal regulations are not—as Trump wants the nation to believe—continuous drags on economic development, job creation or wage growth. They might not even be impediments to future growth. Regulations can and often do bring order to markets, impose safety discipline and create means by which compliance can be checked and enforced. In fact, an early 2018 review by Trump's Office of Management and Budget, which manages rule-making, concluded that federal regulations brought substantial economic benefits.

> The estimated annual benefits of major federal regulations reviewed by OMB from October 1, 2006, to September 30, 2016, for which agencies estimated and monetized both benefits and costs, are in the aggregate between $219 billion and $695 billion, while the estimated annual costs are in the aggregate between $59 billion and $88 billion, reported in 2001 dollars.

In 2015 dollars, aggregate annual benefits are estimated to be between $287 and $911 billion and costs between $78 and $115 billion. These ranges reflect uncertainty in the benefits and costs of each rule at the time that it was evaluated.

At the low end of this spectrum, federal regulations, according to Trump's own rule makers and bean counters, provide 3.6 times the benefit compared to the cost ($287 billion in benefits to $78 billion in costs). At the high end, benefits outweigh the costs by nearly 8 to 1 ($911 billion in benefits to $115 billion in costs). The Trump administration brought no attention to this study.

In his approach to federal regulations, Trump most resembles Ronald Reagan. The two could not be more different in temperament, gentleness, humility or ideological rigor. But they share a visceral hostility to federal rules and an unshakable belief that an unregulated free-market will, over time, achieve more in terms of job creation and safety than any set of federal regulations. Reagan came to it via his ideological transformation from Franklin Delano Roosevelt Democrat to William F. Buckley and Barry Goldwater conservative.

Free-market fans of Trump don't really know why he took after regulations with such zeal. They are pretty sure it has nothing to do with ideology. They don't attribute it to core Republican philosophy because they never have regarded and still largely do not regard Trump as a true Republican. Most chalk it up to availability. Executive power gives him latitude. The Congressional Review Act gave him a simple, smash-mouth legislative tool. Conservative cabinet secretaries were confirmable and could keep Trump's agenda humming with little to no interference.

"I think Trump extrapolates," Norquist, of Americans for Tax Reform, said, referring to Trump's experience as a developer in the 1970s and 80s. "'God damn permits. I know permits!' Some of it comes across as a guy who respects businessmen. He sees entrepreneurs as scrappers as opposed to guys who think deep thoughts, give speeches and write haiku poems or something. He likes business guys. And when they come to him he puts it through his own experience. It's all 180 degrees [from Obama]. It's not just tie goes to the runner. It really is a complete reversing of all of these things."

As I have thought about this I can't forget a man I met in Jackson, Mississippi, on August 24, 2015, as thousands filed into a Trump rally at the massive Mississippi Coliseum. I was interviewing Trump supporters when Lucas Quinn strode by wearing a faded red "Reagan-Bush '84" T-shirt. He had an open, friendly expression on his face and I asked if he would mind answering a few questions. Quinn was from Union, Mississippi. He stood casually with a large Coke cradled in his right hand. The TV camera didn't make him nervous at all. He didn't have a care in the world, or so it seemed. I asked what he liked about Trump.

"He speaks to us. Just normal guys, just normal Joes. He has a lot of good things that he's doing and he seems like he has a little Reagan in him too which is always a good thing because Reagan was probably the best president we've ever had."

"What do you hear or what echoes for you about Reagan in Trump?" I asked.

For the first time Quinn's face clouded over. His eyes narrowed for a second as he paused, then brightened up just as they had been before.

"I don't really know. I wasn't alive when Reagan was president, so I can't speak on Reagan, but Reagan—he was kind of a politician where he was governor of California and then he decided to come on and try the presidency and he pretty much obliterated everybody and he—everything he did made America great."

Quinn had been stumped for a second. Then he realized it didn't really matter. How specifically Trump reminded him of Reagan was irrelevant. *That* he did was all that mattered. I can admit now I chuckled to myself, wrongly assuming that what mattered were the specifics and, as I so often did with Trump supporters, missed the overall. Quinn then talked about Trump's meaning to him.

"Trump is not a politician. We're sick and tired of politicians. We want a guy who is not a politician—just a normal guy—that's gonna come in there and shake the world up and that's what we're hoping for with Trump."

I mentioned Trump was the first billionaire I'd ever heard described as a "normal guy."

"How does he do that?" I asked.

"Maybe it's the charisma," Quinn said. "I don't really know. I know he's going to win."

"How can you be so sure?" I asked.

"Hillary," Quinn said. "She's a liar. She's a manipulator. I'm sick of the corruption. I'm sick of them not doing things just for normal people. They're always doing things for the upper class, but they're not doing things for us."

Moments later I met Jimmy Richard (pronounced ree-shard), from Tylertown, Mississippi. He spoke with a slow, thick drawl that took some getting used to (my editors at CBS said it was too thick to be understood). Richard was emphatic about Trump, among the most belligerently happy of all the many hundreds of Trump backers I met in my travels. "He's a nonpolitician," Richard said with a tiny gleam in his eye. "I think we need to get some of that in there. I think that's what they're afraid of—is getting that in there. You know, kicking over their little honey hole. Republicans and Democrats."

Richard paused for a moment and looked as if he was going to walk away but decided to add one more thought.

"I like who he picked for vice president, Mr. Pence."

I asked why.

"Well, what he did in Arkansas. I mean Arizona."

"Indiana," I said, helpfully.

"Indiana. Wherever it was. I mean he turned it around."

Specifics did not matter to Quinn or Richard; neither did flubbing answers about how Trump was like Reagan or where Pence was from. For the first time, they were involved in politics and didn't feel stupid or self-conscious in their ignorance—the way other politicians and media coverage of other campaigns had made them feel. What mattered to Quinn and Richard and millions of Trump supporters was he was with them and they were with him. What Trump symbolized eclipsed all other considerations. China. Trade. Forgotten middle class. Can't be bought. Businessman. Success. Reagan. Flag. Dreams. Win. What any of those things meant in miniature, how they would translate into legislation or decision-making, was less than irrelevant—it was bothersome and stupid. Trump voters saw what they saw, believed what they believed and knew what they knew. Everyone else could get stuffed.

These voters believed Washington had been screwing them, not protecting them. It was their time now.

As Trump reduces regulations, these voters may see economic benefits but may also find themselves exposed to greater health, safety and environmental risks. When Trump said he wanted to return the U.S. regulatory regime to the size it was during the Kennedy administration, that would mean eradicating almost every environmental protection on the books as well as safety rules for manufacturing, pipelines, refineries, coal mines, nursing homes, hospitals and construction—to name just a few. It's a fanciful goal and utterly unachievable—litigation alone would grind such maneuvers to a halt. But it speaks to the underlying ideology of a rules-free or rules-light economy—one no president has embraced with such fervor since Reagan and one which, with the aid and assistance of a willing Republican Congress, has more of a chance to flourish than at any time in a century.

Quinn saw Reagan in Trump. On regulations he was far-seeing and accurate.

"His appointments are better than Reagan's," Norquist told me. "Reagan had to get 60 votes in a pre-Reagan Senate." That meant Reagan had to nominate Republicans who could be confirmed and, as a result, tended to be far less conservative than Trump's current cabinet secretaries and undersecretaries. "Reagan was holding the building up, he was holding regulations back."

Trump is imposing the government Reagan could only daydream about. Reagan never had a Republican House. He had a Republican Senate for six years but by contemporary standards at least 13 of those Senate Republicans would be unelectable—too liberal or moderate—in the states they represented. Lowell Weicker Jr. of Connecticut, Charles McCurdy Mathias Jr. of Maryland, John Chafee of Rhode Island, Bob Packwood and Mark Hatfield of Oregon, John Heinz of Pennsylvania, Slade Gorton of Washington, Charles Percy of Illinois, John Danforth of Missouri, Rudy Boschwitz and Dave Durenberger of Minnesota, Jake Garn of Utah and Nancy Kassebaum of Kansas (and possibly Bob Dole of Kansas and Howard Baker of Tennessee) would never survive a primary in the modern-day, Trump-infused GOP.

What that meant for Reagan was a perpetually hostile House with subpoena and oversight powers to investigate cabinet actions and possible malfeasance—or both. The House Energy and Commerce Committee, under the dogged leadership of Rep. John Dingell of Michigan, clashed with Reagan's first head of the Environmental Protection Agency, Anne Gorsuch Burford (mother of Justice Gorsuch). Dingell was seeking documents on Superfund management that Burford sought to withhold from Congress, citing executive privilege. Dingell also accused Burford of siding with industry in regulatory matters, and environmentalists fretted as she cut the agency budget by nearly a quarter and reduced the number of filings against alleged polluters. Burford resigned under Dingell's unrelenting pressure.

Such Democratic oversight was one problem for Reagan. Another was that at least 13 and possibly 15 Republican senators (depending on the issue) were demonstrably more liberal than Reagan and his administration on matters of federal regulation. For this reason, Reagan achieved far less than he wanted; fighting rearguard battles through most of his presidency to block and redirect rules and regulatory legislation (it's no coincidence Reagan did not move to reauthorize the Clean Air Act or Civil Rights Act—both tasks were eagerly taken up by George H. W. Bush, and added upon them was another piece of America's regulatory infrastructure, the Americans with Disabilities Act).

Trump and his cabinet met no such resistance. In 1982, one of the issues that tripped Burford up was the revelation that she met with the owner of a New Mexico company concerned about a pending EPA ruling. Burford made no explicit promises but left the owners with the impression they would be spared. That single meeting and the implied reassurance of a light EPA touch became a significant flash point. In 2017, the GOP Congress showed no interest in numerous examples of Trump cabinet officials meeting and conferring on regulatory policy with industry chieftains. The GOP-led Congress similarly looked the other way as numerous Trump cabinet secretaries ran up huge taxpayer costs by misusing charter and military flights or traveling first class. Similarly, there was little or no oversight over government-wide efforts by the Trump cabinet to erase scientific information from websites and erase, for example, references to "clean energy" and "greenhouse gases." Congress also looked the other way when Trump signed an executive order in late January allowing registered lobbyists to join the administration immediately, provided they did not work directly on issues on which they had lobbied the previous two years (Obama's rule, which Trump nullified, required a one-year cooling-off period for any registered lobbyist to work in the administration). The Trump rule also allowed administration officials to begin lobbying their former agency within a year of leaving government service. This is swampy stuff. Trump's first year saw him leave dozens of scientific government positions vacant—another topic Congress ignored. Trump cabinet departments—led by the EPA—were subject to a record number of open records lawsuits, filed under the Freedom of Information Act, seeking access to basic facts about travel, regulatory actions and encounters with industry representatives. From the GOP-led Congress, another bored sigh.

On May 1, the Trump White House, clearly infatuated with the light touch Republicans were providing, formalized its cozy relationship. The Justice Department Office of Legal Counsel (OLC), at the behest of the White House, released a first-of-its-kind opinion declaring that no administration official had to respond to a request for information from any House or Senate Democrat. The administration, the memo said, was only required to respond to majority party requests. Since almost none came, this memorialized the oversight cease-fire. The memo read:

> The constitutional authority to conduct oversight—that is, authority to make official inquiries into and conduct investigations of Executive Branch programs and activities—may be exercised only by each house of Congress or, under existing delegations, by committees and subcommittees [or their chairmen]. Individual members of Congress, including ranking minority members, do not have the authority to conduct oversight in the absence of a specific delegation by a full house committee, or subcommittee. They may request information from the Executive Branch, which may respond at its discretion, but such requests do not trigger any obligation to accommodate congressional needs and are not legally enforceable through a subpoena or contempt proceedings.

The opinion and its potential consequences would have passed without notice if not for Sen. Charles Grassley, Iowa Republican and chairman of the Judiciary Committee. Grassley is one of the most aggressive investigators in Congress and his staff has a near-legendary reputation for chasing down Executive Branch agencies for relevant information—and for not pulling partisan punches. Grassley has given hell to Republicans and Democrats. He was a huge advocate for Trump in probing senior-level FBI political mismanagement of the Clinton email investigation. On this score, however, Grassley sided with Congress and against Trump—though he allowed as to how Trump might have been given erroneous legal advice.

On June 9, Grassley wrote Trump. Since this book is likely to be one of the few widely read places where the tug-of-war between Congress and the Executive Branch under Trump can be given some real estate, allow me the indulgence of quoting Grassley's letter at length:

> *Every* member of Congress is a Constitutional officer, duly elected to represent and cast votes in the interests of their constituents. This applies obviously regardless of whether they are in the majority or the minority at the moment and regardless of whether they are in a leadership position on a particular committee. Thus, *all* members need accurate information from the Executive Branch in order to carry out their Constitutional function to make informed decisions on all sorts of legislative issues covering a vast array of complex matters across our massive federal government.

Farther down in the letter, "For OLC to so fundamentally misunderstand and misstate such a simple fact exposes its shocking lack of professionalism and objectivity. Indeed, OLC appears to have utterly failed to live up to its own standards. You are being ill-served and ill-advised."

Grassley then accused Trump of (gasp!) extending Obama's penchant for ignoring Congress and legitimate oversight.

> Imagine if the Congress took a similar position and refused to voluntarily disclose any information to an Executive Branch official unless the official was capable of compelling an answer. Imagine Congressional legal opinion instructing Members and staff to withhold all information about bills,

nominations, or appropriations from most Executive Branch officials on the grounds that Congress has "no constitutional obligation to accommodate information requests from the Deputy Undersecretary of Legislative Affairs." It's absurd.

Trump supporters might consider this all good-government nonsense. It is not. Grassley is not Trump's enemy, per se, but has built a career around the tedious and unrewarding work of protecting the institutional powers of Congress. Those powers are protected by the Constitution and consistent, at least in theory, with Trump's drain-the-swamp rhetoric. But Trump's industry-friendly cabinet secretaries, his coziness with lobbyists, his hostility to public records releases and his legally indefensible (Grassley's words, not mine) stiff-arming of congressional oversight point, some might reasonably fear, to the outlines of an emerging pro-business autocracy.

There is an unrecognized political peril as well—one that should deeply trouble Trump loyalists. If Democrats take control of the House or Senate, or both, the Trump legal opinion especially empowers them to request all manner of information and legally prioritizes Trump officials to comply in an orderly and timely fashion. This legal opinion may prove among the most politically and procedurally hazardous documents produced during Trump's first year. With it, Democrats can demand—using Trump's own Justice Department memo—all manner of information now locked away about luxurious travel, secret lobbyist encounters, regulatory machinations, scientific erasures and the like. As the saying goes, hubris leads to nemesis.

Trump already had the inclination and the means to cut regulations. A compliant Congress meant no pesky oversight, giving agencies unchecked authority to uproot years and sometimes decades of rules and regulations. Viewed strictly through the lens of Republicanism influenced by Reagan, Trump has the ideological Congress that Reagan envisioned 30 years before. He sits atop a feverishly ideological Congress inculcated in the free-market orthodoxy of Reaganism. What Trump has achieved in terms of changing almost every federal agency is not a departure from Obama—it is a structural repudiation.

Every agency is more conservative ideologically than it has been since before World War II and ones like the Environmental Protection

Agency—born in 1970—have never had a more retrograde bent than they do now. The Interior Department has reversed decades of assumptions about public land use, shifting from a quasi-environmental religion of erring on the side of no use and pristine preservation to mixed use that prioritizes mineral and oil and gas exploitation. The shift is by no means subtle—from, How do we save federal lands? to How do we use them?

The EPA has shifted from finding new ways to regulate to new ways to minimally comply with federal law. Whereas both Bushes used the agency to either protect or slightly enlarge the environmental status quo and the Clinton and Obama administrations used it to push the frontiers forward, Trump's administrator, Scott Pruitt (who resigned in early July 2018), sought to enforce the most crabbed and limited interpretation of existing law. For those weary of EPA overreach this was a long-overdue and welcome return to sanity and predictability. For environmentalists increasingly alarmed by global warming and who feared retrenchment of long-standing policies to reduce air and water pollution, this was the worst form of denial by dicta—bureaucratic belligerence that bordered on malice. There is a self-reinforcing dynamic at play. Appointees like Pruitt, who sued the EPA 14 times as Oklahoma attorney general, brought hostility to the agency. They knew the GOP-led Congress would not ask intrusive questions, allowing them to keep their activities largely hidden. They also knew Congress would not block deregulatory moves and would endorse narrow interpretations of existing law.

Cabinet secretaries also know Trump will not complain or question the use of industry lobbyists inside their agencies. And many, such as Pruitt, Education Secretary Betsy DeVos, Zinke and Chao, have deep relationships with the business interests most likely to benefit from deregulatory actions or agency preferences—in DeVos's case for charter schools and home schooling, and in Chao's case for dramatically reducing the time allocated for environmental reviews or land use decisions on new transportation projects. Under Trump, industry and private markets have the means, motive and opportunity to knock regulatory Washington on its ass. The ass-knocking has begun in earnest. The swamp has not been drained. It's been repopulated—fewer regulatory manatees, gray whales and sponges; more private capital sharks, barracudas and eels.

Substantive interviews with Trump cabinet secretaries are hard to come by. I sat down with Pruitt on January 17, 2018, inside his office on the third floor of EPA headquarters. Pruitt epitomized the free-market exuberance of the Trump deregulatory model. Here are some relevant excerpts with accompanying analysis.

> Pruitt: We had many regulations that this agency had adopted historically that had created confusion and did not serve advancing protection of the environment. So we spent the past year trying to achieve regulatory certainty, regulatory clarity, to make sure that people knew what was expected of them so they could invest, achieve good outcomes in the environment, but also know that there wasn't an agency in Washington D.C. trying to pick winners and losers in the marketplace. So I think the president has done an extraordinary job at impacting the economy in a very positive way. We see that in all markers. And then there's much optimism we—as we head into 2018.
>
> Me: And is the philosophy in accordance with that directive, to protect the environment or protect business?
>
> Pruitt: Well, it's neither.

"Neither" provides vital insight. Pruitt does not believe the mission of the Environmental Protection Agency is to protect the environment. The EPA is the only cabinet-level agency with a specific mandate to weigh environmental concerns above all others because Congress knew every other agency did not and that business interests had the upperhand everywhere else in government.

> Pruitt: The Clean Power Plan was an example of this administration picking winners and losers in the development of electricity, in the generation of electricity—
>
> Me: The loser would be coal.
>
> Pruitt: Choosing renewables at the expense of, what, natural resources that we have—
>
> Me: Meaning coal.
>
> Pruitt: Well, across the whole spectrum, natural gas and the rest. And so this agency shouldn't be in the business of

saying, "We're gonna favor certain sources of energy over others." It should be taking the Clean Air Act and adopting regulations that are an extension of our authority. And—you know this, Major, that the Supreme Court, because the past administration did that wrongly, intervened and issued a stay against that Clean Power Plan because it was so unlawful. So that doesn't achieve any outcomes for the environment or the economy. I believe most companies, most states, most citizens want to comply with the law. They want to do what's right. But—but the regulations that we've adopted in a whole host of areas have not been consistent, so they don't know what's expected of them.

The Clean Power Plan did incentivize power companies to shift to renewable and clean-burning fuels (like natural gas), to move away from burning coal that has higher carbon dioxide emissions linked scientifically to increases in global temperatures. The winners-and-losers formulation is revealing in that the only distinct loser is coal—because Clean Power Plan regulations penalize its use as compared to other forms of energy which, in some but not all cases, would prove more expensive to consumers. The long-running argument in environmental policy is cumulative costs of pollution on public health and safety— balancing the costs of, for example, a utility bill that is $30 higher per year against reduced instances of asthma or more severe weather events. The essence of environmental regulation is to weigh the cumulative win-loss ratio and—at the EPA, at least historically—advocate for a cleaner environment in dialogue/negotiation with other federal agencies.

Me: Would you say that's the environmental history of our country, that people want to comply and don't try to skirt the law, because this agency was created in response to environmental problems that were a result of people not adhering to any kind of basic structures of environmental stewardship at all.

Pruitt: And look at the progress we've made, Major, in that regard. In that same area we were talking about earlier, those—those air pollutants that we regulate under the Clean Air Act that are so essential to our work here, 65 percent improvement reduction in those pollutants since 1980. We've grown our economy substantially, but also reduced those pollutants by 65 percent. And most of that through investments and—new technology and industry from the private sector. I mean, we can achieve a lot through government mandate; we can achieve more, in my view, though investment, cooperation and partnership, through innovation and technologies in the private sector.

Me: You know you have your critics. And some wonder if the people you have placed in leadership positions have the public's best interests at heart. Michael Honeycutt is the head of the EPA Science Advisory Board. He's quoted as saying once, "I haven't seen the data that says lowering ozone will produce a health benefit." He goes on to say, "It might have a negative health benefit." Do you agree with that?

Pruitt: No. Ozone is something that we most definitely have to regulate. It—we're required to do so, and it has—

Me: Linked to asthma and lots of other health effects—

Pruitt: Its impact is very—it's a very important thing to regulate. And we will.

Me: There are others who also wonder about those who have come from industry who are in leadership position here. Nancy Beck, former senior director in the American Chemistry Council, now deputy assistant administrator in the office of Chemical Safety and Pollution Protection. Now, some might listen to that history of work and say, "I'm not comfortable with that." Why should the American public be comfortable with someone coming from industry and into this agency?

Pruitt: See, I don't mind the paradigm, Major. I mean, there's a paradigm that we have—that's been pushed on the American people the last decade or so—that—that we can't be—both about stewardship and—and also development, economic development and growth. And—

Me: This agency can be about economic development?

Pruitt: We should be about administering statutes—that we're required to administer—but we shouldn't come in and

say that the way forward on environmental protection is pro-
hibition versus stewardship.

Me: Environmentalism with industry. Is that right?

Pruitt: We should be about partnership. And I will tell you, if
we have companies, industries, citizens who violate the law,
we're gonna prosecute them and we're gonna hold them ac-
countable. But we should not start on the premise that all
people are that way or all industries are that way. That is just
simply wrongheaded, and it doesn't achieve good outcomes.

Three days after that Pruitt interview, on the one-year anniversary
of his inauguration, Trump tweeted about his regulatory record: "The
Trump Administration has terminated more UNNECESSARY Regulation, in just 12 months, than any other Administration has terminated during their full term in office, no matter what the length. The
good news is, THERE IS MUCH MORE TO COME!"

When I interviewed Pruitt he was not the poster boy for questionable conduct that he would become. By mid-2018, Pruitt faced no fewer
than 10 federal investigations into his spending habits, the dispensing
of large pay raises to political allies, flying first class, building a private
"Cone of Silence"–style private phone booth (look up the 1960s spy sitcom Get Smart for clarity on the "Cone"), and below-market-rate living
arrangements funded by lobbyists or associates of lobbyists. No Trump
cabinet member was the target of more federal investigations. And yet,
Pruitt remained a trusted member of the cabinet, surviving revelations
about waste and extravagance that led Trump to fire his first secretary
of the Department of Health and Human Services, Tom Price, and his
first secretary of the Department of Veterans Affairs, David Shulkin.
When Pruitt resigned he was the subject of 15 audits, reviews or
investigations—and one probe from the House Oversight Committee.
He was replaced on a an interim basis by Andrew Wheeler, a former
coal industry lobbyist and vice president of the Washington Coal Club.

Why did Pruitt survive so much longer than Price and Shulkin?
Because his agency is at the forefront of Trump's deregulatory crusade
and Pruitt carried out the mission with gusto. When Trump touted
deregulatory actions, his agency-by-agency tabulation showed the
EPA at the top, with 16 deregulatory actions in 2017, more than any

other agency or department. Pruitt also backed Trump on leaving the Paris climate accord and canceling the Obama-era Waters of the United States regulation of ground-water use and pollution. He also scaled back standards on tailpipe emissions. In early April Sen. Rand Paul, Kentucky Republican and one-time Trump opponent, tweeted that Pruitt was "likely the bravest and most conservative member of Trump's cabinet. We need him to help drain the regulatory swamp." Note the reference to the regulatory swamp. Not the lobbyist swamp. Not the special interest swamp. Not the industry swamp. "The greatest sin you've committed, if any, is you've actually done what President Trump ran on and won on," Rep. Kevin Cramer, North Dakota Republican, told Pruitt during his congressional testimony in late April of 2018, amid numerous calls, mostly from Democrats but some from Republicans, for him to resign.

Before he resigned, Pruitt was a fixture in the cabinet because he could show Trump he was doing his bidding, scoring his points and turning his agenda into action. Price and Shulkin could not do that to Pruitt's extent because both were hamstrung by legislative resistance from congressional Republicans—Price on Obamacare repeal-and-replace and Shulkin on all matter of veterans spending and bureaucracy (both parties jealously guard veterans policy). Pruitt was empowered by a GOP-led Congress that endorsed his deregulatory approach. In the realm of deregulatory policy, few consequences of the 2018 midterm elections will loom larger. Trump's arrogant legal memo giving congressional committee chairs special oversight power and privilege may prove Trump's undoing if Democrats regain Congress. It will tie Trump and his cabinet secretaries in oversight knots that no pair of scissors will be large enough to cut.

THIRTEEN

Tax Reform

It would be too easy to start this chapter with Trump's "Christmas present" ceremony on the South Lawn of the White House that celebrated his biggest legislative accomplishment—the first structural rewriting of the federal tax code since 1986 as well as permanent reductions to the corporate tax rates and personal tax rates. We will get to that celebration in due time.

One of the fascinating aspects of Trump's first year is its upside-down quality. As was true when Trump was in South Korea, there were times when it looked as if Trump's presidency was falling in upon itself and in danger of unraveling before the public's incredulous eyes. Trump supporters might well say that was never their perspective, only that of media enemies who wished it to be true. Whether you subscribe to that point of view or not, it is true that many in the Trump world and White House felt buffeted by Trump's consistent inconsistency and often felt things were far less stable than they appeared—even when they appeared pretty seriously unstable. Whether because of Trump's own taste for theatrics and publicity or his inexperience and contempt for governing norms, there were more than a few *Perils of Pauline* moments. Trump's push for tax reform had its fair share. But the larger point about tax reform and Trump's first year, and that year's zany unpredictability, is that Trump's biggest defeat led to his most memorable and legacy-shaping victory.

The failure to repeal and replace Obamacare, in an odd sense, created two new realities that led to a more focused, disciplined effort to achieve tax reform. First, Republicans found themselves without a frontline achievement, and the need to land one led them to overcome obstacles that might under other circumstances have slowed or stopped them. Second, Trump dealt with the issue differently, delegated more and used the powers of his office more adroitly to get what he wanted.

"I don't know if we could've gotten taxes if we had gotten health," House Majority Leader Kevin McCarthy said early in 2018. "Health is such a problem. We passed something. And the Senate was off on something else. I don't know if we could have combined them."

McCarthy's point was if the GOP Senate's health care overhaul hadn't fallen one vote short, that bill and the vastly different House measure would had to have been merged and passed. Lounging with one leg draped over a chair in his first-floor Capitol office, McCarthy told me he doubted it would have come to pass. McCarthy winced as he imagined a tortured and ultimately futile House and Senate effort to forge a compromise that he was certain in retrospect would have taken up what remained of the summer and fall and left anger, division and fatigue in its wake. No one I have spoken to in senior House or Senate GOP leadership disagreed. Neither did the White House.

The pursuit of a new tax code and big reductions in corporate and individual rates did not rise out of the ashes of the Obamacare faceplant. The White House had put forth efforts early in 2017 to elicit tax suggestions from conservative groups and free-market think tanks. In this, the effort was more sophisticated and subtle than with Obamacare. Once Trump settled on a fusion of repeal-and-replace, he left the details to Congress and saw his role primarily as cheerleader and pleader.

One of the earliest White House strategy sessions on taxes occurred in early February with Trump and his economic team and key conservative groups.

"They listened, which never happened on health care," said Tim Phillips, president of Americans for Prosperity, the Koch-backed grassroots organization that spent tens of millions in 2016 on Republican candidates not-named Trump. Even at the February encounter, Phillips and other conservatives had grown worried about the GOP drift on Obamacare repeal-and-replace and could sense Republicans were losing their nerve and had no plan. As the process ground forward, plenty of meetings were held in which Trump helplessly pleaded with Republicans to strike a deal; amid this beseeching, he often found policy and political conversations circular and numbing.

"When we were in health care meetings [with Trump] the focus was on let's get this deal done. Let's just get it done," Phillips said.

In mid-March 2017, when Obamacare efforts were unraveling in the House, Speaker Ryan and Ways and Means Committee Chairman Kevin Brady of Texas met with Treasury Secretary Steve Mnuchin and National Economic Council Director Gary Cohn. The subject: tax reform. The goal was to lay the foundation for a unified tax bill. "Clearly with health care there were three or four or five or six different versions," Brady told me. "It was one of the problems and one of the reasons we weren't able to unite. We were not going to be playing that again."

On taxes, Trump was different. Phillips, lawmakers, lobbyists and administration officials all say he was more focused, assertive and knowledgeable. "It was him being fluent on every major issue," Phillips said. "He didn't defer. His ideas. Aggressive. He knew why he believed that. And he would take the lead on it. He would dive in. That was very different. It was a dramatic difference that was noticed."

Failing to repeal and replace Obamacare did not pave the way for tax cuts but it did focus the collective Republican mind—guillotines, real or metaphorical, have that effect. Republicans were in real trouble. The party's biggest and most reliable donors had fled for the exits. When the fat cats started to stray panic set in. When congressional Republicans talk about their "base," part of it is this institutional class of donors. Shoring up that base became a matter of political survival. During the time Republicans struggled to repeal and replace Obamacare, many of them said doing so was an existential imperative for the party. Fake News. The actual existential imperative was cutting taxes and simplifying the federal tax code—and thereby keeping a Trump promise that mattered more to rank-and-file Republicans and big business than anything having to do with Obamacare.

There was another change. Soon after health care failed, Trump hired a new chief of staff. Kelly radically reduced the number of people who saw Trump daily and imposed tight controls on the information, especially news clips and other blog posts (which previously did more to distract, amuse or flatter Trump than inform him) that reached his desk or overnight briefing book. This had a noticeable effect on the information Trump received and, importantly, how he came to process it. Kelly, with Trump's full support here as well, also changed the way the West Wing oriented itself to tax reform—appointing National Economic Council Director Gary Cohn as the single voice to speak on its behalf.

"How we approached the tax issue was infinitely more organized and disciplined," Kelly said. "It's because I got here. It's just the way you do it. Gary Cohn was the point guy. Gary would be the font of all knowledge."

For Short and his entire legislative team inside the White House, Kelly's arrival brought order and discipline. Firing Bannon, which Kelly did shortly after his arrival, also appeared to have been crucial. It reduced discord during the fall push for tax legislation and sent a message, at least for that early part of Kelly's tenure, that he was in charge and had Trump's full backing.

"What was essential to that was being able to push out Bannon and change people's roles," Short said, noting that Priebus had never really been given that chance. "At the beginning, it would have been difficult. There were many different power centers and there were differences between the power centers. It flows from having a stronger chief of staff. The difference was dramatic. Reince was not given the power."

Trump also grew momentarily introspective. He did not do an after-action report on himself of the kind major companies perform after a big event or mistake, but he did take advice on how to proceed on tax reform. When GOP leaders came to him with direct requests on how to handle one aspect or another of the process, Trump complied and thus permitted himself to be put in a role that was at times deferential, sometimes even subservient, to Republican lawmakers at the forefront of writing the tax legislation.

As Phillips said, Trump was more comfortable with the underlying details of tax policy—he knew the ins and outs reasonably well and over time his coterie of wealthy phone pals helped increase his base of knowledge. But, interestingly, those who watched him work on the issue said Trump did not lord that information over his advisors or lawmakers—unless he was trying to prove a point or break a stalemate. Trump was, lawmakers and aides said, helpfully and disarmingly circumspect. He also learned how better to lobby for votes. During the health care debate Trump was so desperate for a deal he would call lawmakers—frequently House Republicans—and ask them what they needed or wanted, how to get them from "No" to "Yes." Armed with that information, Trump would then promise each lawmaker he would make the requested change to secure their vote. Trump gave out so many assurances the bill writers didn't know how to react. Trump's one-on-one lobbying gave each lawmaker an outsized sense of his or her importance. Backbench Republicans began to ask themselves why they had to succumb to pressure from a committee chairman or member of the GOP leadership when they could take their case directly to Trump. "Everybody was looking to gain leverage," Short said. "A call with the president and they thought they could go around leadership. They would think 'How can I engage the White House in a way that I can leverage leadership?' It's like he was out on an island, making himself accessible. Members [of Congress] abused that. We all learned from that."

When it came to tax cuts and simplification, Trump kept working the phones, but instead of acting as chief lobbyist and bill writer, he followed the advice of Ryan and McConnell and deferred to Senate Finance Chairman Orrin Hatch and House Ways and Means Chairman Kevin Brady. On his calls, Trump would listen to a House or Senate Republican, jot down their concerns or ideas and promise only to pass along the information to the chairmen. "He did something very important," Brady told me. "He stepped back, just as he said he would. And he let the tax writers write the bill. We knew the target on the wall and it was the president stepping back, saying 'Hit that target.'" Trump did this from the White House and throughout his trip in Asia, taking calls at all hours and relaying information to Brady, who had the constitutional responsibility of writing the first version (because all tax law must originate in the House). Brady recalled a call he received from Trump from Japan on November 7. It was about 3 a.m. in Japan and, due to the time difference, 2 p.m. in the afternoon of November 6 in Washington. Brady's committee had just begun work on debating and voting to approve the tax bill, a process known as the markup. "He called me at 3 in the morning from Asia," Brady told me, his face and voice still incredulous. "He calls to talk tax reform. He says, 'How is the markup going?' We spent about an hour on the phone before I finally said, 'Mr. President, I'm worried about you.' He said, 'Why?' I said, 'You need to get some sleep. Seriously, you need to go to bed.' He just laughed it off." Trump was heading from Tokyo to Seoul that day for bilateral meetings with South Korean President Moon Jae-in.

To the question, then, "Can Trump learn?," the answer can be reasonably said to be yes. To the larger question of whether those lessons can or will translate to other achievements, nothing in the first six months of 2018 suggested in the affirmative. Yet, in ways important to tax reform but not applicable elsewhere, Trump learned to work with Republicans who were highly motivated—"scared to their political deaths" might be another phrase—to achieve what Trump wanted. Interests and learning, new tactics and new imperatives converged to produce a result that, at least economically, will influence U.S. fiscal and economic policy for a generation.

And it all started with what looked and sounded like a crashing thud.

It was April 26 and Mnuchin and Cohn filed into the White House briefing room to discuss Trump's tax plan. Aides distributed quite possibly the flimsiest policy document in Washington history—a one-page summary consisting of 271 words. As I looked at the piece of paper I thought there was a mistake. This couldn't be the "plan." So much was missing. I thought to myself, a freshman member of Congress would be embarrassed to release a document this vague. It was unworthy of the White House, especially one that considered itself economically sophisticated and familiar with the ins and outs of tax policy.

During a contentious briefing, Mnuchin and Cohn struggled to explain why their plan left so much to the imagination. Mnuchin was involved in terms of Treasury Department calculations of how policy would influence the numbers, but Cohn at this stage was trying to run economic policy (which meant, among other things, fending off Bannon) and beginning to figure out the politics of tax reform for Trump. At the podium in the briefing room it was an unabashed Wall Street moment. For those who remembered Trump's campaign rhetoric about economic populism, his chief advocates were full on plutocrats. Cohn and Mnuchin both came from Goldman Sachs. Cohn was Goldman's president and COO from 2006 to 2017 and received a stock-heavy severance of $285 million before he joined the White House. Mnuchin worked at Goldman for 17 years, rising to chief information officer. He left in 2002 and founded several hedge funds and a movie production financing company that brought *Avatar*, *X-Men*, *American Sniper* and *Mad Max: Fury Road* (among others) to the big screen. During the Great Recession, Mnuchin bought distressed residential lender IndyMac; he rebranded it OneWest Bank and moved it back to profitability before selling it in 2015 to CIT Group and gaining $97 million of company stock in the transaction.

The advisors were asked about rates on repatriation of corporate income held overseas. No answer. They were asked about tax loopholes affecting lower tax rates on dividends and capital gains. No answer. They were asked about pass-through companies and if they would enjoy the lower corporate tax rate. No answer. At one point, Cohn referred to these as "micro-details."

Fair enough, I thought. I'll try something more fundamental.

"On the 10, 25 and 35 percent rate, do you have income brackets established that you are going to propose?"

"Again, we're in constant dialogue with the House and Senate," Cohn said evasively.

"We're holding a bunch of listening groups right now. We have outlines. We have a broad-brush view of where they're going to be. We're running an enormous amount of data on the proposals right now. We will be back to you with very firm details."

The advisors were asked about future deficits.

"Does it pay for itself? Is this plan revenue-neutral?"

"We're working on lots of details as to this," Mnuchin said. "We have over 100 people in the Treasury that have been working on tax and scoring lots of different scenarios. This will pay for itself with growth and with reduced—reduction of different deductions and closing loopholes."

Then came the question about possible revenue shortfalls.

"If it turns out that it actually won't be paid for by growth, it won't keep deficits in check, is the president comfortable with that?"

"When we look at deficits, the deficit has gone from $10 trillion to $20 trillion in the last administration," Mnuchin said, making an embarrassing mistake by confusing annual deficits with accumulated public debt—a jaw-dropping blunder for a treasury secretary. "This plan is going to lower the debt-to-GDP ratio. The economic plan under Trump will grow the economy and will create massive amounts of revenues, trillions of dollars in additional revenues."

Then came the real money question—one any American would ask and expect to be answered.

"Middle-class families who watch this tonight on the news. A family of four, median income of $60,000, what does it mean for them?"

"It's going to be a tax cut," Cohn said defiantly.

"How much?"

"You're asking the same question as asked over here [referring to my question]," Cohn said. "We will let you know the specific details at the appropriate moment. We will continue to give you more details as we have them."

Where was the confidence of conviction? Where was the data? Why weren't there tax brackets? Why couldn't the plan explain itself in dollars and cents?

The lack of detail was breathtaking. When, exactly, was a more appropriate moment than the unveiling of the tax plan to explain what was in the tax plan? Mnuchin's deficit gaffe and the relentlessly sunny predictions of trillions in new revenue were equally problematic. It sounded far-fetched and amateurish. This was not for lack of expertise or will. Cohn could have talked to death about the specifics of tax reform. Mnuchin might have been able to keep up as well. Why didn't they? Two reasons: one unique to working for Trump, the other indecision masquerading as strategy. The first is tied to the jarring unpredictability of Trump. On April 21, at the Treasury Department no less, Trump announced that his "massive" tax plan would be released in a "big announcement on Wednesday." Hours earlier, Mnuchin had no answer to a reporter's question about how long until the tax proposal would be released. "Tax reform is way too complicated," Mnuchin said.

"The importance of that was the president's message," Brady told me. "It was, 'I'm dead serious.' The message to his own White House was 'I'm serious about this, man.'"

Trump's "April Surprise" caught congressional Republicans flat-footed and sent Mnuchin and Cohn scrambling. There had been plenty of discussions and circulated ideas, but nothing had gelled. But Trump was irritated about stories of a puny list of First 100 Days accomplishments. The Wednesday he haphazardly circled on the calendar was April 26, three days before his 100th. The second reason Cohn and Mnuchin were so evasive is they did not know how to proceed on politics or policy. Health care was staggering. Trump was angry and restless. He wanted something *else* to talk about. Taxes! But Mnuchin and Cohn didn't want to overpromise or overcommit. The White House didn't know what it was for in terms of specific tax changes because it wasn't sure yet what it could get. The paralyzed process left Cohn and Mnuchin with a piece of paper, wan smiles and a raft of unanswered questions. Under normal circumstances, tax cuts would have died right there. Among the financial and political press, the rollout made Trump's vaunted tax plan look puny, ill-defined and politically skittish.

Not everyone saw it this way. Conservative activists like Phillips loved it for all the reasons the critics attacked it.

"It was simple and it was powerful," Phillips said. "That was actually the virtue of it. It was exactly what you want: clarity, something big with a wow to it. That was a moment that was overlooked but that was a seminal moment. Outside groups and members looked at that and said 'Yes!' That is the most overlooked moment of that debate."

It was not overlooked as much as it was underappreciated or misconstrued. That happened with some frequency during Trump's first year. The sheer volume of tweets, events, achievements, distractions and personality clashes made it so.

Unmistakably, the next turning point for tax reform was neither overlooked nor underappreciated. Because it happened behind closed doors, it was known only to a select few, its importance at the moment somewhat understood but not deeply appreciated. As is often true in legislative politics, it is only clear which moments matter and which don't after the fact. This one mattered. Big League.

It occurred inside Senate Majority Leader Mitch McConnell's softly lit conference room on the second floor of the U.S. Capitol. It was 2:30 p.m. on September 12, 2017 when Treasury Secretary Mnuchin and top White House economic advisor Cohn arrived to meet with McConnell and top Republicans on the tax-writing Finance Committee and numbers-crunching Budget Committee. The goal was to determine the overall size of the tax cut and develop a strategy to move the legislation rapidly through the reconciliation process. Mnuchin and Cohn filed into the rectangular room and sat at the conference table. Hatch represented the Finance Committee as its chairman. His staff, always nearby to assist, hovered feet away. Every Senate Republican on the Budget Committee sat down. As is always the case, White House, Treasury and Senate staff vied for seats against the wall.

What I am about to describe is incredibly dense and colorless. It must be said, however, that what was decided and how it was handled represented the single most important decision in a legislative process that would eventually yield the Trump tax bill. In short, Trump and Republicans decided to pass a tax cut that allowed a $1.5 trillion deficit over the next 10 years, again using the reconciliation process, which had originally been drafted and historically had been used only to prevent new fiscal policy—be it tax cuts or other new mandatory spending providing social benefits—from increasing the deficit. The irony is self-evident. A process designed to reduce deficits produced, at least on paper, the largest projected deficits in U.S. history. Depending on the long-term economic performance of Trump's tax cuts, this could be one of the most dubious achievements of Trump's first year.

For Mnuchin, Cohn and the assembled senators there was one dominant issue to resolve. That was how best to accelerate consideration of tax legislation to meet the agreed-upon goal of passing a bill by Christmas. The central obstacle was the House budget resolution. It required cuts to Medicare and tax increases the Senate would not accept. For those tax cuts to pass the Republican-controlled House and Senate, both chambers had to agree on a budget resolution. This was vital to the reconciliation process. Reconciliation allows for big changes to tax policy, mandatory spending or debt obligations in the Senate under a time limit (20 hours of debate) and without a three-fifths majority (60 votes). This provides a huge tactical advantage. To seize it, Republicans had to agree on a budget resolution. No resolution, no reconciliation. No reconciliation, no simple majority passage in the Senate and no bill on Trump's desk by Christmas—possibly ever.

The question facing the meeting in McConnell's conference room was how much the Senate was willing to increase the deficit to accommodate Trump's tax cuts. Even before the August recess, Senate Republicans knew the House budget resolution was a political non-starter—chiefly because it envisioned a balanced budget in 10 years with hundreds of billions in budget gimmicks, rosy economic assumptions and those politically unpalatable mandatory spending cuts. What had to be found was new reconciliation language that would make room for tax cuts, meaning language that would allow for an increase in 10-year deficit figures. Budget Committee Republicans met with this goal in mind on September 7 but produced no results. McConnell called his September 12 meeting to break the logjam. He wanted to marry White House goals with emerging reconciliation language. McConnell sensed his members would not be able to agree upon a number or a process until they knew how much deficit spending Trump, the self-proclaimed "king of debt," was prepared to swallow.

Mnuchin looked around the room and said: "Well, we're hoping for 1.5 but would really like 2."

That sentence, depending upon the success or failure of Trump's tax cuts, may go down as the most beneficial or most ruinous in 21st-century tax policy. Mnuchin told the senators, whom he knew were the fulcrum on which future tax policy would turn, that Trump would sign a tax cut even if it raised deficits by up to $2 trillion over 10 years. This was in line with what Republicans hoped for and had been quietly plotting but didn't dare seek. Mnuchin was not so much setting policy as indulging the outer limits of GOP tax cut fantasies. That point was unmistakably driven home when, mere moments later, Mnuchin reached for a piece of paper containing the outlines of specific tax cuts. As Mnuchin began to talk, McConnell interrupted him to say it was unwise for him to discuss specifics. Those, McConnell admonished, are best left to the Finance and Ways and Means committees since they had jurisdiction. Specifics from the White House would only leak and unnecessarily distract from the work ahead. Hatch reinforced McConnell's cautionary words. Chastened, Mnuchin folded the piece of paper and tucked it into his pocket.

The next day Trump, in his own irrepressible way, memorialized the progress on Twitter. He put the tax cut debate in the context of summer hurricanes and the toll they had taken on economic growth. "With Irma and Harvey devastation, Tax Cuts and Tax Reform is needed more than ever before. Go Congress, go!"

One week later, the Budget Committee announced the size of its reconciliation instruction—$1.5 trillion in deficits over 10 years. The Senate set the vote on the budget resolution with this instruction for October 19. That morning, at 5:54, Trump leaned into the vote on Twitter: "Republicans are going for the big Budget approval today, first step toward massive tax cuts. I think we have the votes, but who knows?"

The budget passed late that night and early the next morning—5:11 a.m., to be exact—Trump offered Twitter play-by-play: "The Budget passed late last night 51 to 49. We got ZERO Democrat votes with only Rand Paul (he will vote for Tax Cuts) voting against." Trump, as he frequently did on Twitter, continued the thought: "This allows for the passage of large scale Tax Cuts [and Reform] which will be the biggest in the history of our country." Later that day, Trump also sent a little light toward McConnell, writing just before 1 p.m. "Great news on the 2018 budget @SenateMajLdr [McConnell's Twitter handle]—first step toward delivering MASSIVE tax cuts for the American people."

The House was left with a choice. Pass the Senate budget and ignore its preference for revenue-neutral tax cuts or go to a time-consuming conference committee to try to reconcile the math and politics. Speaker Ryan knew a conference committee would devour valuable time and could easily end in collapse. He had no choice but to accept the Senate budget and force his members to go along with deficit-financed tax cuts—a bitter policy pill for Ryan that amplified an earlier loss he suffered in tax negotiations. The House acquiesced, something it had never done in the history of congressional budgeting, and accepted the Senate bill without a single change.

"That's another spot where the president weighed in on," Brady told me. "No budget, no tax reform. That's the only runway we're going to land on. We were dead in the water without the budget."

In addition to Trump, Brady credits Budget Committee Chair Diane Black, of Tennessee, as a crucial force in winning House approval for the Senate budget. Black knew tax reform depended on a budget resolution and knew the House would get little if anything it wanted out of the Senate budget process. She devoted much of August to phoning committee members and rank-and-file Republicans to prepare them for the necessary and inevitable compromise to come.

There was another crucial moment in September. The White House, House and Senate were scheduled to unveil their "framework" for tax cuts on September 27. This wasn't the bill but the key provisions that had been hammered out during weeks of negotiations. The seven-page document had wide margins and lots of white space. That made it look and feel more substantive than it was. But there was enough policy to chart the road ahead. Even so, it nearly fell apart over one number—20. House and Senate Republicans agreed on a corporate tax rate of 20 percent. Trump had proposed 15 percent and was fixated on the number. When Cohn told Trump the framework called for a 20 percent rate, he threatened to blow up the entire bill. He wanted 15 percent because that was his number. No one else had proposed a rate that low and he frequently reminded outside groups during regular strategy sessions that a 15 percent rate would be historic.

Cohn and Mnuchin talked Trump up to 18 percent but couldn't move him any higher. They pleaded with Ryan to call Trump and get him to 20 percent. Ryan gave it to Trump in art-of-the-deal lingo he could appreciate. We can't hold 15 percent, Ryan said. The votes aren't there and everyone knows it. If we start at 15 percent we will have to move up and each step will mean negotiating with members to get their votes, adding complexity and wasting time. When members see a negotiation happening over what they know is one of your top priorities, Ryan told Trump, they will drive a harder bargain because they know you want it and that time is working against a deal. Under this scenario, the hunt for votes could push the rate past 20 percent as members use that higher rate to bargain for other tax breaks. Trump still wanted to start the bidding at a 15 percent rate. Ryan told him if he did that the corporate rate would become a piggy bank for lawmakers and Trump would be negotiating against himself, trading increases in the corporate rate in a way he might not be able to control. It was shrewder, Ryan said, to hold at 20 percent and work all other policy issues with that as a baseline. Ryan cautioned Trump he might have to budge off 20 percent in the final stages of negotiations. Trump agreed. In the end, Trump also okayed a final 21 percent corporate rate as one of the last revenue-generating concessions.

"He knows where he wants to go and is relentless in pushing people toward that goal and out of their comfort zone," Brady said of Trump's negotiating style. "When he couldn't, he was okay with the give if he knew why and what we were getting in return."

The House passed the budget on October 26, paving the bill's way toward passage, and guaranteeing Trump his Christmas present. The hardest decisions had been made, the toughest votes taken. Having swallowed projected deficits of more than $1 trillion over 10 years, all that was left was to vote to cut taxes. Republicans can literally do that with both arms tied behind their backs. Trump praised Ryan, McCarthy and House Majority Whip Steve Scalise on Twitter. "Congratulations to @SpeakerRyan @GOPLeader @SteveScalise and to the Republican Party Budget passage yesterday. Now for biggest tax cuts."

The tweets during this unglamorous but vital budget resolution process illustrated Trump learning as he was doing. Republicans taught him the process was key to victory and Trump lent the weight of his Twitter feed to the cause, conveying to Republicans he was listening and following their advice. This reinforced a sense of teamwork and trust. It may seem trivial in the grand scheme of things (many of Trump's Twitter spasms were) but these tweets were disciplined and collaborative. They worked.

Trump stood inside the Oval Office on December 20 going over his prepared remarks celebrating the tax cut's passage. The head of legislative affairs, Marc Short, was in his second-floor office reviewing an email he had just received from a friend at AT&T. The company was announcing a $1,000 bonus for each employee because of the reduction in corporate tax rates. Short walked down to the Oval Office and gave the release to Trump.

"Aw, this is awesome," Trump said with a big grin. "I think I'll go out and say it." Improvising, as per his tendency, Trump topped off his prepared remarks on the South Lawn, beaming with Republicans nestled on stage and arrayed prom-night style on staircases flanking him. "This just came out," Trump said grandly. "AT&T plans to increase U.S. capital spending $1 billion and provide a $1,000 special bonus to more than 200,000 U.S. employees and that's because of what we did. That's pretty good. That's pretty good."

The tax cut is now law and Trump and his fellow Republicans are betting it will set the economy on fire. All economic indicators in mid-June 2018 reinforced this belief, with second-quarter growth pegged at 3.7 percent and unemployment at 3.8 percent, the lowest since the late 1990s. Even so, some Federal Reserve studies suggested a slowing of the post–tax cut surge. What's clear and important is the Trump-led GOP abandoned any sense of caution about higher deficits or mounting federal debt. As mentioned, the law projects a deficit of $1.5 trillion over 10 years. That sounds like a lot of money and it is. But Trump's economic team argues it's not as large as it sounds. Spread out over 10 years that is roughly $150 billion a year. The U.S. GDP in 2017 was $19.7 trillion and, barring a recession, is expected to grow by 2.5 percent to 3 percent every year for the next decade, meaning annual increases in deficits *due solely to the tax cut* are manageable.

Budget analysts are not so sanguine.

"The big tax cut enacted in 2017 was such a departure from the past in terms of economic policy and American political culture and put in place such large reductions in revenues that it will likely be used by historians to mark the point when federal fiscal policy made a very sharp turn from the past and began a new normal," said Stan Collender, a leading budget expert and author of the Budget Guy column in *Forbes*. "The new normal includes permanent $1 trillion to $2 trillion budget deficits and the strong possibility the deficit will rise above $2 trillion during economic downturns."

From this Collender and others fear payments to service the national debt will continue to rise and interest rates will also climb, making it more expensive to finance the mounting debt and thereby, possibly, crowding out access to capital which could curtail future economic growth.

"I see no economic or governing philosophy at all," Collender said. "His focus appears to be on very short-term political wins even when the not-quite-as-short-term economic damage could be substantial and long-lasting. The new normal produces a one-time very short-term sugar high in terms of economic growth that is completely unsustainable."

Earlier, I quoted Mnuchin from the tax plan unveiling briefing promising that tax cuts would lower the debt-to-GDP ratio. At the end of 2017 that ratio was 104 percent. That figure is derived by dividing the public debt, $20.493 trillion, by the GDP, of $19.739 trillion. The World Bank considers any debt-to-GDP ratio above 77 percent economically hazardous. The United States has carried a ratio this high only once before, when it fought World War II and carried out Great Recession–inspired social welfare programs. After the war, the ratio fell back below 77 percent and remained there until the Great Recession of 2008–2009.

"What we got was a massive tax cut with detrimental fiscal effects," said Maya MacGuineas, president of the Committee for a Responsible Federal Budget. "We passed a tax cut that was projected to add over $1 trillion to the debt over a decade and that was after accounting for the economic effects of projected growth. It seems to have created a new era of unprecedented fiscal irresponsibility."

Early in 2018, Trump agreed to a two-year budget deal that raised domestic spending $296 billion above existing spending caps. That amount did not count $160 billion for Overseas Contingency Operations, a slush fund set aside for unforeseen military operations or other expenses. The 2019 deficit is projected to exceed $1 trillion and could rise to $2 trillion by 2027. Twin increases in defense and non-defense spending will create higher deficits immediately because the falloff in federal tax revenue will come long before back-end revenue gains are derived from higher growth—if those come at all (the meager economic gains of tax cuts in 2001 and 2003 under George W. Bush offer little statistical basis for optimism). Higher deficits will trigger more federal debt. That will increase debt service payments, increasing pressure on interest rates. Stock market volatility in the first six months of 2018 was linked to these underlying anxieties and may well continue through the year. Trump's tax cuts are not the largest in terms of size or scope, but they are historic when placed in relation to the economy into which the tax cuts were fed. Trump decided to inject fiscal stimulus through lower taxes and increased domestic spending at a time of near-full employment (4.1 unemployment percent when the tax bill was signed) and when deficits were spiraling upward—not from lack of economic growth but for want of fiscal discipline.

When Trump declared his tax cut the biggest in history he was, predictably, wrong. In terms of their relationship to the economy (the value of the tax cut compared with the size of the economy as measured by GDP) tax cuts signed by Kennedy, Reagan, George W. Bush and, most galling to Trump, Obama were larger. Strategically, the law's corporate tax cuts (from 35 percent to 21 percent) were made permanent. The individual rate reductions begin to expire in 2025. Trump and Republicans are betting the corporate tax rates will remain and future Congresses will extend the individual tax cuts—never allowing them to return to Obama-era levels. This is a hidden deficit time bomb in the law. There's ample reason to believe this politically cynical move will work. Days after Trump signed the tax cuts, CNN's Jake Tapper asked Bernie Sanders if it was "a good thing" that "91 percent of middle-income Americans will receive a tax cut." Sanders said: "Yeah, it is a very good thing. And that's why we should've made the tax cuts for the middle class permanent." Sanders opposed all other parts of the Trump tax cuts, but his embrace—permanent embrace—of rate reductions for middle-income earners suggested Republicans were onto something. With Sanders at the vanguard of making temporary Trump tax cuts for the middle class permanent, you may reasonably assume Trump's tax-cutting legacy, possibly lasting decades, is secure.

Epilogue

Too much winging it.

That was the blunt assessment of a trusted White House advisor in the immediate aftermath of Trump's catastrophic press conference with Russian President Vladimir Putin in Helsinki. The repercussions were immediate. Putin crowed. Rank-and-file Republicans, long strangled by self-imposed supplication, began to rebel. Trump back-tracked not once, not twice but three times—first no then yes on Russian interference in the 2016 election; first no then yes on whether Russia was interfering in the run-up to the 2018 mid-terms; first yes then no on letting Russians interrogate Americans on trumped up charges of political fraud. The back-tracking was hemmed and convoluted. Too much winging it.

Trump left for Helsinki with no agenda and no strategy. European diplomats pleaded for information from the White House about what Trump wanted from Putin—knowing Putin wanted plenty from Trump, namely sanctions relief, some acquiescence to Russia's annexation of Crimea and access to Americans for questioning. Putin also wanted to upstage Trump and sow anger in America over election hacking. What Trump secured remained a mystery. In public, Trump gave no ground on these issues but Putin got a White House invitation for some time in the fall—possibly in the middle of the mid-term elections his government would be attempting to destabilize. Before and during Helsinki, Trump undercut his director of National Intelligence, Dan Coats, a former Indiana senator and ambassador to Germany, by appearing to side with Putin over Coats on the uncontestable fact that Putin ordered cyber attacks and bot-driven social media meddling in the 2016 election. As Trump flew back to Washington, Coats issued an emphatic statement about Russian culpability, ignoring the commander-in-chief's equivocation. Later that week at a security conference in Aspen, Colorado, Coats was informed of the White House invitation to Putin.

"Say that again," Coats said to NBC's Andrea Mitchell, who was interviewing him at the Aspen Security Forum. "Did I hear you? Okaaay. That's going to be special."

Coats said that he would have advised Trump against his one-on-one encounter with Putin and said he still knew nothing of its contents. The implications, like the Helsinki summit itself, were hard to fathom. So was Trump's pre-Helsinki criticism of NATO allies, specifically Germany, which he said was "totally controlled" by Russia. And yet, it was all of a piece with Trump's overseas adventures one month before.

Within 72 hours in mid-June 2018, Trump denounced the duly elected leader of Canada and celebrated the dynastic dictator of North Korea. Canada is America's third-largest trading partner and has been a military ally in every armed conflict since World War I. North Korea is a communist outpost of murder, repression and militarism. Justin Trudeau is the youthful face of inclusion, diversity and tolerance. Kim Jong-un is the youthful face of autocracy, torture and state-run economic graft. Trump spurned the former and embraced the latter.

Trump stood near a stage in Singapore before holding a press conference and watched part of that embrace—a White House–produced propaganda video that showed how he and the young Kim could transform the world by achieving peace and bringing economic development—down to drone-delivered packages—to the hermit kingdom. Trump showed Kim the video because, of course, that's how Trump relates to information, though moving pictures, words and hyper-simplified narratives. If the summit with Kim hadn't already bathed the dictator in a favorable new light, this video offered an air-brushed beautification suitable for Vogue. The regime Trump branded as "wicked" and "depraved" before the United Nations in September of 2017 was now fit for "Morning in America" commercial hagiography.

During the post-summit press conference, Trump stunned South Korea and the Pentagon by announcing the suspension of joint military exercises, calling them "expensive" and "provocative." It was the first time an American president had criticized the exercises—long a staple of U.S.-South Korean preparedness—using the same words as the North Korean despots. For an awkward couple of days the Pentagon tried to comprehend the president's intent. South Korea did the same. Then it became clear. Trump really meant it. End the exercises even though North Korea had taken no discernible actions toward disarmament or denuclearization. Trump then declared on Twitter: "There is no longer a Nuclear Threat from North Korea." By mid-July, with negotiations stalled, Trump declared there was "no rush" to denuclearize North Korea. Winging it.

Such was and is the neck-snapping summer of Trump 2018. The Wild Ride continued at the same frenzied pace, in the same unmappable directions, but brought with it a different sense of unease. The White House team around Trump showed signs of fatigue. Daily briefings diminished in number. Trump dusted off his "enemy of the people" Twitter diatribe against the media after Helsinki but it felt defensive and surprisingly dull. June and July, like the previous months of Trump's presidency, were defined by nonstop churn. Only the contested content changed: family separation protests and lawsuits, economic gyrations, Supreme Court "vindication" for the travel ban, a new Supreme Court vacancy, two uneven summits, accusations of "treason," recriminations on trade, damaging revelations about the FBI and Justice Department handling of the Clinton email investigation and 2016 surveillance as well as a jaw-dropping bid to create a sixth branch of the U.S. military—one to patrol space. As work on this book drew to a close, the Wild Ride rattled and plunged. There was, it seemed, no place to remain calm.

Before the post-Helsinki uprising, small though it was, congressional Republican leaders spent the summer in lockstep with Trump on immigration and trade. Amid rumblings of rank-and-file dissent, the leadership refused to challenge Trump's hard-line tactics on either policy. GOP leaders cast their political and legislative lot with a president who in mid-July owned a 90 percent approval rating among self-identified Republicans, the highest rating, according to Gallup, of any time since Trump's inauguration and the highest mark for any Republican president at that stage of his presidency, save for George W. Bush in the aftermath of the 9/11 terrorist attacks.

In proximity came an administration announcement that it would not defend Obamacare protections for people with preexisting medical conditions seeking insurance coverage. Several states had sued over the requirement that insurance companies provide coverage for preexisting conditions while not charging dramatically higher premiums. The lawsuits were made on two grounds: one, that Trump's tax cut law would, in 2019, abolish the penalty for failing to obtain insurance coverage, the so-called individual mandate; two, that without the individual mandate and absent federal subsidies to insurers, which Trump had already abolished, there was no financing mechanism for this Obamacare protection and therefore it should be junked. The Trump Justice Department was bound by precedent to defend a law that had been upheld by the Supreme Court, as Obamacare had been. It refused. The move had no practical effect but did reveal Trump's hostility to precedent and to a central pillar of Obamacare—one Trump frequently extolled during the campaign and promised to defend after winning the election. That raised accusations of hypocrisy and cruelty. Such charges have become so frequent as to border on cliché—at least in the eyes of the Trumpian faithful.

Meanwhile, the administration authorized the construction of tent prison camps along the border and elsewhere to house children and adults to be processed for speedy deportation, or, at least, speedier deportation. To critics, allowing Obamacare to atrophy under legislative, regulatory and legal assault matched the venomous decision to describe all undocumented immigrants—many women and children—as criminals who had to be separated and housed in makeshift prisons. Both were hallmarks, critics alleged, of Trump's snarling 2018 stridency. As the mid-term cycle approached, Trump was popular among Republicans but vilified among Democrats. Independents strongly opposed

the administration's Obamacare and zero-tolerance immigration policies as the GOP clung silently to hopes that the revved-up domestic
economy would shield them from anti-Trump rage.

In mid-June the Federal Reserve raised interest rates one-quarter of
one percent and announced it would begin a steady process of further
raising interest rates because the U.S. economy was so strong and job
prospects so bright. Tighter money supply, the Fed announced, would
not threaten job growth and higher wages would not spur inflation. The
Fed projected that the jobless rate would fall to 3.2 percent—the lowest
in more than 30 years. "The economy is doing very well," said Federal
Reserve Chairman Jerome Powell on June 13. "Most people who want
to find jobs are finding them and unemployment and inflation are low."
In June of 2018, the Bureau of Labor Statistics reported 6.7 million job
openings and 6.4 million potential applicants, the second consecutive
month that available jobs outnumbered available workers—an unprecedented state of economic affairs. Business and consumer confidence
hit all-time highs; manufacturing continued to make gains; and it appeared that the only economic question of relevance was whether the
stellar numbers across almost every economic category could or would
last. The only immediate signs of unease were rising mortgage and bond
rates and some low-level anxiety about what the coming interest rate
increases—the Fed signaled two more in 2018—might portend. Trump
complained about the interest rate increases in mid-July, rattling markets accustomed to White House deference. "I'm not thrilled," Trump
told CNBC. "But at the same time, I'm letting them do what they feel is
best." Letting them. Wild.

At the margins of the economic conversation lurked anxiety about
Trump's toying with a trade war in Asia and Europe and with neighboring Canada and Mexico. In a showdown rich with irony and symbolism, Milwaukee-based Harley-Davidson announced on June 25 it
would move some production overseas to avoid European Union tariffs
sparked by Trump-announced tariffs on steel and aluminum. Trump
had hosted Harley executives and motorcycles on the White House
South Lawn on February 2, 2017, only 13 days into his presidency, to
thank Wisconsin for his victory. "Made in America," Trump said then,
with a double thumbs-up. The day after Harley announced its reaction
to EU tariffs, Trump denounced the company, saying it was using the

trade war as an "excuse" and predicting backlash from employees and customers. "The Aura will be gone," Trump said on Twitter. "They will be taxed like never before." Threats of tariffs and countervailing tariffs started to take on more specificity. A trade war, or certainly a series of destabilizing trade skirmishes, appeared close. Internal administration conflict over how hard to push the threat of tariffs led to high-stress disagreements, with free-traders like Mnuchin and Kudlow losing ground to Trump and energetic and influential trade counsel Peter Navarro.

Meanwhile, news surfaced of more White House defections as Press Secretary Sarah Sanders and Deputy Press Secretary Raj Shah reportedly set their departures in motion. Chief of Staff Kelly, looking exhausted in Singapore and Helsinki, was also plotting his exit. Short, the legislative director, left to teach at the University of Virginia on July 20—his move prompting on-line protest petitions from faculty and students who called the appointment just before the one-year anniversary of white nationalist violence in Charlottesville "unconscionable." Short told Politico the White House "could have done a better job expressing sympathy for the victims and outrage at those who perpetrated this evil." Deputy Chief of Staff Joe Hagin, who engineered the logistics for every Trump overseas trip, worked every detail of the Kim summit and was by acclamation the steadiest of hands inside the White House, resigned for a quieter life in the private sector.

For these and others, the grim reality of working for Trump—his impetuous, undisciplined and ungrateful ways—was too much to endure. What characterized service to Trump was something that I had never seen before: People would enter the White House with a predetermined exit date, rarely more than a year away. Some stayed longer than their imagined one-year punchout date, but not many. I've known many White House aides in other administrations—with exalted and minimalist titles—who imagined a finite time of service but who stayed much, much longer—because they loved the work, the president they served and the unique role, of whatever size, they played in history. That was almost never true with those who worked for Trump. It's not that White House aides under Trump did not believe in him. It's that, for many of those I've spoken to, that was not nearly compensation enough, not practically, not politically, not spiritually. Belief in Trump, for them and so many others now on the scrapheap of the personnel wood-chipper, is easier at a distance. Up close, belief runs headlong into reality—and the reality is that Trump does not share, does not inspire and does not lead nearly so much as he owns, commands, demands, projects and brands. He is in every way exhausting to the soul and corrosive to the spirit. This is hardest for those who still admire him and wish most fervently for him to succeed. The pain and pity of it all is that the common adhesives within the realm of politics—faith, trust, admiration, hope, belief and, yes, ambition—suffer mightily in Trump's acidic world of self-regard. The ranks of the Trumpian vanquished were so large and so conspicuous that by mid-summer 2018 the White House had to resort to a jobs fair on Capitol Hill to attract low- and mid-level employees. In one of the tightest job markets in decades, the White House could not give away jobs in the most powerful building in American government. And yet, the political reality for Trump appeared ever more favorable, signaling a genuinely historic decoupling of a president's team from the president himself—a separation that took on the look of a figure indifferent to political norms, one driven by persona and only minimally inhibited by government checks and balances. These tendencies became more visible in Trump's second year and, at least among voters who identified as Republicans, had no discernible negative consequences.

As for issues of justice, fairness and which investigations and investigators can or should be believed—a recurrent theme in Trump's Wild Ride—the Justice Department Inspector General in mid-June 2018 admonished former FBI Director James Comey for insubordination and improper, though not illegal, conduct. Comey offered a gentle dissent. The same Inspector General report faulted senior FBI investigators and former Attorney General Loretta Lynch in the Hillary Clinton email investigation. No criminal charges surfaced, but the report painted a picture of at least two politically tainted investigators (hostile to Trump), an attorney general who looked too cozy with the Clintons and protocol violations committed by Comey and others that undermined the entire email server investigation. The report found no evidence of illicit spying upon the Trump campaign. It did not suggest a conspiracy within the FBI to harm Trump or undermine justice. In short, the report said people screwed up and their errors cast doubt on the impartiality of the FBI in a high-profile political investigation.

That is a very serious matter. But the disclosures and conclusions fell far short of Trump's histrionic charges and "lock her up" chants of the 2016 campaign and his slightly more muted Twitter diatribes throughout the first year of his presidency. The same applied to Justice Department documents, released in late July, on surveillance of Trump campaign advisor Carter Page. Serious omissions undermined the warrant's credibility, but the errors did not, as Trump insisted, undercut Mueller's investigation. On these topics Trump exaggerated repeatedly. He screamed louder, branded more recklessly and dared the stupefied world to beat him at his own carnival barker act. This has ever been so and is the one part of Trump's life that rarely suffers from too much winging it.

Amid all this came a White House plan to combine the Education and Labor departments, as well as the Trump announcement (one he did not clear with the Pentagon) to create a "Space Force" that would be on equal legal, budgetary and operational footing with the Army, Navy, Air Force, Marine Corps and Coast Guard. "Our destiny, beyond the Earth, is not only a matter of national identity but a matter of national security," Trump said on June 18. Afterward, NASA administrator Jim Bridenstine told me the force was necessary because much of the modern world's electronic conveniences operated via low-orbit satellites that could be in jeopardy if space was not aggressively patrolled. Space, Bridenstine said, was "congested, contested and hostile." The U.S. needed a Space Force, Bridenstine said, to confront threats from China and others. Congress had debated the general question of space security but was a long way from funding Trump's Space Force.

A common refrain among White House reporters covering Trump is "What a long year last week was." All of us feel disoriented by the disruptions. Trump supporters I met during the campaign begged for a disrupting force in Washington. They have that, and most polling evidence suggests they are not only happy but exhaustedly gleeful. Trump's opponents remained as angrily exhausted as Jon Stewart was 11 days into Trump's presidency. In mid-June of 2018, Oscar-winning actor Robert De Niro screamed "Fuck Trump" during a live Tony Awards presentation on CBS (it was bleeped in time for FCC compliance). Days later, the actor Peter Fonda, son of the Hollywood legend Henry Fonda, said Trump's son Barron should be kidnapped and caged to show Trump the inhumanity of his "zero tolerance" immigration policy. (He later deleted the tweet and apologized.)

The zigs and zags of Trump's presidency have been relentless and unignorable. Trump is both. His Wild Ride is ours. His fate as a political figure, the most unique in modern history, is in many ways our own fate. Politically, Trump has defied the forces of gravity so long that many Republicans defending their own jobs (as opposed to the many who have retired in despair) have come to question whether gravity even exists. They act as if in the presence of a strange new force, timid, tight-lipped, tremulous. If Trump falls it will be because of a new political gravity, one of his creation and one that heralds a staunch Democratic backlash and revitalization. It could also suggest buyers' remorse among independents and some Republicans. The office-defending Republicans in Congress may come to rue their hesitancy if Trump crashes back to earth in the mid-terms. But if Trump and his quiet GOP allies survive with House and Senate majorities intact, Trump's re-nomination will be virtually certain and his reelection far more likely than imagined on Inauguration Day; if that comes to pass, a burn-it-all-down rage among disappointed Democrats is likely to seize the party and be very hard to contain.

Such is the stuff of political history—of Trump, of the Republican and Democratic parties and of the nation. Another "Make America Great Again" moment awaits.

Who defines that and who defends that will determine the extent of the Trump legacy. What was unknowable before the 2016 election is knowable now. Trump is real. His role in American life is pervasive. His effect on politics, policies and institutions is far-reaching, testing, taunting and, some fear, poisonous.

As Trump might say, "What have you got to lose?" Maybe a lot. Maybe nothing. After nearly two years of Trump, America at least knows the stakes and value of its lottery ticket.

Mr. Trump's
Wild Statistics

Approval rating for President Trump, by percentage,
    January 2017 (CBS News Poll)   40

Approval rating for President Trump, by percentage,
    January 2018 (CBS News Poll)   37

Growth in Dow Jones Industrial Average, by percentage,
    January 20, 2017 to January 19, 2018   +31.5

Growth in Dow Jones Industrial average, by percentage,
    January 20, 2009 to January 20, 2010   +33.4

Lobbying expenditures in Washington, adjusted for
    inflation, January 2009 to January 2010 $4.4 billion

Lobbying expenditures in Washington, adjusted for
    inflation, January 2017 to January 2018 $4 billion

Registered federal lobbyists,
    in 2009   13,730
    in 2016   11,169
    in 2017   11,444

Number of tweets via @RealDonalTrump account, excluding retweets, from January 20, 2017 to January 19, 2018	2,238
Number of tweets via @POTUS (the official account of the President of the United States), excluding retweets, from January 20, 2017 to January 19, 2018	417
Number of tweets that mention "Hillary"	50
Number of tweets that use the phrase "Crooked Hillary"	27
Number of tweets that use "Make America Great Again"	55
Number of tweets that include an exclamation point	1,381
Number of tweets that refer to North Korean dictator Kim Jong-un as "Rocket Man"	5
Insulting phrases that Trump, while president, has used to describe others	43
Total number of first-year Trump press conferences	21
Of these, total number of solo first-year Trump press conferences	1
Total number of first-year Obama press conferences	27
Of those, total number of first-year solo Obama press conferences	11
Total number of first-year George W. Bush press conferences	19
Of those, total number of first-year solo George W. Bush press conferences	5
Days lapsed from inauguration to formation of "Trump for President" reelection campaign	0
Number of Trump reelection rallies, January 20, 2017 to January 20, 2018	10
Of these, number held in states Trump lost in 2016	0
Executive orders signed by Trump, January 20 to December 31, 2017	55
Executive orders signed by Obama, January 20 to December 31, 2009	39

Executive orders signed by George W. Bush,
    January 20 to December 31, 2001   54

Detentions of immigrants apprehended or ruled
    inadmissible along the southwest border
    in December 2016   58,412
    in June 2017   21,657
    in December 2017   40,513

Deportations, excluding those caught at the border,
    from January 20 to September 30, 2017   61,094

Deportations, excluding those caught at the border,
    from January 20 to September 30, 2016
    (last year of Obama presidency)   44,512

Immigration-related administrative arrests and
    removal operations from January 20
    to September 30, 2017   110,568

Immigration-related administrative arrests and
    removal operations from January 20
    to September 30, 2016 (last year of Obama
    presidency)   77,806

U.S. adults, by percentage, without health insurance,
    December 31, 2016   10.9

U.S. adults, by percentage, without health insurance,
    December 31, 2017   12.3

Federal regulations eliminated in Trump's first year   879
Federal regulations delayed in Trump's first year   700

Number of National Rifle Association national
    conventions Trump has attended in 2016 and 2017   2

Number of National Rifle Association national
    conventions attended the year before or during
    the presidencies of George H. W. Bush, Clinton,
    George W. Bush and Obama   0

First-year firings or resignations of senior Trump
    White House officials   15

Vacancies in the 635 senior Executive Branch
  positions as of January 30, 2018   239

Number of federal circuit court or district judges
  nominated and confirmed in Trump's first year   22
Number nominated and approved in Obama's first year   12

Acknowledgments

Every book is a collaboration. The writer writes but leans relentlessly on others for encouragement, advice and courageous criticism.

Those closest to the book are also called upon to be patient and tolerant through periods of quiet isolation and a writer's corrosive self-doubt. A writer's spirit is fierce but rarely endures alone. My beloved wife, Lara, has given all in support of this project. She believed. Relentlessly. That mattered more than I can describe. Without her this book is a mirage.

Nothing I do in life will matter more than being a father. Mary Ellen, Luke and Audrey, thank you for your love, support and inspiration. All are ever-present and I am blessed to be your dad.

Steve Chaggaris, my dear friend and excellent journalist, has been an indispensable fact-checker, proofreader, cheerleader and advisor. Without his guidance and support, many disjointed chapters would still be searching for a book.

I am thankful to numerous CBS colleagues, starting with my White House producer, Arden Farhi, the finest friend and colleague a journalist could have. I am indebted to many others at CBS: Chloe Arensberg,

Caroline Horn, Susan Zirinsky, Paula Reid, Dean Reynolds, Charlie Brooks, Jaqueline Alemany, Jillian Hughes, Katiana Krawchenko, Steven Portnoy, Jeff Pegues, Brian Gottlieb, Len Tepper, Andy Triay, Pat Milton and Louise Serio. CBS management supported this project and my thanks begin with CBS Chairman and President Leslie Moonves and include CBS News President David Rhodes, CBS News CFO Charlie Pavlounis, CBS News Executive Vice President Ingrid Ciprian-Matthews, CBS News Radio GM Craig Swagler, CBS Washington Bureau Chief Chris Isham and, most especially, cheerful Deputy Washington Bureau Chief Ward Sloane.

A special note of thanks to David Jackson, White House Correspondent for *USA Today*. He provided meaningful advice and suggestions throughout. I relied on his institutional knowledge and gifts as a writer more than he knows.

I am also thankful to those who worked on the Trump campaign and within the Trump White House who assisted me even though the personal incentives were meager and the professional risks pronounced.

Lastly, I am profoundly thankful to my agents, Ann Tanenbaum and Ella Snow. No writer could have better advocates. Also to my lawyer, Robert Barnett: no one has profited more than I from your shrewd and steady advice.

No book exists without an all-seeing editor and task-master. Adam Bellow, my superb editor, was both. He tamed what was unruly, focused what was blurry, excised what was unnecessary and guided what was errant. I am indebted. Thanks also to Kevin Reilly and Alan Bradshaw, whose superb attention to detail and perseverance brought this manuscript across the finish line.

Index